THE
ROMANCE OF THE ROSE
ILLUMINATED

———————

Medieval and Renaissance
Texts and Studies

Volume 223

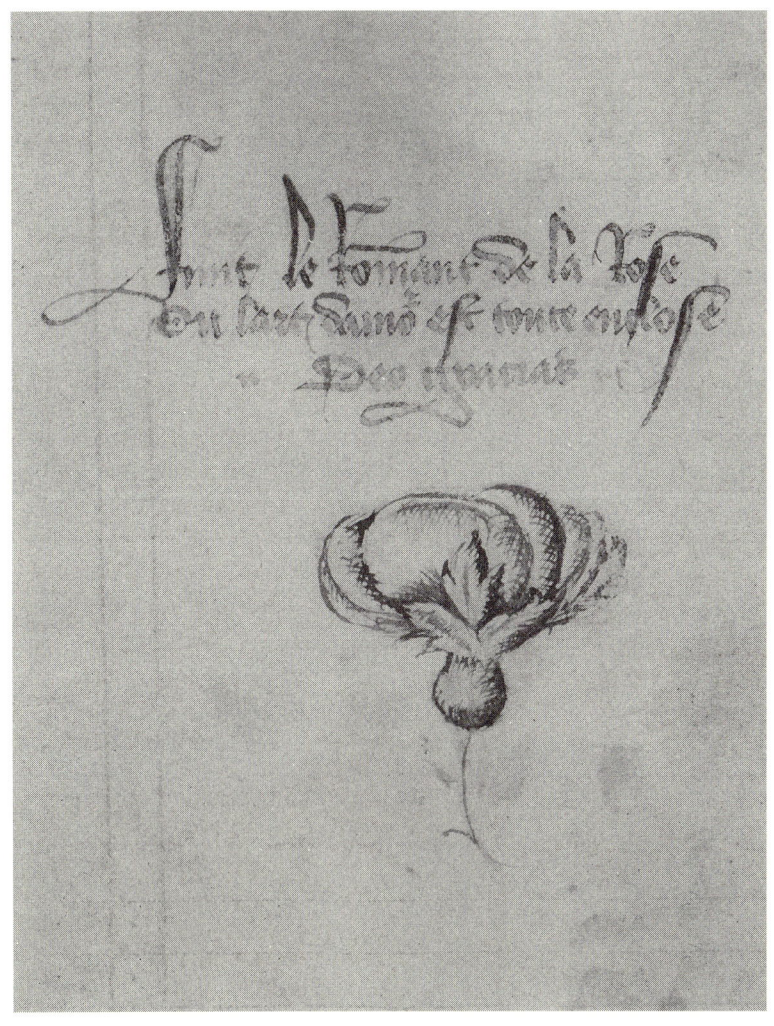

Explicit with scribal sketch of a rose: "Finit le Romant de le Rose ou lart damour est toute enclose. Deo gracias" [Here ends the Romance of the Rose, in which the art of love is wholly enclosed. Thanks be to God]. Aberystwyth, NLW MS 5014D, fol. 146r (mid-fifteenth century). By permission of the National Library of Wales.

THE
ROMANCE OF THE ROSE
ILLUMINATED

Manuscripts at the National Library of Wales,
Aberystwyth

by

ALCUIN BLAMIRES AND GAIL C. HOLIAN

Arizona Center for Medieval and Renaissance Studies
Tempe, Arizona
2002

*A generous grant from the Florence Gould Foundation
has assisted in meeting the publication costs of this volume.*

© 2002
Arizona Board of Regents for Arizona State University

Library of Congress Cataloging-in-Publication Data

Blamires, Alcuin, and Holian, Gail.
　　The Romance of the rose illuminated : manuscripts at the National Library of Wales, Aberystwyth / Alcuin Blamires and Gail C. Holian.
　　　　p. cm.
　　Includes bibliographical references.
　　ISBN : 0-86698-265-5
　　　　1. Guillaume, de Lorris, fl. 1230. Roman de la Rose — Manuscripts. 2. Guillaume, de Lorris, fl. 1230. Roman de la Rose — Illustrations. 3. Illuminations of books and manuscripts, Medieval. 4. National Library of Wales. I. Holian, Gail C. II. National Library of Wales. III. Title.

PQ1530.A3 B53 2001
841'.1—dc21　　　　　　　　　　　　　　　　　　　　　　　　　　2001056183

This book is made to last.
It is set in Bembo,
smythe-sewn and printed on acid-free paper
to library specifications.

Printed in the United States of America

Contents

Acknowledgements	ix
Abbreviations	xi
List of Illustrations	
Color Plates	xii
Black and White Figures	xiii
Preface	xv
Introduction	xvii
A Survey of Iconographical Studies of the *Rose*	1
The *Rose* Illustrated: Commentary on the Plates	
i. Dating the Illuminations	26
ii. The Frontispieces (*Incipit* Illustrations)	31
iii. The Images on the Wall	41
iv. The Garden	64
v. The Continuation	87
Descriptions of the Manuscripts of the *Roman de la Rose* at the National Library of Wales, by Daniel Huws	103
NLW MS 5011E	106
NLW MS 5012E	108
NLW MS 5013D	112
NLW MS 5014D	115
NLW MS 5015D	118
NLW MS 5016D	121
NLW MS 5017D	126
Bibliography	129

Acknowledgements

To address the *Romance of the Rose* and its manuscript illustrations is to engage with a subject that presents many challenges of a specialised nature. In preparing this volume, we are fortunate to have enjoyed the assistance of numerous scholars who have shared their expertise with us. No one knows the Aberystwyth manuscripts better than their erstwhile curator Daniel Huws, whose collaboration has been altogether invaluable. Meradith McMunn gave us access to unpublished materials and brought her considerable knowledge of illuminated *Rose* manuscripts to bear on iconographic details. Domenic Leo enlightened us concerning the affiliations of one Aberystwyth manuscript; François Avril provided invaluable suggestions and corroboration concerning others. Useful hints about dating came also from Anne Sutton and Alison Stones. A tentative inquiry to Mary and Richard Rouse about a named scribe in one manuscript led to an exchange of information from which we benefited much. Kitty Howells and Rose Williams generously assisted us with their language skills, and C. W. Marx with his palaeographical acumen. The academic development of the volume was agreeably encouraged by many others including Allen Samuels, Martha Driver, Flora Lewis, and Renate Blumenfeld-Kosinski.

For crucial support of our project it is our pleasure to thank Sister Barbara Williams (former President, Georgian Court College) and Keith Robbins (Vice-Chancellor, University of Wales, Lampeter), as well as the administrators of the Pantyfedwen Research Fund at the latter institution. For practical assistance in bringing the project to fruition and for generosity in waiving reproduction fees we are grateful to Brynley Roberts and Lionel Madden, former Librarians at the National Library of Wales, and the current Librarian, Andrew Green, as well as Mari Wyn of the Marketing Department. We could not have done without the skill of the Library's meticulous Photographer, Gareth Hughes. We are grateful, too, to the successive General Editors of MRTS who took up our proposal and saw it into print, namely Mario Di Cesare and Robert Bjork.

Our deepest debt, however, is to the Florence Gould Foundation (New York) for most generously underwriting the Anglo-American research collaboration upon which this book is based, and for subsidising the cost of the color repro-

Acknowledgements

ductions. Without the Gould Foundation, and in particular without the good offices of Daniel Davison, John R. Young, and Jay and Anne Harbeck, the book would not have come into existence.

— *Alcuin Blamires and Gail C. Holian*

Abbreviations

BL	The British Library, London
BN	Bibliothèque nationale de France, Paris
Bodl.	The Bodleian Library, Oxford
CUL	Cambridge University Library
EETS	Early English Text Society
Morgan	The Pierpont Morgan Library, New York
NLW	The National Library of Wales, Aberystwyth
ÖNB	Österreichische Nationalbibliothek, Vienna

List of Illustrations

COLOR PLATES

Reproduced from Roman de la Rose *manuscripts by kind permission of the National Library of Wales, Aberystwyth, Wales.*

1. Frontispiece: Aberystwyth, NLW MS 5017D, fol. 1r
2. Frontispiece: Aberystwyth, NLW MS 5013D, fol. 1r
3. Haïne: Aberystwyth, NLW MS 5017D, fol. 2r
4. Haïne: Aberystwyth, NLW MS 5016D, fol. 3r
5. Haïne: Aberystwyth, NLW MS 5013D, fol. 2r
6. Felonie: Aberystwyth, NLW MS 5013D, fol. 2r
7. Vilanie: Aberystwyth, NLW MS 5013D, fol. 2r
8. Vilanie: Aberystwyth, NLW MS 5017D, fol. 2r
9. Covoitise: Aberystwyth, NLW MS 5017D, fol. 2r
10. Covoitise: Aberystwyth, NLW MS 5016D, fol. 3r
11. Covoitise and Avarice: Aberystwyth, NLW MS 5013D, fol. 2v
12. Avarice: Aberystwyth, NLW MS 5017D, fol. 2v
13. Avarice: Aberystwyth, NLW MS 5016D, fol. 3v
14. Envie: Aberystwyth, NLW MS 5017D, fol. 2v
15. Envie: Aberystwyth, NLW MS 5016D, fol. 3v
16. Envie: Aberystwyth, NLW MS 5013D, fol. 3r
17. Tritesce: Aberystwyth, NLW MS 5017D, fol. 3r
18. Tritesce: Aberystwyth, NLW MS 5016D, fol. 4r
19. Tritesce: Aberystwyth, NLW MS 5013D, fol. 3v
20. Vielleice: Aberystwyth, NLW MS 5017D, fol. 3v
21. Vielleice: Aberystwyth, NLW MS 5016D, fol. 4v
22. Vielleice: Aberystwyth, NLW MS 5013D, fol. 4r
23. Papelardie: Aberystwyth, NLW MS 5017D, fol. 4r
24. Papelardie: Aberystwyth, NLW MS 5016D, fol. 5r
25. Papelardie: Aberystwyth, NLW MS 5013D, fol. 4v
26. Povreté: Aberystwyth, NLW MS 5017D, fol. 4r
27. Povreté: Aberystwyth, NLW MS 5016D, fol. 5r
28. Povreté: Aberystwyth, NLW MS 5013D, fol. 4v

List of Illustrations

29. The Lover encounters Oiseuse: Aberystwyth, NLW MS 5016D, fol. 5v
30. The Lover in the garden with birds: Aberystwyth, NLW MS 5016D, fol. 6v
31. Oiseuse leads the Lover to the garden gate: Aberystwyth, NLW MS 5016D, fol. 7r
32. The *carole*: Aberystwyth, NLW MS 5017D, fol. 6v
33. Deduiz (or the Lover) walks among trees: Aberystwyth, NLW MS 5016D, fol. 8r
34. Narcissus gazes at the spring: Aberystwyth, NLW MS 5016D, fol. 11v
35. The God of Love shoots an arrow at the Lover: Aberystwyth, NLW MS 5016D, fol. 13r
36. The Lover's homage; the God of Love locks his heart: Aberystwyth, NLW MS 5016D, fol. 15r
37. The God of Love locks the Lover's heart: Aberystwyth, NLW MS 5016D, fol. 15r
38. Bel Acueil reprimands the Lover: Aberystwyth, NLW MS 5016D, fol. 20v
39. Reason addresses the Lover: Aberystwyth, NLW MS 5016D, fol. 21r
40. The Jalous beats his wife (misplaced): Aberystwyth, NLW MS 5016D, fol. 26v
41. Author writing: Aberystwyth, NLW MS 5016D, fol. 28r
42. Friend advises the Lover: Aberystwyth, NLW MS 5016D, fol. 47r
43. The Lover meets Richece and her partner: Aberystwyth, NLW MS 5016D, fol. 64r
44. Venus aims at the castle: Aberystwyth, NLW MS 5016D, fol. 129v
45. Pygmalion sculpts a female form: Aberystwyth, NLW MS 5016D, fol. 130r
46. Venus and Pygmalion (whole opening): Aberystwyth, NLW MS 5016D, fols. 129v-130r
47. Frontispiece: Aberystwyth, NLW MS 5011E, fol. 1r
48. Frontispiece: Aberystwyth, NLW MS 5014D, fol. 1r
49. *Explicit* with scribal sketch of a rose: Aberystwyth, NLW MS 5014D, fol. 146r

Black and White Figures

Reproduced by kind permission of the British Library, London;
the Bibliothèque nationale de France, Paris;
the Pierpont Morgan Library, New York; and the Bodleian Library, Oxford.

1. "Equité" and "Felonnie": *Somme le roi*, London, BL MS Add. 28162, fol. 7v
2. The Poet dreams of a debating theologian and knight: *Le Songe du verger*, London, BL MS Royal 19 C IV, fol. 1v

List of Illustrations

3. The Duke received by St Peter at the gate of Paradise: The *Grandes Heures* of the Duke of Berry, Paris, BN MS lat. 919, fol. 96r
4. Venus heats Bel Acueil with her firebrand: *Roman de la Rose*, New York, Morgan MS M 132, fol. 30r
5. Pöor and Honte waken Dangiers: *Roman de la Rose*, Oxford, Bodl. MS e Mus 65, fol. 27v
6. Jalousie oversees the building of the castle: *Roman de la Rose*, Oxford, Bodl. MS e Mus 65, fol. 28v
7. Lucretia's suicide: *Roman de la Rose*, New York, Morgan MS M 324, fol. 59r
8. The Lover meets Richece and partner: *Roman de la Rose*, New York, Morgan MS M 324, fol. 68r
9. The God of Love consults his "barons": *Roman de la Rose*, Oxford, Bodl. MS e Mus 65, fol. 82v
10. Faus Semblant kills Malebouche: *Roman de la Rose*, New York, Morgan MS M 132, fol. 90r
11. La Vielle with Bel Acueil in the castle: *Roman de la Rose*, Oxford, Bodl. MS e Mus 65, fol. 98v
12. Dangiers forces the Lover away from the rose: *Roman de la Rose*, New York, Morgan MS M 132, fol. 109v
13. The God of Love instigates the siege: *Roman de la Rose*, London, BL MS Royal 20 A XVII, fol. 125r
14. Nature confesses to Genius: *Roman de la Rose*, London, BL MS Yates Thompson 21, fol. 108r
15. Death and funeral of Esclados: *Le Chevalier au lion*, Paris, BN MS fr. 1433, fol. 69v
16. Pygmalion sculpts: *Roman de la Rose*, New York, Morgan MS M 132, fol. 149r

Preface

Our book primarily discusses the illuminations in a collection of *Roman de la Rose* manuscripts made by Francis Bourdillon, now in the Department of Manuscripts and Records at the National Library of Wales, Aberystwyth. In an ideal world many other *Rose* manuscripts around the globe would have an equal or even prior claim to be the subjects of such a book, so a word of explanation about the inception of this project may be appropriate.

The origin of the book can be traced to the "Medieval Illuminated Manuscripts in Wales" project developed and co-directed by C. W. Marx and Alcuin Blamires, with the assistance of Flora Lewis, in the Department of English at the University of Wales, Lampeter. The aim of that project (pursued with the help of research funding from the University and then, very substantially, from the Leverhulme Trust) was to create reproductions of the miniatures in every illuminated manuscript housed in Wales, and in the longer term to produce a catalogue making the materials more generally known.

When the "MIMW" directors introduced their project to colleagues at a Warburg Institute conference, they were energetically urged that it is always a major priority to get little-known miniatures into circulation through publication in whatever way possible. The prospect of achieving independent publication specifically of the *Roman de la Rose* miniatures in the Welsh holdings was first recognized at the suggestion of Gail Holian of Georgian Court College, New Jersey. But prospect was converted into reality by the enlightened interest of the Florence Gould Foundation in fostering Anglo-American research into French culture. Particular goals of the Gould Foundation are to promote French-American understanding and to provide support for education and the arts in the United States and France. Florence Gould was a tremendous patron of literature — and especially French literature — in the post-World War II years. It happens that she was also linked by marriage to the New Jersey estate which is now the site of Georgian Court College. Since Francis Bourdillon's family was of French extraction and since he was particularly dedicated to collecting manuscripts and early editions of French romances, there seems a special appropriateness in aligning the Gould Foundation with the present analysis of his illuminated *Roman de la Rose* manuscripts.

The book will serve one of its primary objectives if it makes the existence and interest of the illuminations in the manuscripts at Aberystwyth better known.

Preface

Nevertheless, we do not argue that they are of outstanding aesthetic quality. In the past, arguably, cataloguers and illumination scholars have sometimes directed disproportionate attention to aesthetically arresting illuminations. Yet key questions about narrative illustration are, we shall show, raised quite as sharply by the work of illuminators whom the art historian might not place in the "front rank." We are less concerned to calibrate miniatures as artistically superior or inferior than we are concerned to assess the validity of different modes of interpretative strategies that have been applied, or might be applied, to medieval narrative illustrations. What follows is therefore not only a case-study of a particular group of illuminated *Rose* manuscripts in the context of a conspectus of *Rose* illustration: it is also an inquiry into the processes and expediencies of medieval illustration. We like to think that Francis Bourdillon, who himself wrote about the expediency which early printers applied to their production of woodcut-illustrated editions of the poem, would have relished our investigation of the *Romance of the Rose* manuscripts he owned.

This study is collaborative. The Introduction, Chapter 1 and Chapter 2 were written by Alcuin Blamires on the basis of joint research with Gail Holian. Daniel Huws wrote Chapter 3; he also cast a wary eye over the preceding chapters, though of course any infelicities or errors that remain are our own responsibility.

Introduction

To study the reception of the *Rose* is ... to encounter the range of medieval ideas about love and marriage, gender and sexuality, about sin and free will, about language and power, about human society, nature, and the cosmos. And because the *Rose* manuscript tradition is so vast, it yields a rich variety of material: interpolations and abridgements, reworkings of the text on both a large and small scale, extensive programs of rubrication and illumination, a significant body of marginal annotations.[1]

Sylvia Huot aptly describes as "vast" the manuscript tradition of *Le Roman de la Rose* — the allegorical poem about desire, of which the first part was written in France by Guillaume de Lorris around 1235 and the continuation by Jean de Meun in the 1270s.[2] This study attends to a hitherto relatively obscure outcrop in the vastness: namely, to a cluster of seven manuscripts in the National Library of Wales at Aberystwyth. They were acquired from the library of Francis Bourdillon, a gentleman scholar and bibliophile whose life straddled the nineteenth and twentieth centuries and who took a particular interest in early illustrated printed editions of the *Rose* and hence in the manuscript tradition from which such editions derived.[3]

Like most illuminated manuscripts, these of the *Romance of the Rose* have that charisma of uniqueness, each possessing its own "flavor," which characterizes to a lesser extent even undecorated medieval manuscripts of all sorts — including the ugliest. To open a manuscript containing illustrated ("historiated") initials or (as is the rule with the *Rose* when it is illustrated) containing framed miniatures, is to experience a heightened anticipation, a rush of adrenaline, even when you are used to opening them. It is in fact a privilege, one which should be extended to as many people as is consistent with preserving the books themselves. A facsimile

---

[1] Sylvia Huot, *The* Romance of the Rose *and its Medieval Readers: Interpretation, Reception, Manuscript Transmission* (Cambridge: Cambridge University Press, 1993), 9.

[2] For a recent discussion of dating, see Susan Stakel, *False Roses: Structures of Duality and Deceit in Jean de Meun's "Roman de la Rose,"* Stanford French and Italian Studies, 69 (Saratoga, CA: Anma Libri, 1991), 10–11.

[3] Details of Bourdillon's career are given in Chapter 3, below.

Introduction

or a digital image of every page is the next best thing, but is unrealistically expensive. Color reproduction of all the miniatures is a tolerable substitute, which we have chosen as the backbone of this book.

Five of the National Library's *Rose* manuscripts are illuminated, the other two (NLW 5012E, 5015D) being intended for illumination which, however, was never accomplished. The library's illuminated manuscripts seem to us worth discussing and presenting together for several reasons. First, while the manuscripts themselves are in theory known to *Rose* scholars, their illuminations have hardly ever been mentioned, let alone reproduced. Second, although the illuminations are neither artistically outstanding nor iconographically idiosyncratic, that, in our view, is an incentive, not a disincentive. These are competent, pleasurable, iconographically "mainstream" illuminated manuscripts which therefore warrant exploration, as we shall argue, precisely because study of the poem's illustrations has tended both to misunderstand the ordinary and to concentrate too often on the exceptional. In many respects the study of medieval illumination still remains to be established in terms of the unexceptional. Third, the juxtaposition of several cycles of illumination under one roof, as it were, is a compelling way of energizing salient questions about (for example) how the narrative was responded to, what the functions of illustration were taken to be, and who did what, and when, in the production of an illuminated medieval book.

To insert these manuscripts into the vastness of the tradition to which they belong, it is only necessary to mention that at least 310 whole or fragmentary manuscripts of the *Rose* survive, of which some 230 have either miniatures or spaces for them. There are fourteen which have, or in some cases were meant to have, more than a hundred illustrations each, and extensive cycles are present from the time of the earliest manuscripts in the 1280s. These statistics come from Meradith McMunn, who is making a comprehensive study of illuminated *Rose* manuscripts with a view to producing a complete descriptive catalogue and iconographical index, a task constantly extended by the pleasurable discovery of illuminations not previously recorded.[4] Her project is vital if the subject is eventually to be got

---

[4] Interim publications by Meradith McMunn are: "Representations of the Erotic in Some Illustrated Manuscripts of the *Roman de la Rose*," *Romance Languages Annual* 4 (1992): 125–30; "The Iconography of Dangier in the Illustrated Manuscripts of the *Roman de la Rose*," *Romance Languages Annual* 5 (1994): 86–91; "Animal Imagery in the Text and Illustrations of the *Roman de la Rose*," *Reinardus: Yearbook of the International Reynard Society* 9 (1996): 87–108 (with statistics on pp. 96–97); "In Love and War: Images of Warfare in the Illustrated Manuscripts of the *Roman de la Rose*, " in *Chivalry, Knighthood, and War in the Middle Ages*, ed. Susan Ridyard, *Sewanee Mediaeval Studies* 9 (Sewanee, TN: University of the South, 1999), 165–93. We are much indebted to her for letting us see some of these articles before publication, and for encouragement of the present project. The standard cata-

INTRODUCTION

under control. The tendency meanwhile is for scholars to bite off manageable chunks: to concentrate on illustration of a segment of the poem, such as the representations of "vices" depicted on the garden wall near the beginning of the story; or on author-portraits, or on Pygmalion miniatures later on;[5] or, alternatively, to explore particular manuscripts and their affiliates.[6]

The present book explores particular manuscripts, while aspiring to set them within the wider field of *Rose* iconography generally and within horizons of probability in the production of illumination in the relevant period. Before commenting further on what we think that entails, we should like to provide an initial orientation by presenting a narrative résumé of the poem, noting the points at which illustrations would be characteristic of well-endowed manuscripts (though "characteristic" is a provocative adjective, as will be explained afterwards). The résumé will also provide an opportunity to detail the English names which will be used in this book to identify the personifications named in the Old French — there being no consensus about how to translate some of them.[7]

In a characteristic illuminated *Rose* manuscript, then, the beginning of the text might be headed by a substantial illumination showing a man asleep, who then awakes, dresses and walks by a river towards a wall. In the text the narrator (l'Amant, Guillaume, whom we shall call the LOVER) tells of his dream of rising, taking to the meadows, and scanning the outside of a garden wall looking for an entrance. This wall bears depictions of a set of personifications, apparently antithetical to youthful love and therefore described in hostile terms — each one assigned a separate miniature, so that illustrations come thick and fast in these first

---

logue of *Rose* manuscripts by Ernest Langlois, *Les Manuscrits du Roman de la Rose: Description et classement* (Paris: Champion; Lille: Tallandier, 1910; repr. Geneva: Slatkine, 1974) merely signals the presence of miniatures in each manuscript in a sketchy, informal way; e.g., "miniatures," "fine miniatures," "numerous fine miniatures," "37 rather ugly miniatures," etc. (our trans.).

[5] Respectively Philippe Ménard, "Les Représentations des vices sur les murs du verger du *Roman de la Rose*: la texte et les enluminures," in *Texte et Image*, Actes du Colloque international de Chantilly, 1982 (Paris: Les Belles Lettres, 1984), 177–90; David Hult, *Self-Fulfilling Prophecies: Readership and Authority in the First Romance of the Rose* (Cambridge: Cambridge University Press, 1986), esp. 74–93; and Virginia W. Egbert, "Pygmalion as Sculptor," *Princeton University Library Chronicle* 28 (1966): 20–23.

[6] See, for instance, Lori Walters, "A Parisian Manuscript of the *Romance of the Rose*," *Princeton University Library Chronicle* 51 (1989): 31–55.

[7] The two most accessible translations are *The Romance of the Rose by Guillaume de Lorris and Jean de Meun*, trans. Charles Dahlberg (Princeton: Princeton University Press, 1971; 3rd ed., 1995); and *The Romance of the Rose*, trans. Frances Horgan, World's Classics (Oxford: Oxford University Press, 1994). Horgan's version is quoted in the present book, except for some modifications of naming as indicated below.

Introduction

few pages. The images of the wall are at first briefly described. For the sake of consistency, we give the Old French names for these and other characters in the form in which the edition by Lecoy (used in this book) prints them; many critics inconsistently refer to Lecoy's edition but import spellings for the *dramatis personae* from elsewhere.[8] Haïne (HATRED) and Felonie and Vilanie (VIOLENCE and ABUSE)[9] have only thirty lines between them, but the next two, Covoitise and Avarice (GREED and AVARICE), have sixty-five; then Envie (ENVY) has fifty-five all to herself. Tritesce (MISERY) and Vielleice (SENILITY) come next with substantial descriptions (especially the latter), but Guillaume hastens rather more over the last two, Papelardie (HYPOCRISY) and Povreté (POVERTY).

To enter the garden from whose wall these figures look away, the Lover has to go through a small door opened by Oiseuse (we shall call her EASE, though she is often translated as "Idleness" or "Leisure"):[10] equipped in some miniatures with comb and mirror, she is seen confronting him or letting him in. Amidst the woods and birdsong within, the Lover is enchanted to encounter Deduiz (PLEASURE, translated by Dahlberg as "Diversion") and his elegant companions in a circular *carole* dance, illustrated. There can be separate miniatures of one or two of Pleasure's companions, the company of love, who are here described: Amors (the GOD of LOVE), Largesce, Franchise (OPENNESS, rendered "Generosity of Spirit" by Horgan), Cortoisie, etc. Breaking away from the party, the Lover soon reaches a spot containing the spring where Narcissus died. Narcissus, or the Lover, or perhaps one youth for both, is frequently painted gazing at a woodland spring: the roses which the Lover espies through reflecting crystals in the same spring —

---

[8] Guillaume de Lorris and Jean de Meun, *Le Roman de la Rose*, ed. Félix Lecoy, 3 vols., Classiques Français du Moyen Age (Paris: Champion, 1965–70).

[9] Dahlberg's translation leaves "Felony" and "Villainy" as they are. For *Felonie*, Sarah Kay suggests "Treachery" in *The Romance of the Rose*, Critical Guides to French Texts, 110 (London: Grant and Cutler, 1995), 24. Horgan renders *Felonie* as "Cruelty" and *Vilanie* as "Baseness." *Vilanie* is a matrix of social/moral negatives particularly difficult to encapsulate in one modern term. "Villainy" in modern parlance implies crime indulgently perceived: we have preferred "Abuse" to alternatives such as "Baseness" (too tame and anachronistic?) or to possibilities such as "Uncourtliness," "Boorishness," "Barbarism," or "Vulgarity."

[10] Amidst considerable discussion about whether Oiseuse is to be understood as the sin of Sloth or as the leisure which is conducive to courtship, in our view the nuance of the Old French word (cf. Latin *otium*) is best served in modern English by the word "ease," which still retains something of its Middle English equivocation: see **Ease**, sb. (4), "Absence of painful effort; freedom from the burden of toil; leisure; in bad sense, idleness, sloth," *Oxford English Dictionary*, 2nd ed. The Middle English translation of the *Rose* renders *Oiseuse* as "Ydelnesse," but this in turn raises a question about the precise meaning of the latter term; see *The Romaunt of the Rose* (line 592) in *The Riverside Chaucer*, ed. Larry Benson, 3rd ed. (Boston: Houghton Mifflin; and Oxford: Oxford University Press, 1987).

Introduction

and which immediately preoccupy him — are also in the painting. The reader already knows that Amors has stalked the Lover, and the miniaturist now characteristically presents a threefold ensuing drama whereby the God shoots the Lover with arrows, accepts his fealty, and locks his heart.

The God's long ensuing speech on proper loving and on coping with its emotions is pictorially a desert: miniatures restart when action restarts, as Bel Acueil (RESPONSIVENESS, we suggest, rather than the quaint-sounding "Fair Welcome") kindly lets the Lover approach the Rose. The immediate intervention of the thug Dangiers (REFUSAL, perhaps, instead of Dahlberg's "Resistance" or Horgan's "Rebuff")[11] is also illustrated. Upset, the Lover finds himself accosted by, but distinctly uninterested in, Reson (REASON, a queenly figure painted coming out of her tower). The witty psychology of the to-ing and fro-ing of the Lover's subsequent attempts to regain access to the Rose attracts occasional miniatures, to mark his consolation through the strategic advice given in a speech by Amis (FRIEND), then the attempts of allies (Franchise/OPENNESS and Pitié/PITY) to mollify Refusal, and the arrival of Venus to warm up Responsiveness again. But this in turn provokes a counter-campaign because Jalousie (JEALOUSY, meaning the repressive forces around or within the Rose) remonstrates with Responsiveness and with Honte (MODESTY, sometimes rendered "Shame"[12]). Modesty and Pöor (TIMIDITY) hasten away to wake up Refusal from where he has gone to sleep, a visually engaging scene very frequently featured in the illuminated manuscripts. The upshot is the construction of a castle around the rose-plot and a tower in which to render Responsiveness inaccessible, and it is this image (rather than the Lover's forlorn ensuing laments) that usually constitutes the last illustration to Guillaume's part of the poem.

Illuminated manuscripts enforce with rubrics and author-portraits what the narrative itself does not here disclose — the junction between Guillaume's and Jean's parts of the poem.

---

[11] Dangiers' club comes from the forest of *Refus* (15,287). "Refusal" is adopted by Leslie C. Brook, "Jalousie and Jealousy in Jean de Meun's *Rose*," *Romance Quarterly* 41 (1994): 59–70 (here 60). Other alternatives are "Reserve" (cf. "figure de la réserve caractéristique de la dame courtoise," Eric Hicks, "Donner à voir: Guillaume de Lorris ou le Roman Impossible," *Etudes de Lettres* 37 (1994): 93–104 (here 97); or "Aloofness" (Priscilla Martin renders Dangiers as "a woman's sexual aloofness," *Chaucer's Women: Nuns, Wives and Amazons* [Basingstoke: Macmillan, 1990], 59). Perhaps both of these understate the threatening energy of Guillaume's personification as perceived by the Lover, emphasised by C. S. Lewis in a celebrated discussion of Dangiers in *The Allegory of Love* (Oxford: Oxford University Press, 1936), 124. For a recent summary see McMunn, "Iconography of Dangier," 87.

[12] Hence defined in modern French as *pudeur* by Hicks, "Donner à voir," 100.

Introduction

Reason now reappears and lectures the Lover. (Jean compiles massive speeches for his personifications, so a conspicuous function of miniatures in the continuation, even more than in Guillaume's text, is to announce visually the intervention of each new speaker.) Reason's discourse attempting to divert the Lover from his material quest can attract further illustrations where she discusses the instability of Fortune and its exemplification in famous lives such as Virginia's and Nero's. When the Lover abandons Reason and resorts to Friend instead, illuminators usually signal that with another "conversation" image; optionally they go on to represent also Friend's nostalgia for a Golden Age devoid of lordship or sexual possessiveness. Within the harangue of a bullying misogynistic character next imagined by Friend, the Jalous (or JEALOUS HUSBAND), an allusion to Lucretia's suicide may attract representation, though more compulsory is a miniature of the husband abusing his wife.

A new direction is promised and visually represented as the Lover encounters an alternative arbiter of love, Richece (WEALTH), only to be rejected by her. The Lover is running out of options and needs reassurance from the God of Love, which is forthcoming in some miniatures as a kindly patting of the forehead at this point. The God takes action, summoning his "barons," who may appear visually in military panoply. Jean interrupts the poem here — at its midpoint overall — to address the reader, so an authorial picture is sometimes found here. But with ten thousand lines still to go, illustration thins somewhat as Jean's narrative proceeds. The second half of the poem typically commands no more than one-third of the illustrations.

The incipient military siege of the fortress of Jalousie recedes with the intrusion of a new speaker, Faus Semblant (FRAUD),[13] a self-styled friar who is depicted (with or without his mock-pious female associate CONSTRAINED ABSTINENCE) volunteering his services to the God. As Douglas Kelly has observed, the pair of them "personify the increasing degeneration of Amant's love."[14] Illustrators do little with Fraud's satirical revelations of religious hypocrisy: they pass instead to the next action at the castle. They may show the two cronies at the castle gate tackling one of the Rose's guardians, Male Bouche (SCANDAL,[15] thought of as a phenomenon restraining sexual interest). Also, or alternatively, in one of the poem's most coolly bloodthirsty moments, Fraud is represented slitting Scandal's throat while the latter kneels before him as to a confessor.

---

[13] "Fraud" is a translation commended by Stakel, *False Roses*, 81, though the archaic "False Seeming" is widely used for this personification.

[14] Douglas Kelly, *Internal Difference and Meanings in the* Roman de la Rose (Madison: University of Wisconsin Press, 1995), 106.

[15] Often rendered "Evil Tongue" (e.g., Horgan) or "Foul Mouth" (e.g., Dahlberg).

Introduction

The way is now clear to resume contact with Responsiveness if the co-operation of the OLD WOMAN appointed as chaperone can be secured (La Vielle is sometimes translated the "Duenna," but that term surely itself requires translation). She is most often depicted taking a headband of flowers to offer to Responsiveness on the Lover's behalf. On the battlements of the tower the Old Woman subjects her charge to lurid autobiography and to advice on the game of courtship. Exemplary materials in her speech sometimes qualify for illustration — the tragic fate of monogamous women like Dido and Phyllis, and, more bizarrely (in their literal representation), nature's drive for freedom as exemplified in caged birds or trapped fish. The upshot is that Responsiveness becomes open to the Lover again — but only for Refusal to emerge, brandishing his club once more.

The God of Love resorts to all-out war. Illustrators show a general siege, or individual combatants, especially Openness and Refusal who fight each other first. Making no headway, the God sends for the help of Venus. On her arrival a mighty oath is sworn against opponents of heterosexuality, overheard by Nature from the forge in which (as illuminations frequently show) she is at her work of forging creatures. Lamenting the consequences of her role in creating humankind since humanity fails to ensure its perpetuation, she makes ostensibly a "confession" but actually a hugely rambling philosophical disquisition before her priest Genius. The "confession" may be presented in a miniature: sometimes also shown is a couple in bed, illustrating Genius's cynical allegations about wives' ways of discovering husbands' secrets. Nature asks Genius to carry her complaint to the God of Love, and excommunicate any who work against their cause. Manuscripts may next depict the God installing Genius in episcopal robes, though a miniature of the sequel where Genius preaches to the congregation of Love's barons is particularly prominent in the tradition.

Within Genius's "sermon," options for illustration include a contrast drawn between the Rose Garden of Love and the Celestial Park. However, pictorial manuscript tradition in the closing stages of the poem is dominated by two representations: the return to attack, as Venus prepares to shoot a firebrand at a sexual icon in the castle; and the inserted story of Pygmalion's passion for a female form sculpted by his own hands. Just as Venus brought a spark of life to Pygmalion's statue, so she ends the reign of Dangiers/Refusal by applying her torch to the castle. Some manuscripts depict the culmination, whether in terms of the Lover's orgasmic "pilgrimage" metaphor (a pilgrim figure is represented probing the "shrine" of female sexuality), or in terms of a final act of despoliation as he plucks a rose.

We suggested that this résumé would be indicative of illustrations "characteristic" of a fairly extensive cycle of *Rose* illuminations, which on the above basis could add up to sixty miniatures. Yet there is not any such thing as a characteristic cycle. In no two illuminated manuscripts of the poem does the selection of scenes

INTRODUCTION

ever seem to coincide, even where (as McMunn observes) the actual number of illustrations is the same.[16] This becomes very apparent when comparative tables are assembled to show which scenes are illustrated, or not, in which manuscript, as they have been by Lori Walters for four similar mid-fourteenth-century manuscripts; the word "absent" wanders about from column to column disclosing that occasionally even one of the most persistent scenes goes missing — such as that of Oiseuse/Ease and the Lover.[17] Nevertheless, the episodes we have picked out as characteristic do have, so to speak, a high attendance rate in the illuminated manuscripts. That is, there was a core of loci at which miniatures were usually to be found if the manuscript's illustration programme was more than minimal. Evidently where corners were to be cut, some scenes were considerably less optional than others. Just which were dispensed with—if not dictated by purchaser or bookseller — might be up to the whim of the scribe, in conjunction with the selectivity of an illuminated exemplar (unless an unilluminated one was being used). In the other direction, a profusely illustrated manuscript might do little more than multiply "talk" scenes, B speaking to C, X advising Y, C rebuking X. Yet at the same time it is clear that the taste of some buyers or scribes put a priority on the classicising elements of Jean's poem — the stories of Nero, Dido, Lucrece — and made sure to pack in miniatures on such subjects.

So much for the "characteristic" *Rose* cycle, so far as it can be pinned down. What, other than intercontinental travel, are the resources available for studying these materials further?

Rose illuminations can of course be studied by the determined enthusiast in microfilms and transparencies made available by libraries around the world, the Bodleian Library in Oxford being conspicuous for its unparsimonious provision. Generally, so far as availability in printed publications is concerned, the tally must be reckoned "thin, but growing." Not counting discussions involving just a few reproductions, there are really seven substantial published resources to date. Three of these seven are fairly widely accessible. Four others are much harder to obtain. The reader will find further critical discussion of most of them in Chapter One, but a word or two about what reproductions can be found in them, and how the present book differs from or complements their approach, seems timely here.[18]

---

[16] "In Love and War," 169.

[17] BN MS fr. 24388; see Walters, "A Parisian Manuscript," 38, Table I.

[18] For smaller groups of reproductions see: D. W. Robertson Jr., *A Preface to Chaucer* (Princeton: Princeton University Press, 1962), with sixteen miscellaneous miniatures; Guillaume de Lorris and Jean de Meun, *The Romance of the Rose*, trans. Harry W. Robbins, ed. Charles W. Dunn (New York: Dutton, 1963), with fifteen miniatures from three manuscripts in the Pierpont Morgan library, New York; Rosemond Tuve, *Allegorical Imagery: Some Mediaeval Books and Their Posterity* (Princeton: Princeton University Press, 1966), with

INTRODUCTION

In the "hard-to-obtain" group, Alfred Kuhn's sixty-six-page article published in 1914 contains forty-five figures (mostly miniatures from various *Rose* manuscripts, but including some comparative materials) and numerous Plates, of which the most valuable reproduce all sixty-one miniatures from a fourteenth-century Vienna manuscript, which is the special focus of Kuhn's discussion.[19] These reproductions in black and white would be even more helpful if they did not snip the framed pictures hygienically out of their contexts. The consequence is that the viewer cannot retrieve the surrounding rubrication or text.

Simonetta Peruzzi's 1986 study of another fourteenth-century illuminated manuscript now in Florence is of similar length (seventy-six pages) but published as a small book.[20] It includes twenty-nine plates, mostly in color, but only seventeen are from the Florence manuscript, while the remainder exemplify Peruzzi's interest in forging stylistic connections with illuminations of other texts. The Florence miniatures are presented with minimal (sometimes no) surrounding text, but Peruzzi supplies a scrupulous schedule of rubrics and textual locations, within a complete listing of the rubrics throughout the manuscript. More recently still, Eberhard König has produced two studies. The first is a two-volume facsimile and analysis of a Vatican *Rose*, which may be the earliest extant illustrated version. Few libraries in the English-speaking educational world possess this lavish production in the "Codices e Vaticanis selecti" series.[21] More surprising is the similar unavailability of König's thriftier 1992 study of all the illuminated Vatican *Rose* manuscripts, with fifty-four illustrations, many in color, mostly drawing again on the manuscript presented in his earlier facsimile production.[22]

In our category of "more readily accessible" publications containing significant numbers of illustrations, John Fleming's study is the earliest.[23] His full-length

---

fifteen figures including a few woodcut illustrations as well as diverse miniatures; Walters, "A Parisian Manuscript," with eight miniatures including four from Princeton University Library, MS Garrett 126; and several articles by McMunn, notably "Animal Imagery," with sixteen illustrations from various manuscripts, and "In Love and War," with eleven illustrations.

[19] Alfred Kuhn, "Die Illustration des *Rosenromans*," *Jahrbuch der Kunsthistorischen Sammlungen des allerhöchsten Kaiserhauses* 31.1 (1912): 1–66.

[20] Simonetta Mazzoni Peruzzi, *Il Codice Laurenziano* Acquisti e Doni *153 del "Roman de la Rose,"* Società Dantesca Italiana, Quaderno 3 (Florence: Sansoni, 1986).

[21] Eberhard König, *Der Rosenroman des Berthaud d'Achy: Codex Urbinatus Latinus 376*, with an Appendix by Gabriele Bartz, facsimile and commentary, 2 vols., Codices e Vaticanis selecti, 71 (Zurich: Belser Verlag, 1987).

[22] Eberhard König, *Die Liebe im Zeichen der Rose: Die Handschriften des Rosenromans in der Vatikanischen Bibliothek* (Stuttgart and Zurich: Belser Verlag, 1992).

[23] John V. Fleming, *The* Roman de la Rose: *A Study in Allegory and Iconography* (Princeton: Princeton University Press, 1969).

Introduction

book contains forty-two black and white figures representing a wide scatter of manuscripts (twenty-seven in all), but drawing particular attention to a vigorously engaging cycle of miniatures in a manuscript at Valencia. However, manuscript illuminations are not the sole or even chief focus of Fleming's book. They are introduced as contributors to his argument about the meaning of the poem. The supplementary use of illuminations is found again in the back of Charles Dahlberg's 1971 modern English translation. Dahlberg's illustrations are intended to assist the reader towards "an approximation of the perspective" operative in the poem's time, particularly an approximation of "thirteenth-century assumptions about the use of imagery."[24] His sixty-four figures comprise: all twenty-eight miniatures illustrating Guillaume's narrative and including the start of Jean's, in a rather early *Rose* at Paris (Bibliothèque Nationale MS fr. 378); thirty miniatures from a contrasting late fifteenth-century text at Oxford (Bodleian Library, MS Douce 195) indicating how moments in Jean's narrative were represented; and six more from four Paris manuscripts, to "illustrate special points" in the notes to the translation. Given the wide dissemination of this translation and its author's self-conscious concern with illustration, it is awkward that some errors of identification await the unwary viewer. Dahlberg is fooled by the thirteenth-century artist's use of a stock male figure into thinking that the Lover appears in two miniatures where, in fact, another character is intended.[25]

Also readily accessible is a 1992 article in the journal *Word and Image* by Suzanne Lewis.[26] She opens fresh directions in her discussion of forty-nine miniatures. These run the gamut of date and style and are investigated from an exploratory postmodern point of view, but it is perhaps mildly disappointing that the majority (thirty-nine) are from already well-known manuscripts in Oxford and London libraries.

What, then, is distinctive about our own venture? First, it concentrates on a restricted corpus of unpublished *Rose* miniatures at one library: not as restricted as the single-manuscript presentation in Peruzzi's and König's (1987) publications, but

---

[24] Trans., *The Romance of the Rose*, Preface, ix. Dahlberg's further comments on illustration are on pp. 22–26.

[25] Despite Dahlberg's caption, figure 23 represents not "Jealousy and the Lover," but Jalousie rebuking Bel Acueil in the speech immediately following. Similarly figure 24, captioned "Shame and the Lover," must represent Honte's answer to Jalousie's remonstrations. In both cases Dahlberg's mistake comes about through an erroneous tacit assumption that the illustrator cannot be representing Jalousie as a masculine figure who looks just like the Lover: but for male as well as female depictions of Jalousie, see Fleming, *Study in Allegory*, 46.

[26] Suzanne Lewis, "Images of Opening, Penetration and Closure in the *Roman de la Rose*," *Word and Image* 8 (1992): 215–42.

INTRODUCTION

akin to König's (1992) survey of Vatican texts in offering scope for comparisons within the corpus. Second, it reproduces in color every miniature from the relevant manuscripts. Third, its analysis of miniatures is not founded upon a commitment to locate them in a holistic interpretation of the poem like Fleming's and Dahlberg's, nor upon a thesis about the early evolution of the poem's iconography like König's, but upon sympathetic and skeptical inquiry into the extent and consistency of the illuminators' interest in the poem. Of course we do have our own interpretative agenda. We share Huot's reservation that medieval readers "may have been more susceptible than [Fleming] tends to acknowledge to the erotic suggestiveness of Jean's audacious language, and to the sheer entertainment value of an art of love,"[27] but while reaction against totalizing moralistic interpretation may itself amount to an ulterior holistic interpretation on our part, such reaction is not a guiding principle of our approach to the illumination. Rather, we seek to blend a knowledge of comparable representations in many other *Rose* manuscripts, and a knowledge of medieval iconography generally, with a realistic attempt to acknowledge the illuminators' *procedures*. In our view their procedures do not characteristically enable them to be deeply in touch with complexities in the text for which they are furnishing miniatures.[28] The craft in which medieval illuminators were steeped was not a craft of literary criticism, and their working practices were probably not conducive to extended textual analysis. Any introduction to *Rose* illumination properly begins with reflections upon those practices.

If the practices of medieval book-painting so far as they are knowable are not assimilated, it is only too easy to begin to assume that illustrations "form an important part of the poem's critical apparatus," that "there is an intimate relationship between the painted picture and the written text," or, in sum, that "it is one of the functions of manuscript illustrations to gloss their texts." These confident assertions by Fleming[29] are based on two slender pieces of evidence. One is a passing remark about the walls of the dreamer's room in Chaucer's *Book of the Duchess*, "peynted, bothe text and glose," with the *Romance of the Rose* (333–34), which Fleming takes as a "reference to painted textual illustrations as a gloss."[30] Yet if *peynted bothe text and glose* means more than "painted with the whole story," or if it is not a deliberate fantasy (appropriate to a dream) confounding the concept of pictorial mural with that of glossed manuscript text, it is most likely to be an imprecise reference to a pictorial mural narrative in compartments, with accompanying descriptive "gloss" (explanation of the pictures) in verses beneath each com-

---

[27] Huot, *The Romance of the Rose and its Medieval Readers*, 13.
[28] In this we diverge from the opinion of McMunn, that the illustrators were "consistently familiar with the text of the poem": "Iconography of Dangier," 86.
[29] Fleming, *Study in Allegory*, 8–12.
[30] Fleming, *Study in Allegory*, 9.

Introduction

partment, as found in medieval panel paintings such as those in Carlisle Cathedral.[31] It is inadequate to support a contention that illuminations themselves were thought of as a commentary or "gloss." Fleming also supports his contention with an observation found in St. Bonaventure, that the illumination of a manuscript both makes it bright and illustrates or throws light upon its meaning.[32] Here, however, Bonaventure is rhetorically exploiting the ambiguity of the Latin term *illuminare* ("to throw light").[33] Perhaps some illuminators did think in terms of throwing light on a manuscript's meaning, but they were not in a position to fancy themselves commentators compiling glosses, that is, compiling interpretations of the poetic discourse.

Several reasons why it is unrealistic to expect medieval illustrations to enact a "gloss" converge on the question of functionality. One is that, arguably, illustrations have always been functionally supplementary to written discourse — even in an epoch which labeled pictures "the books of the illiterate." Suzanne Lewis puts this starkly: "The text is already there before the reader — hence there is no need to replicate its content in images." She also maintains that "there is a profound gap between the capacity of images to convey meaning and the complex textually driven demands of allegory."[34] We shall have to keep returning to this vexed question of images vis-à-vis textual meaning, but for the time being we shall confine ourselves to querying, from the point of view of functional economics, what Suzanne Lewis calls "the prevailing assumption that text illustration is visual representation functioning as a substitute for the text" — in other words as the text's "'unwritten' exegesis."[35] Our reservations are based on the economics of book-trading, and the practicalities of illumination production.

In the book trade, pictures can impart attraction and prestige to a book; they can help sell it. If we drop for a moment the sentiment with which a post-industrial age views an era of handcrafted products, we may wonder whether the

---

[31] The editor in *The Riverside Chaucer* (p. 969) wonders whether *text and glose* is "perhaps simply a formula meaning 'the whole story'," but goes on to toy with the possibility that *glose* could mean "illustrations." When Jean de Meun himself speaks of "glossing" his text, he may be referring to explanations lodged *within* the poetry; Kelly, *Internal Difference*, 146–47 and n. 43.

[32] Fleming, *Study in Allegory*, 11.

[33] Fleming's source is a footnote on Bonaventure's discussions of *lux* ("light") and *lumen* ("illumination") in Ananda K. Coomaraswamy, "Mediaeval Aesthetic II: St. Thomas Aquinas on Dionysius, and a Note on the Relation of Beauty to Truth," *Art Bulletin* 20 (1938): 66–77 (here 72–73, n. 9). Coomaraswamy's note aims to show that Bonaventure and Aquinas share a theory of aesthetics in which brilliance of expression is synonymous with perspicacity.

[34] Lewis, "Images of Opening," 215.

[35] Lewis, "Images of Opening," 215.

INTRODUCTION

basic desiderata have actually remained the same. Nowadays, the design of a book's jacket is a perceptible factor in securing its purchase. In the Middle Ages, bookbindings might be fine or not but were not usually pictorial: in any case, many books were probably sold unbound. It was the presence and impact of an *incipit* miniature on the first page (the manuscript frontispiece, as it were) which fulfilled the function of today's book jacket. Medieval manuscripts are legion in which there is just one, perhaps superb, *incipit* miniature but no ensuing cycle of further miniatures, whether or not spaces were left for them. In the domain of romance, a manuscript of *Melusine* at the National Library of Wales is a good example,[36] and, as we shall see, two of the library's *Rose* manuscripts fall into this category.

Even where several miniatures were budgeted for, there was a tendency for business considerations to affect their overall distribution and relative quality: the advisability, for example, of assigning the frontispiece miniature to a superior artist,[37] and of locating the rest early in the volume. McMunn has drawn attention to "practical salesmanship" as one reason for "putting most illustrations at the beginning of a manuscript to make it appear fuller." As she points out, illustrated *Rose* manuscripts give greater visual emphasis to the early (Guillaume) part of the poem.[38] It would be tempting but implausible to attribute this to a recognition of what has been termed an "impulse to the pictorial" in Guillaume's writing, the impression that he deals not so much in narrative as in a series of *tableaux*.[39] Two other explanations come to mind. The fact that Guillaume's poem was in circulation before Jean continued it could have given the first Guillaume narrative a head start in illumination. Alternatively, scribes copying texts from extensively-illuminated manuscripts for commissions designated to have lesser numbers of miniatures could have taken the easy way out and simply left spaces from the beginning until the designated number was reached. But the retail explanation is probably sufficient. Two of the Aberystwyth *Rose* manuscripts (NLW 5013D, and 5017D) start with a flourish, offering an impressive abundance of miniatures to catch the attention in the first half-dozen folios; then no more.

In order to deflect inappropriate analytical pressure from *Rose* miniatures, some further demythologising of the process of picture production may be necessary. Hard information on this is notoriously scarce, and doubtless practices varied within regions, let alone in different countries. Yet some facts are known or can be

---

[36] NLW MS 5030C.

[37] Kuhn, "Illustration des *Rosenromans*," 50; Elizabeth Salter and Derek Pearsall, "Pictorial Illustration of Late Medieval Poetic Texts: The Role of the Frontispiece," in *Medieval Iconography and Narrative: A Symposium*, ed. Flemming G. Andersen et al. (Odense: Odense University Press, 1980), 100–23 (here 114 and n. 17).

[38] McMunn, "In Love and War," 169.

[39] Kay, *The* Romance of the Rose, 73.

INTRODUCTION

deduced about professional practice here and there; something can be learned from pictures of miniaturists at work; something more from the structure of the manuscripts themselves and occasional surviving instructions in them; and a surprising amount again from the kinds of errors that illuminators make.

Where professional practice is concerned, one difficulty is to decide what reality lies behind habitual modern reference to "designers" or "planners" of miniature cycles in books, and to illuminators' "workshops" or "ateliers" or "paintshops." Such terminology readily carries an implication — intended or not — that miniaturists worked together in sizeable congeries of some sort and that their productions were intricately thought through by someone with overall responsibility for the whole of each decorated book. The "person who oversees the work" on an illuminated manuscript, whether or not that person is also its rubricator or illuminator, may be designated its "planner" or "conceptualizer" according to Lori Walters.[40] But who did oversee the work? Certainly, booksellers or entrepreneurs called *librarii* are documented for thirteenth- and fourteenth-century Paris, and they could have been in a position to farm out and supervise the work on illuminated manuscripts. But the "workshop" concept may be misleading unless we are prepared to envisage a workplace generally confined to one master and an apprentice (though apprentices were expensive), or master and spouse and apprentice. The illuminators named in medieval tax documents in Paris and in London seem to work singly in small premises or "shops," adjacent to each other and able to collaborate, but independent.[41]

---

[40] Lori Walters, "Illuminating the *Rose*: Gui de Mori and the Illustrations of MS 101 of the Municipal Library, Tournai," in *Rethinking the* Romance of the Rose, ed. Kevin Brownlee and Sylvia Huot (Philadelphia: University of Pennsylvania Press, 1992), 167–200 (here 189, n. 3).

[41] For a summary of the Parisian situation see Jonathan Alexander, *Medieval Illuminators and their Methods of Work* (New Haven: Yale University Press, 1992), 22–23. The same production conditions are implied for late fourteenth-century London by C. Paul Christianson, "Evidence for the Study of London's Late Medieval Manuscript-Book Trade," in *Book Production and Publishing in Britain 1375–1475*, ed. Derek Pearsall and Jeremy Griffiths (Cambridge: Cambridge University Press, 1989), 87–108 (esp. 94–96); and forcefully asserted for early fourteenth-century Paris by Joan Diamond, "Manufacture and Market in Parisian Book Illumination around 1300," in Elisabeth Liskar (ed.), *Europäische Kunst um 1300*, Akten des XXV. Internationalen Kongresses für Kunstgeschichte, Wien, 4–10 September 1983, vol. 6 (Vienna: Bohlau, 1986), 101–10. Ann Hedeman, identifying seven artists in a group of three illuminated manuscripts of the *Grandes Chroniques* (late fourteenth/early fifteenth century) deduces that the artists worked in separate gatherings without seeing one another's work; *The Royal Image: Illustrations of the* Grandes Chroniques de France, *1274–1422* (Berkeley and Los Angeles: University of California Press, 1991), 149.

Introduction

It is realistic to suppose that in this context the individual illuminator actually worked on stacks of unbound sheets arranged as for quires, but from which bifolia with script complete and spaces ready for illumination could be extracted. The reason for extracting single sheets like this was that it is much more difficult to apply paint or gold leaf to the surface of a folio when it is folded in with others than when it is separate. But a moment's thought reveals that, if a sheet were extracted thus from its companions, a miniaturist working on it would generally have in front of him or her a folio of text on the left discontinuous with the folio of text on the right, unless it were the middle bifolium of a gathering. And medieval representations of illuminators at work confirm that an illuminator's unit of production was indeed the unbound sheet. This is particularly clear in a mid-fifteenth-century view of a miniaturist's workroom which shows him seated, with a bifolium upon which he works across his lap, while an open bound volume lies on the table in front of him. The bound volume would be a model or exemplar for the book he is illuminating.[42] Painting the bifolium on the lap would, however, be hazardous. The more normal use of a writing-desk is shown in the case of a marginal scene in a *Rose* of the 1330s, where a man and a woman are shown entering decorative initials into loose sheets of parchment, while other manuscript bifolia hang on horizontal rods behind them. This is reproduced by Sylvia Huot in the course of a discussion of the scheme of decoration in a Parisian manuscript of the *Rose* whose marginal narrative scenes, Huot demonstrates, are systematically linked not according to the reading order of the folios but across the front and back of the individual bifolia.[43]

Such a working practice limited the illuminator's scope for reacting in an extended way to narrative text, unless he or she were carefully following the text as well as pictures in an exemplar (copy-text). But the latter possibility raises the question, how long could an illuminator monopolize an exemplar — an existing illuminated book of sometimes considerable value, probably owned by someone else? The most likely scenario is that a customer would ask a *librarius* (in France) or a stationer (in England) for a new illustrated *Rose* with a certain number of miniatures like those in a friend's or institution's copy. An existing illuminated copy could be briefly borrowed, or perhaps viewed at someone's house, by the il-

---

[42] BN MS lat. 4915, fol. 1r; see Alexander, *Medieval Illuminators*, 32, figure 49.

[43] Huot, *The Romance of the Rose and its Medieval Readers*, 286–322, discussing BN, MS fr. 25526. For the man and woman at work, see pp. 321–22 and black and white reproduction in plate 21; color reproduction in Alexander, *Medieval Illuminators*, figure 204 (p. 120). A classic demonstration that the open bifolium was "the consistent unit of work" in the production of a 1430s/1440s religious manuscript in the Morgan Library is Robert Calkins, "Stages of Execution: Procedures of Illumination as Revealed in an Unfinished Book of Hours," *Gesta* 17 (1978): 61–70 (here 63).

Introduction

luminator when ready to work on a version which had been supplied by a scribe with spaces sufficient for the commission. But the borrowing or viewing of the exemplar might only be long enough to enter, either on separate scraps of parchment or paper, or next to the spaces for miniatures in the new manuscript, those quick marginal sketches or those laconic marginal instructions concerning what to paint which have tantalized manuscript scholars in this century.[44]

The point of this excursion into circumstances of production is to temper preconceptions about how absorbed medieval artisans such as the *Rose* illuminators might be in the inner literary dynamics of the texts on which they worked. Like most artisans, they were paid by the piece and hence were pressed for time, and their most efficient solution would be to gauge a miniature's requirements from the briefest and most local information — a rubric, the memory or notes of an existing miniature in an exemplar, a quick look at adjacent text. Jonathan Alexander strikes a suitably wary chord: "Sometimes artists may themselves have read a text, though often, it seems only the first few words."[45]

Moreover, as Lesley Lawton has suggested, the kind of *mistakes* they make militate against notions of intimate textual involvement. Lawton mentions a comical enormity whereby the illustrator of the story of a ring swallowed by a fish painted a fish with a sheep in its mouth instead, having confused Old French *annel* ("ring") with *anel* ("lamb").[46] Less hilarious but striking in another way is the case in a National Library of Wales prose *Tristan* manuscript of a historiated initial in which a queen is shown standing, dictating to a tonsured scribe who writes on a parchment roll. The artist did not read far enough into the folio's right-hand column, where the text specifies that Queen Yseult wrote her letter to Tristan "in her own hand." Or if the artist did read it, a preconceived image of how queens

---

[44] Robert Branner, "The 'Soissons Bible' Paintshop in Thirteenth-Century Paris," *Speculum* 44 (1969): 13–35 (here 16), argues that marginal written instructions in Bibles "are never in the same hand as the text," and is inclined to attribute them to workshop masters. For more discussion see C. E. Pickford, "An Arthurian Manuscript in the John Rylands Library," *Bulletin of the John Rylands Library* 31 (1948): 318–44, and Alexander, *Medieval Illuminators*, 54–71, 112–14. Hedeman thinks in terms of a "master list" of illustration instructions being maintained by a *librarius* for regular commissions: but an instruction might do no more than specify "clerks and nobles speaking and arguing together": *Royal Image*, 149.

[45] Alexander, *Medieval Illuminators*, 53.

[46] Lesley Lawton, "The Illustration of Late Medieval Secular Texts, with Special Reference to Lydgate's *Troy Book*," in *Manuscripts and Readers in Fifteenth-Century England*, ed. Derek Pearsall (Cambridge: D. S. Brewer, 1983), 41–69 (here 46).

INTRODUCTION

"write" letters has overridden the text.[47] For an example of how preconception can also triumph in *Rose* illumination, we may cite the case of the representation of Haïne in the Vatican manuscript studied by König. An instruction on the bottom edge of the relevant folio reads "Here we should have Haine." Instead of turning to the textual description for assistance, however, the painter resorts to a figuration *not* adopted by Guillaume: two men stand animatedly facing away from each other, their back-to-back relation signifying mutual loathing.[48]

Other kinds of muddle are also instructive. The standard scenes for the First and Second Book of Kings are reversed in one French Bible, according to Robert Branner, "probably because both show beheadings."[49] There are mistakes in one Aberystwyth *Rose* manuscript which suggest a similar kind of inattention. Particularly interesting is the fact that an episode of "Jealousy" is there confused with an episode of the "Jealous Husband." In the space where comprehensive precedent would make us expect to see the commanding figure of Jalousie overseeing the construction of a tower as a barrier to the Lover's yearning for the Rose, the miniaturist of NLW 5016D has instead painted the possessive husband abusing his wife — an image which precedent locates nearly six thousand lines further on, in Jean's part of the poem. It would take an act of faith to hypothesize a "deliberate" mistake here, an interpretative choice creatively collapsing one "jealousy" within the other. A much more credible explanation is either that the miniaturist was too cursory in checking through an exemplar, and adopted the second version because he or she missed the first; or that there simply was no picture in the exemplar at line 3797, so he or she substituted the later format of the Jalous as the best of a bad job.

Although other evidence in NLW 5016D discussed in the Commentary below will tend to corroborate the impression of a slippery relationship between miniaturist and text, we would not go as far as Lawton in disowning the communicative potential of narrative miniatures of this period. Lawton has emphasized almost mercilessly the impediments to individual interpretative function in medieval illustration. She notes the sway of the exemplar; the power of preconception (which, for example, imposed pictures of marvelous creatures in a book about eastern travel even where the text expressly distanced itself from traditional notions about extraordinary races thought to live there); and the resort to standardized pictorial

---

[47] NLW MS 5667E, fol. 288v. On preconceived visual schemata prevailing over textual detail see further Alexander, *Medieval Illuminators*, 113–14.

[48] Vatican, MS Urb. lat. 376, fol. 1v (König, *Die Liebe*, 24).

[49] Branner, "'Soissons Bible' Paintshop," 17, referring to the Metropolitan Bible and scenes which should be, respectively, the beheading of Ophni while a Philistine takes the Ark, and the Amalekite beheaded.

Introduction

forms or *moduli*, which, as we have seen in the case of Yseult's letter overcome specifics of the text.[50]

Such considerations enable her to cast doubt on nuances of irony which literary scholars of the *Rose* like Rosemond Tuve have been inclined to discern in visual echoes both within a manuscript and beyond it, and the doubt is right because an illuminator was indeed liable to repeat the design of, say, a courting couple in very distinct contexts within the poem for no more reason than that a useful familiar visual module was involved. Although the poem's narrative entailed various scenes unique to itself, illuminators characteristically deployed the stereotypes of the painting trade, the lexicon of their practiced *moduli*, wherever they could. Visual modules for archery, homage, gift-giving, one person rebuking another, etc., were pressed into service. Whole importations were possible: illuminators faced with the task of representing Jalousie supervising the construction of a tower needed to look no further than the familiar requirements of historiated Bibles in which Cyrus is always seen building a tower at the beginning of the First Book of Esdras. We shall have more to say about the resultant phenomenon of "intervisuality" in Chapter One.

Yet if Lawton is correct in her contention that when a medieval artist consulted the text "he seems to have done so only in a local and sporadic way," and that it is therefore risky to claim "a direct interplay between text and image," she is too grudgingly minimalist when she discusses the fourteenth-century *Rose* illuminations in the Vienna manuscript reproduced by Kuhn:

> The generalized style of visual narration adopted by these miniatures relies heavily on simple groupings and stereotyped gestures. They provide the barest skeleton of events in the text: for example, fol. 26r shows Venus interceding for the lover with Bel-Acceuil. The artist has chosen to depict the kindling of desire in Bel-Acceuil by symbolic means: the goddess holds flames in her left hand. Otherwise this miniature could be one of the many scenes of undifferentiated figures in colloquy with one another that appear in this manuscript. It would be perverse to claim that these miniatures present an interpretation of the text; they seem designed, since they are distributed throughout the manuscript, to break it into readily accessible units.[51]

---

[50] Lawton defines *moduli* as "the stock of motifs involving undifferentiated figures and simple gestures which could be recombined at will": "Illustration of Late Medieval Secular Texts," 45. Similarly, Diamond suggests that individual early fourteenth-century Parisian miniaturists "exploited the narrow repertoire of standardised pictorial forms" in order to respond readily to diverse types and levels of commission: "Manufacture and Market," 103.

[51] Lawton, "Illustration of Late Medieval Secular Texts," 46 and 43–44.

INTRODUCTION

How many of the Vienna codex scenes contain entirely "undifferentiated" figures is a matter for dispute. The figures are perhaps undifferentiated only to the glancing eye. A sympathetic appraisal would reveal what we are able to reveal about the formulaic-looking figures in NLW 5016D and 5017D: that minor details — a handclasp, unbraided hair, perhaps even the relative height of the figures — can signal meaningful difference when one is prepared to seek it. The vocabulary of medieval gesture was simultaneously both circumscribed and important. It should no longer be necessary to apologize for these simple-seeming pre-fifteenth-century configurations as did Branner, writing in 1969 of Bibles around 1240 that "a rather naive emphasis was placed upon gesture and expression" yielding "an apparently unending repetition of standing figures with one hand raised."[52]

Nevertheless, Lawton has a point. Miniatures, as she rightly insists, enacted certain functions that had little to do with nuances of narrative discourse. They were neon-lit stopovers on the narrative route. Generally they imposed plausible formal halts. Paradoxically, the more self-conscious the halt, the less radically it may affect the reader's consciousness. In some texts where miniatures always coincide with new structural blocks — the next chapter or book of the work — their power to affect a reading may be diminished precisely because they are like grandiose chapter headings. In a text like the *Rose*, which lacks the full formality of chapter-divisions, they may conversely appear more interventionist. Some of the miniatures declare a visual pause whether or not we could have predicted one, preparing us abruptly for an imminent incident or change of speaker.[53] It is not, as Lawton has said, that the moment selected would necessarily (in an unilluminated manuscript) seem hugely significant to the reader in itself. Rather, "significance is conferred upon it" by its election for painting.[54] But although that is worth something as an index of local emphases confronting readers of the illuminated manuscripts themselves, it is no excuse for building a medieval interpretation of the poem out of these local emphases which, in Lawton's memorable phrase, "aided the process of reading rather than of understanding" because they articulated the narrative into sections and clarified changes in its *dramatis personae*.[55]

In any case, the number of miniatures varies considerably from manuscript to manuscript, according to the price allowed for in each commission. The bottom

---

[52] Branner, "'Soissons Bible' Paintshop," 18.

[53] The relatively increased impact of miniatures which do not coincide functionally with structural divisions announced in the text is discussed by Peter C. Braeger, "The Illustrations in New College MS 266 for Gower's Conversion Tales," in *John Gower: Recent Readings*, ed. R. F. Yeager (Kalamazoo, MI: Western Michigan University, 1984), 275–310 (here 277).

[54] Lawton, "Illustration of Late Medieval Secular Texts," 15.

[55] Lawton, "Illustration of Late Medieval Secular Texts," 51.

Introduction

line is that the miniatures in NLW 5016D and in most other *Rose* manuscripts are less the result of an artist's meditation on what is important in the text than the result of a compromise between the payment agreed and the scribe's skill in budgeting slots for miniatures in an appropriate way. So far as commercial production was concerned, key decisions about illustration may be presumed to have been taken between the patron and bookseller or scribe (as Christopher de Hamel reminds us) "long before the illuminator was sub-contracted into the operation."[56]

Can there be some way of negotiating between the conviction that narrative miniatures are not a guide to understanding and the conviction that they furnish an interpretative commentary — even that they amount to a kind of *research* on the text, anticipating modern analytical endeavors? In our view the weakest point in the latter case is the difficulty of ascribing interpretative rigor to pictures in a situation where factors such as the book's budget as a determinant of its number of illustrations, the habit of adapting from exemplars, the scribe's function in assigning spaces, and the discontinuous state of the text in the sheets which constitute the unit of production, defeat one's sense of an illuminator's capacity to develop and impose an interpretation. It is from this point of view that we would have to disagree with Sandra Hindman, who, writing on illustration of the poems of Chrétien de Troyes, states that in her experience "pictorial subjects were nearly always chosen carefully instead of randomly" and that "omissions count for as much as inclusions."[57]

What we therefore propose, bearing in mind the cautionary possibility that most illuminators consulted texts only in a local and sporadic way, is that miniatures can yield a kind of *accidental* interpretative profit. If the miniatures have no inherent interpretative authority, they can nevertheless trigger significant interpretative questions for the reader, medieval or modern. Most often they do so for reasons having to do with an illustrator's knee-jerk response to the visual conventions entailed in a particular rubric. But if the result is a purely accidental problematization or elucidation of the text for the reader, the fact that it is adventitious does not invalidate its usefulness. It is from such a point of view that we would be able to agree with another formulation by Hindman — that "the miniatures, when read with their texts, prompt distinctive and sometimes highly inventive readings"[58] — only our sense of this process is that the "prompting" is an *ad hoc*

---

[56] Christopher de Hamel, *Medieval Craftsmen: Scribes and Illuminators* (London: British Museum Press, 1992), 48; and see Kathleen L. Scott, "Design, Decoration and Illustration," in Griffiths and Pearsall (eds.), *Book Production and Publishing*, 31–64 (here 42).

[57] Sandra Hindman, *Sealed in Parchment: Rereadings of Knighthood in the Illuminated Manuscripts of Chrétien de Troyes* (Chicago: University of Chicago Press, 1994), 130.

[58] Hindman, *Sealed in Parchment*, 6.

INTRODUCTION

event between miniature, text and reader, not a premeditated consequence of an illuminator's response to the whole poem.

The event is accidental in several possible ways. It may be that illuminators, casting around in the text in the vicinity of the assigned space, present some detail (in the *Rose* an example would be the appearance of a male partner who is sitting with Richece/Wealth when the Lover meets her) whose narrative implications — when activated by the power of visual representation — engage our interest in the poem's deeper structures. The process is "accidental" in the sense that a configuration that is locally determined so far as the artists are concerned triggers structuring possibilities concerning the larger span of the text in the mind of the reader/viewer. Therefore, it may be that an illuminator's representation of particular incidents, such as the Lover's rite of homage or Venus's use of her torch, accidentally galvanizes the viewer into quite fresh speculation about, say, large gender issues in the narrative. Or it may be that an illuminator's formulaic treatment of, say, certain female or male figures is accidentally productive of insights into the economic, social, and sexual presumptions of the text.

Our Theory of Accidental Meaning in Illumination might come as a shock or an affront to some readers. The theory is not meant to exclude the powerful meditational and mnemonic purposes which illuminations in religious manuscripts could serve, or to deny a pressure of profound textual involvement which illumination achieved in exceptional cases: nor does it deny that medieval art is ubiquitously committed to sign-systems which are far from haphazard. Yet it does mean to define a credible basis from which analysis of secular narrative illustration can operate. Because medieval miniatures have the visual excitement of hand-crafted work, and because they frequently leap from the page in their high colors and their shimmering gold sharply outlined in black, it is very natural for a reader to want them to contribute importantly to the process of narrative analysis. They *can* contribute, as we shall try to demonstrate, but the often fortuitous nature of the contribution should be recognized. The miniatures in a *Rose* manuscript do not constitute a coherent interpretation of the poem so much as they constitute (and constituted) a series of pleasurable *ad hoc* visual stimuli whose generation of interpretative questions was substantially a matter of chance.

The miniaturists' choices were controlled by many factors other than reading the poem, not least by the authority of convention that gave an element of skeletal consistency to the designs produced for various moments in the poem. It is proper to speak of a combination of the fixed and the fortuitous in a particular illuminated manuscript. There is a certain fixity about the configuration conventionally governing a given textual moment: thus, to an extent, something is visually shared and conventional from one manuscript to the next, which ought to approximate an agreed "response" to a given stage of narrative. In practice, the nature of that agreed visual response may be so bland as to resist verbalisation: and

Introduction

in any case the element of stability is attenuated by the fortuitous particularities of a miniaturist's way of producing the received configuration. It is often (but it is not only) the particularities which accidentally harness a reader's thoughts.

The better to understand this phenomenon, more *Rose* images need to be made available in an informed context. Sylvia Huot has described the challenge of the need to provide a comprehensive survey of *Rose* iconography, a survey

> that would finally enable us to place individual miniatures in the context both of the complete manuscript where they appear, and of the iconographic tradition for the passage that they illustrate. In the absence of such a survey, any study of *Rose* iconography is necessarily somewhat selective.[59]

The present volume remains by definition somewhat selective, but nevertheless makes a move, if only a modest one, in the direction suggested by Huot.

---

[59] Huot, *The* Romance of the Rose *and its Medieval Readers*, 15.

Chapter One

A Survey of Iconographical Studies of the *Rose*

Study of medieval *Rose* illustrations was impressively launched in 1912 by Alfred Kuhn, though subsequently there was a hiatus in development of the subject until the 1960s.[1] In retrospect Kuhn's exploration, based on over a hundred illuminated manuscripts of the poem, seems governed by an over-optimistic desire to impose order on an essentially erratic phenomenon. For instance, he sought to define and to assign approximate dates to six "groups" of illustrated manuscripts on the basis of variant frontispieces or *incipit* miniatures. Group I (from the late thirteenth century onwards) depicted the Lover in bed, with a rosebush as backdrop and Dangiers/Refusal at the foot of the bed, while Group II (from the early fourteenth century) presented the Love Garden with some of its occupants. Group III (also beginning in the early fourteenth century) combined the preceding configurations to include Lover, Dangiers, garden wall or tower, and sometimes Oiseuse/Ease. Lover and rosebush alone comprised Group IV, whose allegedly baneful proliferation Kuhn attributed to Parisian mass-production in the mid fourteenth century. A shift towards logical introductory pictorial narrative — excluding Dangiers — characterized Groups V and VI. In the first of these the Dreamer moves across the picture from bed to meadow to garden entrance; in the second (in vogue from the mid-fourteenth century) the same movement is articulated into a sequence of four compartmental scenes within an overall frame (22–50).

This organisation by group is vulnerable because too much of it is leaky. Almost every element in Group III turns out to be optional — sometimes present and sometimes not. The four-compartment scheme in Group VI is sufficiently stable, but two-compartment schemes (incorporated in the Aberystwyth manuscripts) require more than incidental mention; and inevitably some designs elude the grouping altogether. In one New York manuscript, a Lover-with-Dangiers

---

[1] Kuhn, "Die Illustration des *Rosenromans*." Page references will be given in the text in our ensuing discussion.

Chapter One

scene is juxtaposed with twin compartments on the right. In the lower compartment the Lover kneels to a lady: he is transfixed by an arrow shot by the God of Love, who is pictured above enthroned and armed with his bow.[2]

The most disconcerting aspect of Kuhn's grouping is his unconcealed enthusiasm for the transition from the first four "groups" aiming at abstract or symbolic representation, to Group V where the "nonsense" of continuous space between bed and garden is replaced by a "truer" form of narrative illustration (32–33). Yet whatever the shortcomings of this evolutionary preference (almost inevitable in his time), his discussion was both thorough and productive. He acknowledged that the facts were in reality untidy. He knew that Parisian artists moved around, hence undermining attempts to localize manuscripts on the basis of "Parisian" style (42). He also knew that, despite his additional attempt to divide *Rose* illustration into four typical cycles — comprising frontispiece only, Guillaume part only, Guillaume part plus a few further miniatures in Jean's part, or fuller Guillaume part and much more substantial illustration of Jean's — this was a simplification of a situation in which manuscripts might be unpredictably "peppered" with varying numbers and distributions of miniatures according to patronage and price (59).

Although stylistic factors took precedence in Kuhn's study, he made a significant start on iconography. Admittedly, he proposed a slippery general distinction between routine designs reproducing simple visual models, such as persons in conversation or representations of kings or queens, and narrative scenes "distinctive" to the *Rose*, such as Narcissus at the well, or Amors locking the Lover's heart (51). It is slippery because "distinctive" medieval configurations are often composites of familiar visual models or *moduli*. Lesley Lawton argues that medieval illustrators' narrative images were usually evolved out of moduli, that is, standard figures and simple gestures "which could be recombined at will."[3] Although a division between "stock" scenes and "distinctive" (or "new") scenes is still accepted by Meradith McMunn,[4] Kuhn's robust assumptions in this regard are due for revision.

Nevertheless, Kuhn laid a good foundation for iconographic study. He had a salutary respect for minutiae of costume and gesture. Where gesture was concerned, for example, he carefully distinguished between a gesture with both hands which can be deployed "senselessly" and instances where the same gesture aptly communicates "agitated dialogue" (15). In addition, he had an eye for the wider visual context. He noted the apparent influence of Nativity and Jesse-tree conven-

---

[2] Morgan, MS M 120 (c.1370), fol. 1r. This configuration is conspicuous for "translating" the rose into a woman, hence also deleting the rosebush behind the bed.

[3] Lawton, "Illustration of Late Medieval Secular Texts," 45.

[4] McMunn, "Animal Imagery," 97.

tions over the design of frontispieces representing the Lover and Dangiers (20–22). He devoted extended attention to further adaptations from pre-existing models in visual tradition: from "vice" representations, from the "occupations of the months," and from author portraits such as those of the Evangelists. We shall come back to specific examples of these in relation to the Aberystwyth images. In general, Kuhn may be said to have observed but not to have interpreted such parallels, beyond suggesting that they demonstrate the transference of visual cliché.[5]

Into the interpretative void which Kuhn thus left, later scholars have zealously and sometimes rashly plunged. The literary mind finds it difficult to accept that medieval illustrations to the *Romance of the Rose* may borrow images pragmatically, in casual and unsophisticated relation to the text. One honorable exception is Rosemond Tuve. Her 1966 book *Allegorical Imagery* includes a section on the *Rose* that pays some incidental attention to its illuminations, albeit within the complicating context of discussion of allegorical interpretations imposed upon the poem by Molinet at the end of the fifteenth century.[6] She carefully acknowledges the practicalities re-emphasized in the Introduction to the present book. "We must bear in mind," she insists, that miniatures "were most often turned out by workers following models or rubrics, not by artists reading a text"; she urges that miniatures should not be thought of as "individually conceived 'illustrations' "; and that it would be "unusual," though "not unknown" for an illuminator to read the text.[7]

Tuve's pragmatic estimate of the degree of textual awareness among illuminators goes hand in hand with her suspicion that the kinds of ironies and subtleties of meaning which interest her in the poem (especially in Jean's continuation) are mostly not replicable in the visual medium. Although this results in an emphasis on deficit — on what illustrations allegedly cannot do rather than on what they can — it does at least prompt Tuve to attempt to articulate the impediments which she senses. The language of narrative, she suggests, is cumulatively able to embed evaluations (by which she apparently means the poem's ironizing hints towards a governing moral perspective) with "unobtrusive deftness." The visual medium cannot, it seems, match this "deftness." Where the narrative evolution of a metaphor gradually controls the capacity of ostensibly innocent words and things described so that they "betray hidden meaning" effortlessly to the reader, a visual illustration of a metaphoric incident works only by "giving away some of the secret hidden by the metaphor." Her leading example of this is the illustration of Jean's personification of Nature. Nature is seen in many manuscripts at her

---

[5] Kuhn, "Illustration des *Rosenromans*," 50–68 (section entitled "Die Vorbilder").

[6] Tuve, *Allegorical Imagery*, 237–330.

[7] These and the following arguments are to be found in Tuve, *Allegorical Imagery*, 321–29.

CHAPTER ONE

"forge," zealously hammering out a baby example of the human species on her anvil. In the full verbal context, the poem's forging metaphor participates in a redefinition of Love in terms of an ostentatious (and arguably semi-facetious) Campaign for Incessant Procreation. Tuve feels that the usual illustrated Nature yields little more than a conventionalized impression of the perpetuation of the species by a female personification. The point of Nature's role is perhaps better illustrated when the symbolism is abandoned (in Tuve's terms, "giving away the secret") and a manuscript presents a miniature of a naked couple in bed at the point where the text introduces Nature at her forge.

Tuve mentions — but with tantalizing brevity — some variation in the problem of allegorical communication. She implies that difficulties may subside where pre-established iconography exists for abstractions, such as the "vice" of Avarice with her treasure chest, or for exemplary characters such as Delilah, or for familiar concepts such as Fortune and her wheel. But the garden illustrations in her view remain "frankly representational." Her conclusion is that even where attempts are made to recreate the text's metaphors, such as that of the siege of the castle in which the rose is immured, they confirm "how difficult it was to suggest visually the simplest allegorical intent of the author, his psychological and physiological double meanings couched in metaphor."

In our view this despondent thought begins from the wrong premise: that illustration exists to copy narrative on narrative's own terms. It is better to begin with the proposition that, rather than complementing or completing the text, a miniature constitutes a separate representative space in which an image is offered that, however loosely, *arises from* the text.[8] Art historians have nevertheless noticed Tuve's cue. One who does so fruitfully is Michael Camille, whose discussion of Venus and Pygmalion we shall consider in detail later. He echoes Tuve when he remarks that a miniature which aims to illustrate the Lover's final insertion of his pilgrim staff into the sanctuary within the female statuette "can never suggest more than a small range of the poetic metaphor and allusion available in readings of the text." If an artist responds to the wordplay by representing the sanctuary as a woman's vagina, this produces a visual explicitness which risks collapsing the poem's "parodic sacral discourse" whereby shrine and vagina remain in continuous suspension in the reader's mind.[9] Camille shows how such reductiveness is especi-

---

[8] We agree with Stephen J. Nichols that the medieval miniature is a "representative space in its own right," but we believe that the procedures of illumination call in question his further identification of it as a "space of interrogation": "Ekphrasis, Iconoclasm, and Desire," in Brownlee and Huot (eds.), *Rethinking the* Romance of the Rose, 133–66 (here 154).

[9] Michael Camille, *The Gothic Idol: Ideology and Image-Making in Medieval Art* (Cambridge: Cambridge University Press, 1989), 323–24.

ally fraught in the case of Jean's poem because the fact that words do not resemble the things they signify (so that it is arbitrary whether what are named "relics" are renamed "testicles" instead) has itself become a focus of the text long before we reach the sanctuary episode.

Tuve's own understanding of the *Rose* is driven by a conviction that it is shot through with irony, and she therefore lays emphasis on one mock-trinitarian miniature of a fountain in the "heavenly park" described by Genius, which appears to confirm an ironic reading. Yet she quite clearly does not find general confirmation of this among the poem's illustrations, and in this respect she differs signally from John Fleming, whose book on the *Rose* appeared three years later.

All recent iconographical discussion of the poem has been indebted to John Fleming's 1969 Princeton monograph *The Roman de la Rose: A Study in Allegory and Iconography*, which was the fruit of his 1963 doctoral thesis on the poem and its manuscript illustrations. There is no doubting the influentiality of Fleming's supremely confident and adversarial book. In the absence of any other full-length English iconographic account of the poem, and with the added allure of forty-two reproductions from rarely-seen manuscripts, it was destined to become a landmark study. Driven by the twin impulses of a deeply-held belief that the *Rose* had a fundamentally moral intention, and of a belief that the miniatures, rightly read, would serve to corroborate that moral intention, the book sharply contested the view propounded in an earlier study by Gunn,[10] that the poem is a hymn to sexuality and procreation. Such a view may have deserved revision, but with hindsight Fleming's determination to correct it can be seen to have led towards extravagant misapprehension in another direction. It led towards a totalizing conviction about moral meanings, admitting no equivocality in the text, and it entailed a corresponding preference for miniatures capable of reinforcing suitable moral meanings.

Fleming's book was full of laudable ambitions. In general, he wanted to stimulate fresh critical reading of the *Rose* rather than mere lip-service to it, by challenging conventional perception (for example, by declaring that "the great Lady" of the poem is "not the rosebud" but Lady Reason, and by proposing that its meaning transcends "phallicism").[11] Other laudable objectives were to suggest that an allegorical poem does not have to be hard to read, and to draw attention to evidence about early responses to the text.

Again, so far as the poem's illumination was concerned, he properly questioned Kuhn's "evolutionary" thinking. As we have seen, Kuhn had presumed that increasingly naturalistic fifteenth-century techniques paying new attention to plausi-

---

[10] Alan M. F. Gunn, *The Mirror of Love: A Reinterpretation of* The Romance of the Rose (Lubbock, TX: Texas Tech Press, 1952).

[11] Fleming, *Study in Allegory*, 45 and 134. Further page references are given in our text.

bility of space and movement necessarily constituted superior illustration of the poem. Fleming exposed the banality and anachronism of this progressive theory of illustration. In the process, he cogently described major features of the earliest period of illustration:

> Characteristically, the illustrations of the earlier fourteenth century present frozen abstractions against a tight, unyielding, panchromatic background composed of geometrical designs. Such illustrations are idealized in that they present concepts in the abstract rather than in exemplification in a spatial continuum. (39)

Whatever reservations one might have about the epithet "frozen" here, Fleming argues persuasively that this earlier technique was well suited to the concise allegorical methodology of Guillaume, and he absorbingly suggests that if the greater verisimilitude of later fourteenth- and fifteenth-century illumination was "closer" to anything, it was closer to Jean's tendency to give some allegorical figures a veneer of verisimilitude — though the crux, for Fleming, is that Jean remained committed to representing abstract ideas and morals, not lifelike individuals.

It is this conviction that informs the use of the term "iconography" in the title and body of his book. The reader anticipating a substantially visual study on the basis of the typical dictionary definition of *iconography* as "the study of artistic images or symbols"[12] may be disappointed to find that for Fleming, illustrations are ancillary to "icons," that is, they are ancillary to the underlying and abstract concepts assumed to govern the poem's meaning. Thus the judgements required to evaluate figures such as Venus or Nature, he argues, are "pre-eminently iconographic — that is, they involve the correct identification of the significant content of icons" (185). Occasionally he seems to use "iconography" to denote the way in which something is illustrated (207): but mostly he is committed to a theory that an "iconographic" technique — whether textual or pictorial — is one which invokes "discursive concepts" familiar in the culture and existing independently of the immediate narrative (236). (For example, the significant content of the icon articulated through the Pygmalion episode near the end of the poem is allegedly "idolatry.") The theory is somewhat elusive, and its doorway for traffic in external "concepts" is wide open for the importation of moral significance on a grand scale.

Fleming's *a priori* instinct is that the poem must be read as a systematic moral structure about sin. On the moral issue he is "insistent" (his own word for it, 79), schoolmasterly, even propagandist. The propaganda appears in studied assertion of

---

[12] *The Concise Oxford Dictionary of Current English*, 9th ed., ed. Della Thompson (Oxford: Oxford University Press, 1995).

the poem's "interest in abstract moral reality" (35) or of its "theological drift" — in his view "there is always a theological drift" (37) — but also appears more insidiously in coded allusions and turns of phrase. Turns of phrase aim at premature defeat of the reader's neutrality, as when Fleming emotively describes the "handshaking of the Lover and Oiseuse" in one miniature as "lubricious" (34) even though the handclasp depicted there is not negatively marked in any clear way.[13]

Fleming's moralizing iconographical interpretation invites two kinds of critical observation. In a moment we shall see that one of these concerns his theory of how the miniatures support the morality. But first, there is the question of the *irony* that has to be systematically detected in the poem if — when the text ostensibly invites the reader into empathy with its sensual, this-worldly narrator and his quest — it is to be adjudged as having "always a theological drift." Fleming's first chapter concludes by underlining the "ironic" intent of the poem (50–51): behind the fable of its hero's amorous yearnings and exploits we are to diagnose an archetypal foolish figure of humanity, "a Hercules at the crossroads who consistently chooses the wrong road" (53) and therefore presents an ironic spectacle to the reader's superior judgement.

The crux is not whether one is prepared, as most readers are, to find an intermittent vein of irony in some of the Lover's (or other characters') postures, or to see the poem as a debate about relations between passion and morality, between the sexual and the sacral. Rather, Fleming demands that we read in terms of total irony and comprehensive moral intent.[14] This actually produces an extraordinary paradox, because it entails that one of the most moral and eminent of the earliest critics of the *Rose*, the Parisian Jean Gerson, writing around 1400, according to Fleming failed to get the joke, did not spot the irony, and so attacked the poem for its gross *lack* of morality. This qualifies Gerson to be (in Fleming's loaded phrase) "the first modern critic" (47) of the poem — that is, the first instance of unmedieval critical incomprehension. It is a curious spectacle, watching Fleming erect his own moral reading maintaining that the text everywhere promotes Christian morality through irony, over (as it were) the dead body of Gerson who thought that every salacious copy of the *Rose* should be burnt.

The truth is that Fleming has pre-decided the moral design of the poem and has determined that everything has to give way to it. Accordingly he holds that the illustrations as well as the text demonstrate "an interest in abstract moral reality" (35); and that the "content" of the miniatures "suggests and supports" a moral

---

[13] In another prejudicial moment, Amors and Amis and all the rest except Reson are dismissed as "the whole sordid and disreputable gang who would banish Reason to make war on Chastity," Fleming, *Study in Allegory*, 147.

[14] "Jean depends upon his readers to bring to the poem a set of fairly rigorous if commonplace theological concepts against which his ironies can play," 199.

interpretation (14, 53). Moreover, as we saw in the Introduction, the miniatures are implausibly alleged to be designed as a "gloss" (a kind of commentary) on the poem (20). Yet curiously, miniatures which are "close to the text" in the sense of providing "literal illustrations" (a terminology, incidentally, which is surely more problematic than Fleming assumes) are not the "glosses" which are most significant: these are characterized as those "which depart most of all" from the literal, those which use independent visual emblematic devices to illustrate "what the poem means, not what it literally says" (22–26). On such a basis an opening miniature which includes foxes jumping at fleur-de-lis trees — emblematic of the threat posed by friars to institutional Parisian theology in the 1250s, according to Fleming, and therefore responsive to a key element in Jean de Meun's figure Faus Semblant/Fraud (25) — acquires more interest than a miniature which merely shows the Lover in bed, or the Lover with the rosebush and Dangiers/Refusal.

Fleming's adversarial thesis was rooted in a crusading and controversial school of moralizing criticism associated with Princeton during the 1960s, and it is not surprising that eventually opposition began to appear. David Hult, for instance, articulates some of the criticisms we have expressed, emotively describing Fleming's approach as one which

> manifestly avoids the persistent traits of the manuscript tradition in order to concentrate on eccentric iconographic treatments at variance with what is to be found in the text of the poem. What results is a certain disdain for the manuscript tradition as a whole . . . Fleming makes it clear that, paradoxically, those illustrations striking closest to the text are the least interesting by way of explaining the poem's "significant content." The reader quickly understands that the real point behind Fleming's study is to interpret the iconography of a series of doctrinally oriented manuscripts, far and away a minority. . . .[15]

To these strictures a feminist might justifiably add more. When Fleming dismissed Gerson's reaction to Jean de Meun, he had to dismiss Gerson's ally Christine de Pizan too. Demeaning her as a "minor poet," Fleming had the cheek to generalize that her role in the early fifteenth-century literary quarrel about the *Rose* "has been rather inflated . . . by modern feminists and should probably not be taken too seriously" (47).

When it comes to corroborating his moral thesis from analysis of illustrative cycles, Fleming is almost always in difficulties. His exegetical disposition persuades

---

[15] Hults, *Self-Fulfilling Prophecies*, 75–76. Fleming's approach is also dismissed in Salter and Pearsall, "Pictorial Illustration," 104.

him that Guillaume's Garden of Deduiz is not the image of the courtly life C. S. Lewis took it to be, but an Eden-like locus in which action reminiscent of the Fall takes place when the Lover becomes obsessed with the garden's "dangerous" sensual allure. Yet he immediately concedes that the early illustrators cannot render, like Guillaume, a *landscape* of allegedly spiritually dangerous allure, because their technique precludes Guillaume's "suggestion of depth":

> the garden is reduced to a couple of flat trees, mere swaying trunks with bulbs of foliage attached.... The characters are pressed out against a two-dimensional background of solid gold or, more commonly, against regular patterns of brightly colored squares or lozenges. (71–72)

(Less apologetically put, this could serve as an apt description of the representation of the garden and occupants in NLW 5016D, e.g., in Plates 33 and 36.)

Making a virtue of the perceived deficit, Fleming argues that the lack of distracting topographical ornament enables these early artists to "strip" Guillaume's garden narrative to its "iconographic skeleton," that is, to its central moral action. The skeleton is visually expressed through the iconography of three scenes frequently depicted in illuminated manuscripts, and indeed exemplified in the Aberystwyth collection: the Lover's encounter with Oiseuse/Ease, the Dance of Deduiz or Pleasure, and the Well of Narcissus.

Characteristically, Fleming utterly polarizes the possibilities in Oiseuse. The possibility that she embodies a concept of "courtly relaxation" is opposed by the contention that she embodies the vice of Sloth or Idleness, a vice identified in Chaucer's *Second Nun's Prologue* as "ministre and the norice unto vices" (VIII. 1–2). No multivalence or creative confusion or rapprochement between the possibilities is admitted.[16] Fleming finds second-hand evidence for a strictly moral significance in a solemn commentary on a character derived from Oiseuse in a later French poem, which calls her the "queen and nurse of all evils" (p. 79), and in the claim that the vice of Lechery or Luxuria is generally depicted in Gothic art as a woman with mirror and comb. Guillaume's Oiseuse carries a mirror, and her only occupation, the text remarks, is to comb her hair. Illustrators of the Lover's encounter with her, Fleming observes, present mirror and comb "in selective conjunction" (76) while ignoring most other textual details of her description. They therefore choose to represent her as the "quintessence of lust" (75), though such is the moral authority of the mirror/comb iconography that neither Guillaume nor

---

[16] Kay's contrasting openness to multivalence is salutary: is Oiseuse a *Luxuria* figure, or "can she be identified with the love object? Is her beauty meant to imply that leisure is a beautiful experience, or that leisured individuals can cultivate their beauty? Is there some connection between leisure and femininity?" Kay, *The Romance of the Rose*, 25–26.

they allegedly need to signal her depravity in any other way — it can be left to speak for itself.

A number of important and contentious issues are raised in this discussion. Some of them were picked up in a counter-publication by Earl Jeffrey Richards published in 1982.[17] Richards objected that, in identifying the mirror-attribute with Lust, Fleming had overestimated the familiarity (in the later thirteenth century) of what was perhaps a comparatively new model among the range of received models for portraying Lust then current, such as a woman whose sexual organs are assailed by toads, an embracing couple, a woman holding chains, and a girl on a ram or goat. Without the defining context of, say, a discourse on the vices, the mirror is in Richards's view too weak a sign to signify lust at that date. Richards further observes that the mirror attribute is far from universal in miniatures which present Oiseuse. He then adduces various literary and lexical arguments, of which the most important in our view is the simple reminder that Guillaume's description of Oiseuse as a whole epitomizes contemporary stereotypes of female beauty: this enthusiastic portrait is above all, he contends, influenced by "the program of female beauty found in the classic texts of twelfth-century Old French literature."[18]

Richards did not get away with his temerity unscathed. Fleming exercised a right of riposte two volumes later in the same journal.[19] He sought to reclaim the "Luxuria" argument by declaring that the existence of other lust iconography was not pertinent: what was pertinent was that the "principal" significance of "a woman with a mirror *and a comb* [which Richards had passed over] in Gothic art" was that of Lust. Fleming's ensuing discussion explores literary evidence to conclude that medieval readers would "naturally" have recognized in Guillaume's de-

---

[17] Richards, "Reflections on Oiseuse's Mirror: Iconographic Tradition, Luxuria and the *Roman de la Rose*," *Zeitschrift für Romanische Philologie* 98 (1982): 296–311. For other noteworthy discussion of Oiseuse see H. Kolb, "Oiseuse, die Dame mit dem Spiegel," *Germanisch-Romanische Monatsschrift* 15 (1965): 139–49; Robertson, *Preface to Chaucer*, 92–93; John B. Friedman, "L'iconographie de Vénus et de son miroir à la fin du Moyen âge," in *L'Erotisme au Moyen Age*, ed. Bruno Roy (Montreal: Aurore, 1977), 51–82; J. Batany, "Miniature, allégorie, idéologie: 'Oiseuse' et la mystique monacale récupérée par la classe de loisir," in *Guillaume de Lorris, Études sur le* Roman de la Rose, ed. J. Dufournet (Paris: Champion, 1984), 7–36; Carlos Alvar, "Oiseuse, Vénus, Luxure: Trois dames et un miroir," *Romania* 106 (1985): 108–17.

[18] Richards, "Reflections on Oiseuse's Mirror," 307. His ensuing suggestion that *oiseuse* in French of the early thirteenth century might (for a short time) have meant "verbal frivolity" is somewhat strained.

[19] J. Fleming, "Further Reflections on Oiseuse's Mirror," *Zeitschrift für Romanische Philologie* 100 (1984): 26–40.

scription of Oiseuse an emblem of "Ovidian idleness" (by which Fleming means idleness conducive to lust)[20] "cognate with the capital vice of Sloth."[21]

In our view, neither Fleming nor Richards seems altogether convincing, for reasons which warrant exploration here. For one thing (as Fleming's last-quoted argument hints) this whole discussion about the "lustful" attributes of Idleness — or Ease — slides confusingly between two of the seven capital vices. Given the meticulousness with which medieval moral thought was disseminated through confessional treatises, there is something fundamentally peculiar about the proposition that either Guillaume or his illustrators would consciously have wished to submerge Ease, a relative (at least) of Sloth, in the guise of Lust. To be sure, in the collage of vice-figures from a British Library manuscript much alluded to in this debate, a woman with mirror and comb is identified in the text below as *luxure*; but, standing next to her is the personification of *pereisce* or Sloth: a woman idling, as it were, with the distaff which in proper use would be an icon of activity.[22] If the chief point about Guillaume's Oiseuse is that she has nothing to do except to attend to her hair and is therefore to be connected with the vice which Chaucer's Parson calls "Accidie or Slewthe" (X. 388), would illustrators really have been so ready to muddle her up with Lust as Fleming suggests? And, if they did not wish to envisage her as a figure of Sloth, this would tend to confirm that they actually interpreted *oiseuse* in a non-moralistic way, as that form of leisure which enables love to thrive: for according to Chaucer's Pandarus, those "expert in love" say that

> It is oon of the thynges fortthereth most,
> A man to han a layser for to preye,
> And siker place his wo for to bywreye.[23]

---

[20] He has in mind a famous Ovidian remark, that if one avoids ease (or idleness) one breaks Cupid's bow; Ovid, *Remedia amoris*, 139, in *The Art of Love and Other Poems*, ed. and trans. J. H. Mozley, 2nd ed. revised by G. P. Goold (Cambridge, MA: Harvard University Press, 1979); and medieval sayings deriving from this such as *Otia si queris, luxuriosus eris* ("if you cultivate leisure you will become a voluptuary"): Fleming, "Further Reflections," 30.

[21] Fleming, "Further Reflections," 32.

[22] The miniature illustrates the *Testament* of Jean de Meun in BL, MS Yates Thompson 21, fol. 165r, referred to both by Richards, "Reflections," 302–3 and plate 5, and by Robertson, *Preface to Chaucer*, 207 and figure 68. The masculine variant for the woman with "idle" distaff as indicator of Sloth would be a vignette of a laborer lounging in the fields: Tuve, *Allegorical Imagery*, 97 and figure 19.

[23] *Troilus and Criseyde*, II. 1368–70. Chaucer's *leyser* or *layser* is variously glossed by editors as "opportunity" or "time" or "leisure." But its defining context is a reference to having "leyser and vacacioun / From oother worldy occupacioun," *Wife of Bath's Prologue*, III. 683–84.

CHAPTER ONE

More doubt is thrown on Fleming's certainties if one pursues Richards's observation that illustrators are by no means unanimous in supplying Oiseuse with mirror and comb. The point is not so much (as Richards thought) that another attribute sometimes used is the key, with which she is to open the garden gate. It is, rather, that a very large number of miniatures give her *no attribute at all*.[24] They simply represent her as a beautiful woman.[25] In pondering this we may initially recall the suggestion that Guillaume imagines her chiefly as an icon of beauty, but we should go on from there to interrogate afresh what Fleming clearly believes to be the moral monopoly on the meaning of mirror and comb. That is, we should ask whether these attributes are able in various moral contexts to signify lust (sometimes vanity), precisely through an appropriation of the *primary* significance of these attributes, which has to do with a positive or neutral phenomenon, the creation of female beauty. In other words, it is possible that those miniatures which present Oiseuse/Ease with mirror and comb adopt an iconic means of signifying the concept of female beauty; their motive simply converges with that of miniaturists who paint Ease without attributes — it is above all a matter of representing female beauty.

The very dominance of Fleming (and behind him Robertson) in thinking about *Rose* iconography has prevented this sort of speculation from being explored and has foreclosed the evidence which might support it, except in a brief discussion by Carlos Alvar. Alvar contends that Guillaume sets out without moralizing undertone to describe an extremely beautiful woman, "and Beauty habitually carries a mirror: the reason why Luxuria appears with this symbol is that she is identified with the goddess of love — the most beautiful woman."[26] (Indeed it is true that Venus had long been characteristically associated with the mirror: the late classical writer Philostratus describes a picture of her in which she uses a silver mirror.[27])

---

[24] Our analysis suggests that some fifty percent of Oiseuse miniatures include no attribute; among the rest, the mirror and comb predominate, but some miniatures adopt either mirror alone or key alone. We are most grateful to Meradith and William McMunn for confirming in a personal communication that, of 120 manuscript which illustrate Oiseuse, 38 show her with either mirror and comb or mirror only, while 60 show her without any attribute.

[25] For examples, see BN, MS fr. 378, fol. 14v; Vatican, MS Urb. lat. 376, fol. 4v; BL, MS Royal 20 A. XVII, fols 7r and 7v; Morgan, MS M 132, fol. 6r; BL, MS Stowe 947, fol. 5v; BN, MS fr. 25526, fol. 6r; Bodl., MS Douce 332, fol. 7r.

[26] Alvar, "Oiseuse, Vénus, Luxure," 113–14 (our trans.). Alvar suggests that Guillaume would have been prompted to connect Oiseuse/*otium* with Venus by Ovid's remark that Venus "loves leisure" (*otia amat*): *Remedia amoris*, line 143.

[27] *Eikones* (or *Imagines*) I. 7, a second/third-century Greek text cited in Friedman, "L'iconographie," 66. Friedman also mentions (68–69) that a comb is an addition found in

Chapter One

However, mirrors and combs had for long been accoutrements of beauty. In the *Ars amatoria* Ovid instinctively resorts to them in order to express the futility of Pasiphaë's cultivation of her beauty when its object is to impress a bull, not a human:

> What use is it wearing your purple robes, when such a lover has no interest in your clothes? What are you doing with a mirror, in quest of wild mountain herds? what on earth is the point of attending to your braided hair? (I. 303–6, our translation)

For Fleming, the link with Pasiphaë automatically contaminates the conventional beautifying gestures. By virtue of mirror and comb Pasiphaë becomes, in her "bestial lust" the probable "literary ancestress" of Oiseuse.[28] In both cases, does this not invert the iconographical logic? Ovid, Guillaume, and the Oiseuse miniaturists all call upon inherited images for the cultivation of beauty. It is these images (morally neutral ones) that Ovid calls into play in projecting Pasiphaë's mock-courtship; the whole idea is that she is using standard concepts of beautification in a grossly alien context. These same concepts can be seen in neutral visual configurations spanning antique and medieval culture: from Venus handling her tresses while holding up a mirror in a third-century Roman mosaic, to the marginal illuminators of the Luttrell and Peterborough Psalters who offer images of ladies braiding their hair while either a maid or a knight dutifully holds a mirror; and again to the miniaturist of a prose Arthurian cycle in the British Library who presents Sir Gawain coming across a pavilion where a beautiful woman views in a mirror the braiding of her hair by the *pucele* who attends her.[29]

In short, the reason why the Church was able to — and wanted to — appropriate the mirror and comb to signify Lust was that these were culturally en-

---

some Venus descriptions, as when Claudian in his fifth-century *Epithalamion* (lines 99ff.) imagines the Graces arranging her hair with an ivory comb.

[28] Fleming, "Further Reflections," 27 n. 4.

[29] Respectively, Musée national de Bardo, Tunisia, reproduced in Warren Kenton, *Astrology: The Celestial Mirror* (New York: Avon; and London: Thames and Hudson, 1974), figure 12; BL, MS Add. 42130, fol. 63r, reproduced in Janet Backhouse, *The Luttrell Psalter* (London: The British Library, 1989), figure 62; Brussels, Bibl. Roy. MS 9961–62, fol. 74r, reproduced in Lucy F. Sandler, *The Peterborough Psalter in Brussels and Other Fenland Manuscripts* (London: Harvey Miller, 1974), figure 56; and BL, MS Add. 10293, fol. 83r. If it is objected that unlike the last three, Oiseuse/Ease herself (rather than a maid) carries mirror and comb, the answer is that illuminators do not generally interpose redundant characters in the *Rose*.

Chapter One

trenched as the apparatus of beauty. The Church eagerly translated mirror and comb into Lust *because* that was an emotive way of demonizing the cultivation of sexual appeal. That the beauty and the sexual appeal and the Church's moralization of it all focused on a woman's hair is something that feminists today would find entirely predictable as a symptom of masculine objectification of women. (Nevertheless there were medieval contexts, such as the representation of Adolescence in "Ages of Man" pictures, where a male can be found admiring himself in a mirror while combing his hair.[30])

Returning to the *Roman de la Rose*, there is an interesting supplementary piece of evidence for the kind of re-assessment of Oiseuse iconography — and by extension of much other allegedly moral iconography — that we are urging. The poem brings the Lover back to Oiseuse again after his initial encounter with her, when he rediscovers her among the occupants of the garden. Some manuscripts offer another miniature of her at that point. Somewhat perversely, it is a miniature from this *later* location in a Bodley manuscript that Fleming reproduces as a classic version of the mirror/comb iconography. Yet the earlier Oiseuse miniature in the same manuscript, inserted within the formal description in which the mirror and the combing are mentioned, is of the type that simply presents her as a beautiful woman. As it happens the later picture rubricated "Ouseuse portraite," which Fleming has selected, is situated before the text line "La belle Oiseuse fu apres. . . ." The illuminator, who did not illustrate the combing action in the first portrait of Oiseuse (even though in this manuscript that portrait immediately precedes a line praising her blonde hair), offers comb and mirror to represent "The Beautiful Oiseuse" in this second portrait. What we are arguing is that the impulse for her visualization with mirror and comb here and elsewhere may be as much that she is beautiful ("la belle") as that she is idle ("Oiseuse").

At the same time, her beauty is aligned with that of the sirens, who in medieval art also bear mirrors and combs. It may strike the viewer as a dangerous beauty, as it struck the moralistic person who incorporated a rubric in one manuscript signaling "how Oiseuse, who is not wise, gives passage to evil-doing."[31] In NLW 5016D the rubricator likewise prepares the reader — and conceivably encourages the illustrator — to think of Oiseuse in terms of youthful frivolity. The narrative beginning at line 81 is introduced, "How spring prompts youth to leisure

---

[30] Lucy F. Sandler, *The Psalter of Robert de Lisle* (Oxford: Harvey Miller, 1982), 40 and figure 47, showing a Wheel of the Ten Ages of Man on fol. 126v.

[31] "Comment Oeseuse qui n'est pas sage / A mal fere donne passage," BN, MS fr. 1574, fol. 5r, cited in Huot, *The Romance of the Rose and its Medieval Readers*, 280.

and foolishness."³² But this is a far cry from interpretation of Ease/Oiseuse simply as lust.

To claim that moral or religious iconography need not be assumed to have a stranglehold over medieval visual meaning is relatively unusual. It is usually assumed that the appearance, for instance, of a woman with mirror and comb as the "whore" of the Book of Revelations in medieval tapestry "proves" that these attributes have negative sexual valence.³³ The present contention is that the Church was attempting to *impose* negative valence on the more undogmatic cultural significance of such attributes in more open contexts. "One must respond with tact to the courtly tone of the poem," Fleming concedes,³⁴ but on the whole his book mercilessly abuses courtliness and ascribes superficiality to all beauty but the beauty of medieval religious doctrine.

It has seemed worth pausing over his polemic on the iconography of Oiseuse/Ease, both because major questions about relationships between secular and religious culture are raised by it, and because Oiseuse miniatures come closest — which we have argued is not very close — to supplying visual support for the moral reading of the poem. Fleming maintains that the Oiseuse incident introduces the first stage of sin (the stage known in the Middle Ages as "suggestion"), but visual iconography supplies little to buttress the notion that the Lover's introduction into the Carole dance of Deduiz/Pleasure or his involvement with the well of Narcissus are further calibrations of sin. Although Fleming tries to drag in a theological concept of the "old dance" of cupidity, he has to confess that since it is a "purely intellectual" concept, "the moral meaning of the dance is not reflected in the surface detail" of the dance miniatures (84).

As for the "perilous mirror" of the spring of Narcissus wherein the Lover sees crystals and thence the rosebud, this ought, for Fleming, to constitute a warning about self-love and about mortal commitment to material objects of sight. He considers illustrations useful in this regard because they often show Narcissus's or

---

[32] "Comment prin temps esmeut ieunesse / En oyseuse et en follesse," fol. 2v. These lines, followed by "L'Aucteur," are prominent because they occupy only part of a seven-line space left here in the script: possibly this was intended as an illustration space but was assigned for a rubric instead either for lack of a visual exemplar or because it fell short of the size of space (eight to ten lines) assigned to completed miniatures in the manuscript. This rubric parallels one in BN, MS fr. 1574, fol. 1v: see Huot, *The Roman de la Rose and its Medieval Readers*, 29; and eadem, "The Scribe as Editor: Rubrication as Critical Apparatus in Two Manuscripts of the *Roman de la Rose*," *L'Esprit Créateur* 27 (1987): 67–78 (here 68): but other moralizing rubrics in BN, MS 1574 are not matched in NLW 5016D.

[33] Tapestry of Angers, reproduced in Richards, "Reflections on Oiseuse's Mirror," plate 8, and Friedman, "L'iconographie de Vénus," figure 19.

[34] Fleming, *Study in Allegory*, 73.

CHAPTER ONE

the Lover's own reflection rather than the rose. Hardly surprising, one might retort. The entire point of the Narcissus legend, which such miniatures aim to absorb into the Lover's situation, is that Narcissus beholds his own image. Illustrators can only signal that it *is* the spring of Narcissus by pointedly showing the youth's reflection and shifting the rosebush to the side.

When Fleming relaxes into description of visual details and stylistic effects he is tremendously instructive, a pleasure to read: but he is not a good guide to the iconographical "content" of the *Roman de la Rose*, and an underlying reason for that is, perhaps, that he does not like the poem Guillaume began. Its narrative bores him. Complaining that "Amant's description of the psychomachic warfare is painfully tendentious" (98), he has imposed verbal and visual meanings more congenial to his own theological training. It is a training that produces a distorting and reductive moral glare, under which the combined poem's flair and mischievous attraction wither into predictability. Bearing in mind the distribution of subjects found in the Aberystwyth miniatures and the possibilities which we shall suggest that they may raise, it seems worth extending this critique to warn against two sorts of reductive distortion in particular.

One distortion concerns Venus and Amors. According to Fleming (191–92) these two "clearly" have to be seen in terms of the "moral categories of the mythographers": that is, categories which assimilate them into the framework of medieval Christian analysis. Given that such analysis fragments Venus/Cupid into either beneficent figures of celestial harmony or figures of anarchic libido — into either a positive force productive of lawful sexual unions or a negative force driving unlawful sexuality — Fleming declares that their role in the *Rose* marks them out as a negative force. They represent immoderate carnality: in a word, lechery (196). Building on this certainty, Fleming then suggests what distinction between Venus and Cupid/Amors is allegedly implied in the poem by their respective "dramatic" functions:

> Venus ... is the general force of "concupiscence of the flesh," considered as a moral defect ... Her son, Amours, as used by Guillaume and Jean, incites specific incidents of venereal love. Any lecher is a worshipper of Venus; but the man who has "pathologically fallen in love," that is, one who has cultivated a *passio*, has become Cupid's man. ... Venus makes the lover burn with concupiscence, and Cupid counsels him to keep his heart set on a specified object. ... Venus and Amours are specific moral ideas; as iconographically qualified in the *Roman*, they are serious vices. (196–97)[35]

---

[35] C. S. Lewis had earlier stated that Venus "belongs to quite another realm than Cupid," on the basis that she is the sexual appetite and "generative force in nature" as op-

CHAPTER ONE

Apart from the difficulty that the poem's language studiously avoids moral categories such as "concupiscence," the especially curious thing about this analysis is that it actually wanders miles away from the "dramatic function" of the two deities in the poem. Their function clearly splits along gender lines. Amors, who presides over the Lover's initiation into love and over his progress at strategic intervals afterwards, epitomizes male desire. Conversely, Venus first appears when Bel Acueil/Responsiveness cannot be stimulated in the female love-object. Venus epitomizes female desire,[36] and her torch is to women what Amors's arrows are to men, a point emphasized by one illustrator who shows the deities juxtaposed at a moment when they are on the brink of besieging the rose-castle: they each "choose their weapons."[37]

This division of labor is emphatically sustained throughout the poem. Amors is never in direct contact with the Rose or even with Responsiveness: the woman is Venus's responsibility. At her first appearance it is the breath of her torch (a *brandon flambant* whose flame has "warmed many a lady," 3406–8, Horgan 52) which softens Responsiveness into allowing the Lover a kiss (see figure 4). Later the Old Woman speaks of "the bath in which Venus makes women bathe" (12, 721–22, Horgan 196). When Genius intervenes to exhort Love's followers to heterosexual action, it is a candle supplied by Venus which he throws down to incite the company and the world — and from which a smoky flame is so spread by Venus "that no lady could protect herself from it" (20,640–48, Horgan 318).

It is difficult to be precise about the significance of the "torch" adopted as Venus's instrument by Guillaume and Jean, and frequently included by miniaturists, as in NLW 5016D (Plate 44). A torch had been associated with Cupid in classical and late antique literature: thence it had been borrowed as an emblem for Libido (*Luxuria*) in Prudentius's allegory of the combat of vices against virtues, the *Psychomachia*.[38] Is it essentially a phallic concept? If there is an implied phallicism, Venus nevertheless seems to govern its effect on women: heat, smoke, even "odour" (20,648) is imagined irradiating women like a divine emanation whenever she wields the torch: the torch's effect on women is therefore entirely within the goddess's agency. Hence Venus remains an independent arbiter of female de-

---

posed to Cupid's "refined sentiment," *Allegory of Love*, 121.

[36] See Horgan 338, n. to p. 52. Daniel Poirion defines Venus as "la sensualité féminine," *Le Roman de la Rose*, Connaissance des Lettres (Paris: Hatier, 1973), 79, and Kelly defines her as "female sexuality," *Internal Difference*, 104.

[37] Malibu, Getty Mus., MS Ludwig XV 7, fol. 100v, reproduced in McMunn, "In Love and War," figure 6.

[38] Lines 43–45; torch references are gathered by Alvar, "Oiseuse, Vénus, Luxure," 115.

sire. Fleming's claim that the role of the deities projects Venus as *general* fleshly concupiscence, and Amors as controller of specific incidents of love, is eccentric in light of these precise, gendered emphases; and his generalization that both are "serious vices" enormously simplifies the morally elusive strategies of the poem which its illustrators respected.

The same simplification undermines Fleming's view of the climactic Pygmalion episode in Jean's continuation. Pygmalion's love for a stunning female statue which he creates, courts, and at last successfully begs Venus to bring to life, sours under moralistic scrutiny into an exemplification of lust and idolatry, the negative spiritual implications of which are allegedly brought out in illuminations.[39] Fleming suggests that miniatures showing the sculptor's act of creation disclose an underlying obscenity, if not morbid necrophilia, in the way they frequently show Pygmalion hacking at the middle of a defenseless female body recumbent before him (figure 16), sometimes in the posture of a tomb effigy (233–34). But instead of joining him in finding here "the projection of the carver's fetid imagination upon a lifeless form," or "attempted sexual intercourse with a graven image" (234), we would see in text and images an enthusiastic exploration of, and problematization of, masculine fantasy. Jean is engaging critically with the fantasy of conjuring up a form of compliant female beauty.

Conventional masculine desire, Jean seems to suggest, imagines and objectifies female beauty as inert form. Michael Camille has rightly insisted that the illuminators draw on the associations of tomb sculpture in order to communicate that the sculptor's inert statue has the chill of death, is not alive; to communicate that the miracle needed here will be to give life to the inanimate.[40] Pygmalion's own effort of will (the egocentric male attempt to cast the female as sex-object) is futile, without the instigation of reciprocal female *desire*, over which masculine subjectivity really has no power. "It is not masculine art but the power of Venus, that is, of feminine desire, which can achieve consummation," remarks Sarah Kay; so the episode "derides the inadequacy of masculine art, and masculine fantasy, when they join forces to confine women in the role of object."[41] The poem shows desire arising in the woman, autonomously, only after the suitor Pygmalion subjugates himself in prayer to Venus. Fleming labels this prayer Pygmalion's "literal idolatry" because addressed to a pagan deity (235), but in light of our preceding discussion of Venus we would argue that the prayer functions as an invocation of

---

[39] Fleming, *Study in Allegory*, 232. Further page references to this discussion are given in the text.
[40] Camille, *Gothic Idol*, 327.
[41] Kay, *The Romance of the Rose*, 47.

the principle of female desire and subjectivity. (It is interesting that although what Venus actually does, in a parody of deific grace, is to *ensoul* Pygmalion's statue, those who illustrated her action gave pride of place to the torch as emblem of desire.[42])

Camille argues along similar lines but reaches a different conclusion. He posits that, while Pygmalion comes to recognize the otherness of the woman in his statue, he is nevertheless still involved in a power-relationship with her, after she yields by becoming flesh and blood for her maker in "a metaphor for the 'yes' of acquiescence."[43] Camille is curiously unimpressed by the "mutual awareness" which he himself discerns in the conclusion of the episode, where in Jean's words "she refused [Pygmalion] nothing that he wanted. If he raised objections, she yielded ... if she commanded, he obeyed; under no circumstance would he refuse to gratify her every desire" (21,147–51, Horgan 326). Yet surely this minuet of alternating compliance and demand between the two is as striking as the famous mutual accord between Chaucer's pair Dorigen and Arveragus in *The Franklin's Tale* (to which perhaps it contributes).[44] Pygmalion pointedly shares the obeying and gratifying in his new relationship, precisely because he has understood that the Venus-principle in the woman of his dreams must sometimes overrule, sometimes complement, his own desire.

In this absorbing myth Fleming finds only that "a sexual *passio* whose object is an image is satirically explored as a kind of humbug religion"(236). We have given an extended critique of Fleming's book because it has been so long influential, especially among English-speaking readers. In continental Europe it has commanded much less attention. Poirion's classic study of the poem, which appeared in 1973, four years after Fleming's, sidelines Fleming's preoccupation with irony and derision. There is no derision, writes Poirion, though there is "anxiety" about

---

[42] Venus "a l'image anvoia lors ame" (21,087), i.e., "sent a soul to the image" (Horgan 35). Thus in BL, MS Yates Thompson 21, fol. 138r, whose rubric is "How Venus gave life to the image," Venus is a Madonna-like figure who holds her torch close to the statue with one hand while her other hand makes the Christian gesture of blessing. The "blessing" distinguishes this representation — but not much — from the frequent representation in *Rose* manuscripts of Venus holding out her torch to incite Bel Acueil to allow a kiss (e.g., Morgan, MS M 324, fol. 24v).

[43] Camille, *Gothic Idol*, 333.

[44] The mutual interaction of desire between Pygmalion and his partner has been emphasized and interpreted as part of a concluding dialectic in the poem by Kevin Brownlee; "Pygmalion, Mimesis, and the Multiple Endings of the *Roman de la Rose*," in *Rereading Allegory: Essays in Memory of Daniel Poirion*, ed. Sahar Amer and Noah D. Guynn, *Yale French Studies* 95 (1999): 193–211.

the "perils" of love and the "force" of desire: the tonal appropriateness of Fleming's reading is summarily challenged: "Irony is one thing, a smile is another."[45]

Yet Fleming's shadow hangs still over more recent publications in English. Suzanne Lewis continues to maintain that Fleming's (together with Tuve's) work constitutes "a solid base from which most of us now view the *Rose* cycles."[46] True, it has been demonstrated by Sylvia Huot that one can discover in Flemingesque territory more smile and less derision. She emphasizes the varied thresholds of tolerance implied by a gamut of reactions to the audacious erotic/sacral interface of the *Rose* among the poem's medieval scribes and readers, including someone who supplied an intricate series of both phallic and sacred scenes in the margins of a fourteenth-century manuscript.[47] Huot conducts a remarkable exploration of what manuscripts can tell us about positive and negative responses to the moral challenges in the poem. However, in the very process of confirming the ambivalence which some readers felt towards the *Rose*, it may be that she has overplayed the moral issue once more, however judicious her presentation of it.

The problem of how to estimate moral and biblical allusion within iconography has emerged in our case-study of Oiseuse/Ease in this chapter and will resurface in our remarks about *Rose* frontispieces vis-à-vis the Nativity in Chapter Two. Huot stresses the need for caution, since artists "could have drawn on familiar patterns in designing new iconography without intending the new scenes to be associated with those on which they were modeled."[48] Camille, too, has sought to escape from the notion that secular imagery redolent of sacred art has to be read from the sacred point of view. He argues for a more fundamentally dialectical relation between the two, whereby "competing discourses existed" and non-religious art could "redeploy and not just borrow" formulas used in the sacred realm.[49] In an article about the kiss as a medieval sign, Camille explores the phenomenon further and coins the term "intervisuality" to describe it. Intervisuality designates

---

[45] Poirion, *Le Roman de la Rose*, 39 and 64 (our trans.).

[46] Lewis, "Images of Opening," 215.

[47] Huot, *The Romance of the Rose and its Medieval Readers*, 286–322 (for the marginal scenes of BN, MS fr. 25526), and 11–15 (for comments on Fleming).

[48] Huot, *The Roman de la Rose and its Medieval Readers*, 275 n. 6. Cf. Salter and Pearsall's position: "it is not that any underlying religious significance is being brought out, but that the availability of appropriate compositional models is an important consideration for the professional illustrator," "Pictorial Illustration," 104.

[49] Camille, *Gothic Idol*, 310.

a process in which images are not . . . stable referents in some ideal iconographic dictionary, but are perceived by their audience to work across and within different and even competing value-systems.[50]

Camille is interested in how, for instance, the medieval depiction of the kiss can signify both the prohibition of desire and its proper fulfillment. He decides that images were "malleable" forms, material signs which could serve certain social groups and define them against others.[51] Redeployability, instability of referent, malleability — these seem to us to be more useful criteria to bear in mind when studying *Rose* illustrations than the deceptive certainties that have often characterized discussion of the subject.

Modern scholarship is beginning to register the usefulness of making less ambitious, exploratory forays into the poem's iconography. Besides Hult's analysis of the nuances yielded by a range of author-portraits, and besides Camille's subtle interrogation of Venus and Pygmalion images near the end of the *Rose*, one can point to fresh work on representations of Guillaume's "vices" by Philippe Ménard and Herman Braet, and to topic-centered projects pursued by Meradith McMunn.[52] McMunn surveys the presence of the erotic, and also the deployment of animal imagery, in *Rose* illustrations.[53] In a further discussion she exposes the variations (apart from the constant attribute of the club) in representations of Dangiers/Refusal, a figure for whom many students of the poem might expect more consistency. It transpires that Dangiers may be gray-haired and bearded *or* young; he may display peasant *or* nobler status.[54]

Pending the fruition of McMunn's iconographic index, there still remains much scope for scholars working from more limited resources, as Eberhard König and Suzanne Lewis have shown. König has made an intensive study of the ninety-three miniatures in a particularly early Vatican *Rose* manuscript, perhaps as early as 1280, which he is able to juxtapose with three other later illuminated copies in

---

[50] Michael Camille, "Gothic Signs and the Surplus: The Kiss on the Cathedral," in *Contexts: Style and Values in Medieval Art and Literature*, ed. Daniel Poirion and Nancy F. Regalado, *Yale French Studies*, special number (New Haven: Yale University Press, 1991): 151–70 (here 151).

[51] Camille, "Gothic Signs and the Surplus," 168.

[52] Ménard, "Les Représentations des vices"; and Herman Braet, "*Le Roman de la Rose*, espace du regard," *Studi Francesi* 35 (1991): 1–11.

[53] McMunn, "Representations of the Erotic in Some Illustrated Manuscripts of the *Roman de la Rose*," and "Animal Imagery in the Text and Illustrations of the *Roman de la Rose*."

[54] McMunn, "Iconography of Dangier," 86–87.

the Vatican.[55] Together they reveal the evolution of *Rose* illustration over some two hundred years. While König acknowledges that this process partly involves liberation from early conventions and that later artists cultivate more rational canons of time and space, he avoids the Kuhn fallacy and sees no necessary improvement in that: for there is correspondingly an erosion of the symbolic strength, a reduction in the "value of the imagery" evinced in the poem and sustained by its early illustrators (59, 20).

In terms of symbolic density the iconography of the manuscript on which he chiefly concentrates[56] is vigorous but puzzling. It presents the "rose" drama with pleasing energy: yet as König explains, it intermittently seeks to clarify or interpret the symbolic action, as if not trusting the reader to get the point. Thus in several miniatures the Rose is displaced by a girl, or is juxtaposed with one in an expository move, a visual equivalent of saying "a rose; i.e. this girl."[57] Similarly, near the end the artist seemingly paints the Lover, not Venus, setting ablaze the castle of Jealousy (49). König works such substitutions hard. Venus *becomes* the Lover, he suggests, just as differences between Lover and Pygmalion, Lover and Friend, and even between Lover and Reason are blurred in allegedly purposeful ways (36, 47–49). In our view such blurring may owe more to simple error or to a ruthlessly thrifty deployment of stock figures: so, where analogous instances arise in the Aberystwyth manuscripts, we remain more skeptical about subtleties of intention.

In some other ways too our skepticism exceeds his. Whereas he would insist that the manuscript evidence shows that the poem was assumed by very early audiences to treat the love of a "young *cleric*" for the Rose (15, 19), we find the "clerical" option for representing the Dreamer or Lover to be both more complex and less chronologically significant than that, as will be shown. Nor can we trust another generalization, on the strength of a variant illustration of lovers kneeling to Amors in a fourteenth-century Vatican manuscript, that the *Roman de la Rose* gradually became a book for pairs of lovers who used it to honor their own mutual love (54).[58] The image in question is a variant of the normal representation of Amors firing an arrow at the Lover. Instead, in this miniature a young man and

---

[55] In our discussion, page references are to Eberhard König, *Die Liebe im Zeichen der Rose* (Stuttgart: Belser, 1992).

[56] Vatican, MS Urb. lat. 376, signed by the illuminator Berthaud d'Achy. The other Vatican illuminated *Rose* manuscripts are Reg. lat. 1522 and 1858 (both fourteenth century), and 1492 (fifteenth century). In a further manuscript, Ottoboni 1212, the illuminations remained unexecuted.

[57] Juxtaposition, in fol. 12r (*Die Liebe*, 28). Displacement, according to König, in fols. 10r and 13r (*Die Liebe*, 26 and 29).

[58] Vatican, MS Reg. lat. 1522, fol. 12r, at line 1679; reproduced by König, *Die Liebe*, 54.

CHAPTER ONE

young woman kneel, one each side of a tree on which the God sits. König confuses the issue by suggesting that Amors's arms are outstretched "as if to bless" both of them. Actually his arms are outstretched ready to hurl a dart or arrow at each of the supplicants. The artist probably includes the woman in the design for no better reason than that she belongs to a familiar visual model which has here been drafted in, a model which appears elsewhere ubiquitously in ivory carvings and manuscript marginalia. Its use as an illustration at this juncture remains interesting (it develops suspense from the God of Love's posture, along the lines "will-he-won't-he strike the woman, as much as the incipient Lover?"); but it simply doesn't sustain the weight of König's generalization about the developing readership of the poem.

Despite these reservations, König presents the images in the Vatican manuscripts with care and unpartisan appreciation. We have emulated his approach more often than we have been able to emulate Suzanne Lewis's poststructuralist *tour de force* on "opening, penetration and closure" in *Rose* illustration, even though her article gives an invigorating and provocative turn to iconographical study of the poem. It is a *tour de force* because it moves with heady freedom amidst every kind of "opening" or "closure" that can be extracted from the miniatures. The sexually penetrative trajectory of the action, whereby the Lover has to invade "liminal" barriers and enclosures repeatedly thrown up, is merely one of Lewis's concerns (though one that is powerfully presented). Around it she gathers a constellation of analogues: for instance, the Lover penetrated by Amors' arrow; "Bel Acueil" as a name which *means* "accessibility, opening"; the allusion to Nero's macabre opening up of his dead mother's womb; even, bafflingly, a suggestion that Fortune's Wheel "opens" onto the future yet remains a "closed" image of the world.[59]

This methodology, shifting restlessly among discrete conceptual categories and also among discrete illuminated manuscripts, is liberating and exasperating by turns. It is protected by the observation that the illustrations can be studied not as *representations* of the narrative but as "spaces of potential meaning." They "engage the reader in the interpretive process" (215), and Lewis primarily shows how they might engage us in ambivalent psychoanalytical inferences. She does not claim to affirm specific medieval interpretations, and indeed at one point doubts that medieval readers interpreted miniatures with any more certainty than we can (216).[60]

---

[59] Lewis, "Images of Opening," 227–28 and 235–36. Further page references to her discussion are given in our text.

[60] However, medieval readers would probably have known that the crowned head visible in a tree above the Lover at Narcissus's well in Morgan, MS M 245, fol. 11r, is not Charlemagne as Lewis guesses ("Images of Opening," 226 and figure 20) but the God of Love, who haunts a tree in Rennes, Bibliothèque Municipale, MS 243, fol. 14r and in

CHAPTER ONE

Since there is some similarity between this response and what we have claimed in our Introduction to be an "accidental" interpretative function in medieval illustrations, it is appropriate to use an example here to show where the similarity ends. Among Lewis's suggestions, a particularly ingenious and beguiling one is the argument that the representation of the building of Jalousie's tower or fort is frequently the last miniature found in the Guillaume section of the *Rose* because an unfinished building amounts to a concluding icon of Guillaume's unfinished structure. According to Lewis, the illustrated manuscripts avoid visual closure and create an image of incompletion, which serves as "a striking . . . visual metaphor for the fragmentary, open end of the text" (229–30).

To be sure, a narrative might readily be likened to a building in medieval rhetoric.[61] Yet it is implausible to suppose that illustrators were conscious of executing a "last" image of incompletion on (say) folio 30 amidst a book extending to some 160 folios, even if they knew that a depiction of a follow-on author was imminent. The building is of course represented as under construction in some examples because its function is specifically to introduce a new narrative phase announced at line 3779: "Now it is time for me to tell you about what Jealousy was doing . . . ," namely, to tell us how she oversees the process of fortification. Such construction was also a favorite medieval visual motif. On closer inspection, the *Rose* fort here is usually depicted in an advanced stage of completion; to all intents and purposes built, but with workmen putting the finishing touches to it (see figure 6).[62] Hence it does not bespeak "unfinishedness."

The truth is that the reader has been prepared by the narrative and by preceding illustrations to dwell here on retrenchment and attempted enclosure, on locks and bars and crenellations and precautions, on society's attempted hoarding up or seclusion of virginity. Speculation on the likely futility of the masons' strenuous labor may be invited. More subtly the image prompts reflection on certain gender paradoxes, for we shall ask ourselves why, if this is a fortress enclosing the Rose and defending female virginity, it is conspicuously instigated by a woman (Jalousie) to immure a male (Bel Acueil/Responsiveness) who is in some instances already visible within.[63] These are accidental lines of thought that we might take

---

some other *Rose* manuscripts such as Vatican, Reg. lat. 1522 discussed above; see McMunn, "Animal Imagery," 100 and plate 13. In the Morgan example, the God (like King Mark in *Tristan* iconography) risks betraying his presence to his prey because his reflection is visible in the water below.

[61] See Chaucer, *Troilus and Criseyde*, I. 1065–71, and the note to these lines in Benson (ed.), *Riverside Chaucer*, p. 1030.

[62] An exception is ÖNB, MS 2592, fol. 28v (Kuhn, "Illustration des *Rosenromans*," plate VIII), where a laborer digs foundations.

[63] E.g., Morgan, MS M 324, fol. 27r.

Chapter One

back into the text after looking at an illustration which in itself (let us remind ourselves) simply executes a rubric or instruction such as "Jalousie has a tower built to imprison Bel Acueil." It is rather more opportunistic, in fact even an imposition of interpretation, to assert that such illustrations advertise narrative incompletion. Lewis is an excitingly imaginative iconographical analyst, whose stimulus will be apparent in the commentary in the present book. But where does an imaginative response end and an opportunistic one begin? It is a central question in study of *Rose* iconography, and the reader will have to judge our own sensitivity on the matter in what follows.

Chapter Two

The *Rose* Illustrated: Commentary on the Plates

I. *Dating the Illuminations*

Although a detailed codicological description of the Aberystwyth *Rose* manuscripts will be found in Chapter Three, we shall isolate for attention here what can be conjectured about the affiliations and therefore the dating of the illuminations in these manuscripts.

NLW 5017D is the earliest of the Aberystwyth *Rose* manuscripts, on the evidence of both handwriting and illumination. It is a production of the second quarter of the fourteenth century. Its scribe identifies himself at the end as "Stephanus Arnulphi clericus." The same man is recorded as a *librarius* or bookseller in Paris in 1348, and named again as a booktrader in 1368.[1] It is not unlikely that he graduated from a scribal to a bookselling career, and that his work on NLW 5017D therefore antedates 1348. Details which tend to confirm that the manuscript is not much later in that century include the hairstyles and beards in the frontispiece (Plate 1). It ought to be possible to date other details too, such as the fashion of the striped bedcover in the same picture. We have not been able to discover when this fashion arose, though examples of it are conspicuous in the 1330s.[2] But it is instructive that in the frontispiece Dangiers'/Refusal's combination of wavy swept-back hair with a neatly trimmed beard can be matched in a Brussels *Rose* manuscript, also of the 1330s, as well as in English manuscripts like the Luttrell Psalter of this time.[3]

---

[1] For this information about Etienne Ernoul we are indebted to Mary and Richard Rouse. See further p. 128 below.

[2] E.g., *Grandes Chroniques de France*, Brussels, Bibl. Roy. MS 5, fol. 72v, in Hedeman, *Royal Image*, figure 57.

[3] Brussels, Bibl. Roy. MS 9576, fol. 1r, reproduced in Patrick M. de Winter, *La Bibliothèque de Philippe le Hardi Duc de Bourgogne (1364–1404)* (Paris: Éditions du Centre National de la Recherche Scientifique, 1985), figure 91; and BL, MS Add. 42130, fols. 61r and 161r, reproduced in Backhouse, *The Luttrell Psalter*, figures 51 and 69.

CHAPTER TWO

Further corroboration in the case of 5017D is the length of the dangling sleeve extensions worn by the leader of the *carole* in folio 6v (Plate 32). A fashion for dilated sleeve-endings hanging from the elbow arose in Europe sometime around 1330. One can see attenuated versions of it in some Parisian manuscripts associated with the 1330s, but sleeves of the fuller elbow-to-knee length are also visible in manuscripts of the 1330s/1340s.[4] Since the women's dresses and headdresses in the manuscript are also consistent with this period, it is to these decades that, we conclude, the miniatures of NLW 5017D should be assigned. Stylistic considerations reinforce this dating. The artist of the frontispiece and of the "vice" miniatures in NLW 5017D has affinities with the Parisian illuminator Richard de Montbaston, whose work can be traced from the 1320s to the late 1340s when he signed a copy of the *Golden Legend*. However, the *carole* miniature is apparently painted by another artist, more talented but not yet identified.[5]

Chronologically the next of the Aberystwyth manuscripts is NLW 5016D, and here attribution can be more precise. One key to this attribution is in the miniaturist's trees. The trees in the illustrations of Poverty, the Garden (Plates 27, 33), and elsewhere match those in a Bern manuscript of the works of Machaut.[6] The Bern artist in turn can be seen as an imitator of the extremely talented "Master of the *Remède de Fortune*" (as François Avril calls him) who produced Machaut illustrations of great modernity in the 1350s. Prominent features of this Master's style were beautifully stippled trees "in the form of toadstools" (which were to become a characteristic element in Parisian work of the later fourteenth century), and also

---

[4] Attenuated: see Morgan, MS M 185 (Paris, 2nd half fourteenth century), fol. 3v (Nichols, "Ekphrasis," figure 5); Tournai, Munic. lib. MS 101 (1330), fol. 5r (Walters, "Illuminating the Rose," figure 2); also Peruzzi, *Codice Laurenziano*, plates II, XIII, etc. Fuller length, BL, MS Royal 20 A. XVII, fol. 9r (Fleming, *Study in Allegory*, figure 21) and fol. 14v (Lewis, "Images of Opening," figure 14), dated early fourteenth century in George Warner and Julius Wilson, *Catalogue of Western MSS in the Old Royal and Kings' Collections*, 4 vols., vol. II (London: British Museum, 1921), 357–59. Stella Newton explains how, during the 1330s, the "hanging hollow oval" of the sleeve grew longer, until in the 1340s it was "narrowed and flattened into a long strip": *Fashion in the Age of the Black Prince* (Woodbridge: Boydell and Brewer, 1980), 4. Backhouse notes that one young lady at Sir Geoffrey Luttrell's dinner table "is wearing the newly-fashionable hanging sleeves," *Luttrell Psalter*, 9 and figure 48 (fol. 208r).

[5] The *Golden Legend* illuminated by Richard de Montbaston is BN, MS fr. 241. We are extremely indebted to François Avril (personal communication of 14 October 1998) for generous observations about the stylistic affinities of NLW 5017D.

[6] Bern, Burgerbibliothek MS 218, identified in Machaut scholarship as manuscript "K"; see Lawrence Earp, *Guillaume de Machaut: A Guide to Research* (New York and London: Garland, 1995), 97–99.

a way of making his figures glance sideways — with pupils consistently at the corners of the eyes.[7]

Both features are emulated, though with less skill, by the Bern Machaut illuminator who is also the NLW 5016D illuminator and has been christened the "Maître aux arbres ocellés" by Domenic Leo.[8] This designation alludes to the formation of the trees' foliage in alternate bands of pale and deep green, dotted with gold; the trees further parallel each other in that sinuous lines of alternating ochre and pale green are used to fashion the trunks (see Plates 27, 33). Other evidence for the identification is that the palette for the figures' clothes is common to both manuscripts, and that the pupils are set in the corners of the eyes, where they protrude somewhat unnervingly. It can be deduced that this illuminator has attempted to imitate aspects of the work of the *Remède* Master, but with a lesser and more conservative talent. (Avril, with more spectacular materials in mind, supposes the Bern Machaut to represent the work of a Parisian workshop "of secondary importance."[9]) The work in both the Bern and Aberystwyth manuscripts could be dated approximately, but with some confidence, to a latish part of the century by the swelling chests which were in vogue then — seen for example in the representation of Bel Acueil/Responsiveness and the Lover in Plate 38. But greater confidence is made possible by the fact that the Bern Machaut manuscript is dated 1371 by its copyist Guiot de Sens.[10] Notwithstanding that an artist's career might be quite long, there seems no reason to date NLW 5016D very differently, so we propose to situate it approximately in the years 1365–75.

The next Aberystwyth manuscript for consideration, NLW 5013D, is of Parisian origin and has hitherto been guardedly dated on palaeographical grounds as late fourteenth or early fifteenth century. The artist's figures appear distinctive in their unusual height and in hints of facial expressiveness, so identification of an individual's work should ultimately be possible (the facial modeling, in particular, bears some resemblance to that of a *Rose* of c. 1400 owned by the Duke of Berry).[11] There are two features which incline us to date this Aberystwyth manuscript in the 1380s/90s. One is that the youth in the Vilanie/Abuse miniature (Plate 7) whose courtesy provokes Vilanie's vicious reaction is dressed accord-

---

[7] François Avril, "Les Manuscrits enluminés de Guillaume de Machaut, Essai de chronologie," in *Guillaume de Machaut: Colloque — Table Ronde* (Paris: Klincksieck, 1982), 117–33 (here 120).

[8] Domenic Leo is working on the transmission of iconography in Machaut manuscripts, and we are much indebted to him for allowing us to use some of his findings.

[9] Avril, "Manuscrits enluminés de Guillaume de Machaut," 124.

[10] Earp, *Guillaume de Machaut*, 98.

[11] BN, MS fr. 380: a parallel for which we are again indebted to François Avril.

ing to the high fashion of the latish fourteenth century: that is, he wears a low-slung ornamental belt over a thigh-length doublet, and hose elaborately pointed at the toes. His doublet has the padded breast shape and the buttoned front which became fashionable from the 1370s to the 90s (at any later date his sleeves might be expected to be wider).[12] Shoes with unwieldy lengthened points (called *cracowes* or *poulaines*) were thought of as a scandalous innovation in the England of the 1360s.[13] This mad fashion lasted until the early years of the next century when the length of the point eased back — much to the relief of men's feet, one would imagine.

The other clue to a fourteenth- rather than fifteenth-century date for NLW 5013D is the hairstyle of the Dreamer (soon to become the Lover) in the frontispiece (Plate 2). He wears his hair brushed down from the top each side but styled in a thick but orderly bunch at ear level. This style was available from about 1380 and persisted for at least twenty years, to judge from illustrations of the chronicles of France and from other *Rose* manuscripts.[14] Such evidence can be very slippery, but the conjunction of these factors would perhaps be sufficient to warrant a dating around 1380–90.

As it happens, the design of the succession of "vice" miniatures in MS 5013D discloses an interesting affiliation with another *Rose* manuscript, Pierpont Morgan Library M 132, whose dating supports our hypothesis. This New York manuscript as a whole has many more illuminations than NLW 5013 and its figures are squat, rather than commandingly tall; but its "vice" sequence tallies with that in the Aberystwyth manuscript not only in a highly distinctive presentation of Envie but also in systematic rehearsal of particularities of other more stereotyped images, including the folds of Tritesce's/Misery's cloak, the nuance of Povreté's posture, and the presence of Papelardie's/Hypocrisy's rosary. At the one point where the affiliation is breached — because there is no Felonie miniature in Morgan 132 — the Aberystwyth miniaturist produces a picture having an uncanny resemblance to an illustration from later in the Morgan manuscript, as we shall show. The Morgan

---

[12] See Newton, *Fashion*, figures 18–20, and Margaret Scott, *Late Gothic Europe 1400–1500*, The History of Dress Series (London: Mills and Boon; and New Jersey: Humanities Press, 1980), 76–78. For examples from the 1370s see Hedeman, *Royal Image*, figure 70, and the dedication scene for the *Bible historiale* of 1371, The Hague, Musee Meermanno-Westreenianum MS 10 B. 23, fol. 2r, in François Avril, *Manuscript Painting at the Court of France: The Fourteenth Century* (London: Chatto and Windus, 1978), plate 36.

[13] Newton, *Fashion*, 54.

[14] Hedeman, *Royal Image*, figure 91; *Rose* manuscripts such as Morgan, MS 132 (c. 1380), fols. 7v, 71v, etc., or Bodl., MS e Mus. 65 (c. 1390), fol. 3v, etc., or MS Douce 332 (end fourteenth century), fol. 95r, etc.

CHAPTER TWO

manuscript is thought to be of Parisian origin, and has been dated c. 1380.[15]

The other two illuminated *Rose* manuscripts at Aberystwyth are of the fifteenth century. NLW 5011E is the earlier of the two. Its frontispiece (Plate 47) displays features which point to a date well before the middle of the century. The style of the bed and the flat landscape both supply clues in this respect. The Dreamer sleeps on a curiously avant-garde bed: it is molded as an abstract gray shape, as if cut from polystyrene. This distinctive chunky shape, together with the dipping near corner and the uncompromising bolster, can be paralleled in a miniature of "Joseph dreaming of the sun, moon and stars" produced by the Apocalypse Workshop around 1418.[16] Then, the warm flat landscape of stubbly yellow-green grass stretching up to a darker horizon is not unlike that displayed in Terence manuscripts in the slightly earlier work (c. 1410) of the Roman Texts Master, though the latter's horizons are lower.[17] So far as we can determine, these possible connections with the earlier part of the century are substantiated by the handling of the grisaille technique in the left compartment, and the modeling of the figure in the right compartment. We propose a tentative dating c. 1420–30 for this illumination.[18]

The frontispiece in NLW 5014D (Plate 48) also gives clues for a tentative dating, though not one that matches the handwriting. Features such as the hat worn by the Dreamer as he washes on the right prove to have a long history in the fifteenth century, as is also the case with the cultivation of an all-black gown.[19] However, in the representation of the young attendant, the combination of the peculiar cut and shade of the tunic with the style of his carefully swept auburn-blonde hair can best be paralleled rather late in the century. Details of the setting help to confirm a dating somewhere in the 1480s or 90s, for it is in those decades that marbled pillars are especially fashionable to frame interiors. For example, such pillars are found, together with the type of gold statuette featured in NLW

---

[15] William M. Voelkle, *The Pierpont Morgan Library; Masterpieces of Medieval Painting* (Chicago: University of Chicago Press, 1980), 8–9.

[16] BL, MS Egerton 912, fol. 46r; in Millard Meiss, *French Painting in the Time of Jean de Berry: The Limbourgs and their Contemporaries*, 2 vols. (London: Thames and Hudson, 1974), ii, plate 783.

[17] Meiss, *The Limbourgs and their Contemporaries*, ii, plates 192, 198.

[18] We are grateful to Anne Sutton and François Avril for confirming the likelihood of a date early in the fifteenth century for this illumination.

[19] On the prevalence of black in fifteenth-century fashion, from about 1410 onwards, see Scott, *Late Gothic Europe*, 30, 32, 73–74, 100.

5014D, in the Hours of Louis de Laval around 1489.[20] Since at the same period miniaturists produce gold arches inset with decorative panels and roundels like those in Plate 48, this frontispiece should be assigned to the last quarter of the fifteenth century. However, given that the text is written in a script which one would expect to date significantly earlier than that, it is probable that in NLW 5014D we have an example of a manuscript in which the illumination of the frontispiece was left unexecuted for a while.

II. The Frontispieces (Incipit Illustrations)

Of the five illuminated *Rose* manuscripts at Aberystwyth, four have a frontispiece miniature, and the fifth perhaps once had one; its lost or damaged *incipit* folio was replaced in the sixteenth century, and the substitute (now folio 2r) leaves space for a two-column illustration in the upper part of the folio.

The earliest of the remaining four frontispieces is in NLW 5017D (c. 1330–50), and it exemplifies some dominant conventions in the iconography of the poem's *incipit* miniatures. The text commences with a discussion of dreams and with the beginning of Guillaume's/the Dreamer's/the Lover's dream. (It seems preferable to refer to this figure as "the Dreamer" when discussing the frontispieces.) Medieval representations of dreamers often juxtapose the contents of the dream with the sleeping individual, so that the image encompasses dreamer and dreamed incident(s) within a spatial continuum. The dreamer's posture is subject to minute adjustments, but one classic format (as in NLW 5017D, Plate 1) is for the body to be lying with the feet extending to the viewer's right, the body twisting slightly at the waist so that the shoulder and the head (at the viewer's left) are raised against a pillow; the head faces downwards into the left corner of the miniature and is part-supported on the cheek by the dreamer's right hand, and below that by the elbow of the right arm.

This format survives into the fifteenth century, as NLW 5011E and 5014D show (Plates 47, 48), though an interest in presenting the bed in perspective by that time translates it into a less horizontal, more diagonal plane. What the Dreamer's left arm is doing can make a difference. In NLW 5017D (Plate 1) it drops down the front of the torso so that the left forearm and hand are relaxed along the bed and form a little square with the other arm which supports the

---

[20] BN MS lat. 920, fol. 116v, in François Avril and Nicole Reynaud, *Les Manuscrits à peintures en France, 1440–1520* (Paris: Flammarion, and the Bibliothèque nationale de France, 1995), 328 (no. 179). The NLW 5014D frontispiece may be Parisian, or provincial French work. We are indebted to personal communications from François Avril and Anne Sutton corroborating our estimate of its date.

Chapter Two

head. This model is common among *incipit* variants in *Rose* manuscripts,[21] and it may be said to enhance the private world of the sleeper by enclosing or withholding the space defined by his arms, shoulders, and head. When by contrast the left arm is stretched out above his body along the bedcover the effect is quite different, especially if his head faces in the same direction; it then begins to shift towards an image of "wakefulness."[22] In the latter case the Dreamer becomes more of a participant in his dream — exists in closer relation to Dangiers or any other figures facing him. The difference is radically confirmed outside *Rose* illustration by a thirteenth-century miniature which pairs an image of Charlemagne "open" to a vision of the stars, with one in which he is accosted in the "closed" sleeping posture by St James.[23]

NLW 5017D adopts a configuration which reads off three key elements of the dream, which in effect constitute its narrative essence. The first is the rosebush, its pink blooms burgeoning against a superb gold leaf background from a stem behind the bed and extending tantalizingly close to the Dreamer's pillow and body. (In 5017D there is no sign that the painter uses the swirling stems to contrive heart-shapes, as seems to be sometimes the case.[24]) Second, confidently approaching (it seems) past the foot of his bed and gesturing towards the roses is their guardian and the Dreamer's chief opponent, Dangiers/Refusal. From his elbow dangles a tremendous iron key. The third element is the forbidding tower, rising above solid steps and with iron-bound doors locked tight against intruders. It will obstruct the Dreamer's (the Lover's) suit to the Rose's Responsiveness. The tower exudes power in its massive sandstone castellation and in its dark domed roof, which thrusts forcefully through the miniature's thick border: penetration of this fortress will become in the narrative the obsession of the Lover and his allies.

This configuration is a variant of what Kuhn termed the "Group III" model of prefatory illumination showing Lover, rose, Dangiers, and a tower gate set in the garden wall. In Plate 1, however, the tower has more the character of a keep

---

[21] E.g., Vatican, MS Urb. lat. 376, fol. 1r (König, *Die Liebe*, 23); BN, MS fr. 378, fol. 13r (Dahlberg, trans., figure 1) and MS fr. 800 fol. 1r (Fleming, *Study in Allegory*, figure 1); BL, MS Royal 19 B. XIII, fol. 5r, and MS Add. 31840, fol. 3r (Fleming, *Study in Allegory*, figure 15), and MS Yates Thompson 21, fol. 3r.

[22] The arm is stretched out but with head still downwards in Brussels, Bibl. Roy. MS 4782, fol. 1r (de Winter, *Bibliothèque de Philippe le Hardi*, figure 61); with head facing outwards, in Vatican, MS Reg. lat. 1522, fol. 1r (König, *Die Liebe*, 51). The latter posture illustrates wakefulness (*Vigilie*) in ÖNB, MS 2644, a 1390s manuscript of the *Tacuinum sanitatis*; see *The Four Seasons of the House of Cerruti*, trans. Judith Spencer (New York: Facts on File, 1984), 133.

[23] Paris, Bibl. Ste-Geneviève MS 782, fol. 141r (Hedeman, *Royal Image*, figure 5).

[24] König, *Die Liebe*, 22–23.

such as later incarcerates Bel Acueil/Responsiveness than that of a wall gate, so the ensemble really presents a symbolic paradigm of the whole poem — what Kuhn termed its *Grundakkord*.[25] As Kuhn also saw, it allowed illuminators to draw on visual archetypes from religious art. First, the siting of the rosebush behind the contours of the Dreamer's limbs in the bed gives an impression that it somehow grows from his own body; this invokes more than a hint of the established iconography of the "Jesse tree" (a genealogical tree of the generations from Jesse, father of David, to Christ). In medieval art that tree typically sprouts from Jesse's loins as he sleeps and it spreads above and to the side, but with human figures inhabiting its foliage to signify the generations.[26] Apart from the conspicuous absence of those figures, a small (but perhaps discreetly deliberate) variation from the Jesse model in most *Rose* miniatures of this type is that they situate the rose-stem near the knees rather than the crotch of the Dreamer. This detail acknowledges difference even as it makes the visual connection. But, if this amounts to a Jesse *allusion*, why was it initiated? Not, we suggest, as some sort of arch satire directed at the Dreamer's sexual impulse by contrasting it with a holy dynasty. Rather, the allusion simply highlights the concept of growth and procreation itself, which is integral to the text both in terms of the Dreamer's subsequent excitement over the growth of the rose (e.g., 3339–60) and in terms of a pervasive textual preoccupation with procreation, emphasized particularly by Nature and Genius.

There is another underlying visual connection which has teased scholars ever since Kuhn proposed it, namely with medieval representations of the Nativity of Christ. The head-on-cheek posture, the left-right alignment, and the formal juxtaposition of the figure on the bed with a bearded figure on the right, is reminiscent of a favorite early medieval Nativity format as evinced, for instance, in the Harley Hours. In the Harley manuscript the place and function of the "tree" is taken over by a column rising behind the middle of Mary's half-recumbent body; atop the column is a floor on which the Christ child's crib rests. Behind the foot of the bed to the right a grizzled and bearded Joseph stands or sits in profile, hand on staff,

---

[25] Kuhn, "Illustration des *Rosenromans*," 21. On the proleptic tower-prison in such frontispieces, see König, *Die Liebe*, 52.

[26] Cf. Psalter of Ingeburge of Denmark, Chantilly, Musée Condé MS 9 (*A History of Private Life*, vol. 2: *Revelations of the Medieval World*, ed. Georges Duby, trans. Arthur Goldhammer [Cambridge, MA: Belknap Press of Harvard University Press, 1988], plate I); and the early fourteenth century Gorleston Psalter, BL, MS Add. 49622, fol. 8r (Richard Marks and Nigel Morgan, *Golden Age of English Manuscript Painting, 1200–1500* [London: Chatto and Windus, 1981], plate 19). König pursues the Jesse analogy and provides a thirteenth century illustration: *Die Liebe*, 22–23.

staring at his wife.²⁷ But since the Dreamer in NLW 5017D is not the Madonna, a rosebush is not a column, and the location is no stable, one is forced to conclude that the Nativity precedent was of purely formal use to the illuminator. There is no pressure in the analogy, since what Kuhn called the "Madonna-like pose" of the Dreamer was in reality widely disseminated as a sleeping posture. In fact the reclining figure was so standardized in medieval art as to become, in Ringbom's words, "a kind of pictorial quotation mark, an index telling the beholder that the picture deals with a dream."²⁸

It is instructive to compare Plate 1 with sister miniatures. The Dreamer-rosebush-Dangiers configuration (even Dangiers' gesture) matches that in some late thirteenth- and early fourteenth-century examples, but there are significant variations. The relevant miniature in one of the Vatican manuscripts considered by König is particularly close in that it includes the tower at the far right — yet it differs too in adding a row of "vices" painted on a wall to the rear.²⁹

Variations in the Dreamer's and Dangiers' appearance are worth pausing over. In NLW 5017D the Dreamer has a full, youthful head of hair and a trim beard. There is no sign of a tonsure: when the tonsure is present it must signify that the Dreamer is also the author (Guillaume), imagined as a clerical figure who should perhaps have better things to dream about.³⁰ Dangiers, meanwhile, is a surprisingly dapper personage for the *vilain* role he plays in the text. He, too, has well-brushed hair and a tidy beard, as well as a slim build not redolent of visual clichés for peasantry. König argues — we are less sure — that examples showing him wearing a coif (a cap tied beneath the chin) represent him as an aristocrat and thereby reinforce the courtly ambience.³¹ It was mainly among the earliest *Rose*

---

[27] BL, MS Harley 928, fol. 3v. For a reproduction see Claire Donovan, *The de Brailes Hours: Shaping the Book of Hours in Thirteenth-Century Oxford* (Toronto: University of Toronto Press, 1991), figure 92. The model was still common in the thirteenth century, and clung on occasionally later: see Robert Branner, *Manuscript Painting in Paris during the Reign of Saint Louis* (Berkeley and Los Angeles: University of California Press, 1977), figures 213–14, and Meiss, *The Limbourgs*, plate 809.

[28] Sixten Ringbom, "Some Pictorial Conventions for the Recounting of Thoughts and Experiences in Late Medieval Art," in Andersen et al., eds., *Medieval Iconography*, 38–69 (here 45). The contrary view that the Nativity and Jesse allusions carry strenuous moral significance is argued by Charles Dahlberg, "Love and the *Roman de la Rose*," *Speculum* 44 (1969): 568–84 (pp. 578–81).

[29] Vatican, MS Reg. lat. 1522, fol. 1r (König, *Die Liebe*, 51).

[30] See Vatican, MS Urb. lat. 376, fol. 1r (König, *Die Liebe*, 23); BN, MS fr. 378, fol. 13r (Dahlberg, trans., figure 1); BL, MS Royal 19 B. XIII, fol. 5r; and numerous instances among other frontispiece models.

[31] König, *Die Liebe*, 23, commenting on Vatican, MS Urb. lat. 376, fol. 1r; cf. BN, MS fr. 378, fol. 13r (Dahlberg, trans., figure 1). However, the evidence on this style of cap

cycles that his menace and his gruffness were muted to this extent — and even then miniaturists might supply him with a heavy club rather than a smaller knobby stick.[32] Later manuscripts often leave him out of the frontispiece but tend to present him in the subsequent scenes where he challenges the Lover as a gross, rough-bearded, heavy-booted figure, even a caricature of oafishness (see figures 12–13).[33] As we have seen, Meradith McMunn has noted variations in Dangiers iconography, including a "fluctuation between representing [him] as peasant or a figure of higher social status."[34] The shortness of the tunic in Plate 1 cannot be taken as a sign of peasant status, since a tunic scarcely any longer is worn by the leader of the dance in folio 6v of the same manuscript (Plate 32).

It is impossible to know what reason some *incipit* illuminators had for toning down the uncourtly nature of Dangiers, but the nuance in such a modification is of real consequence. As Felicity Riddy has finely explained, in courtly literature the "gentil" man is characterized by his capacity for "sexual deferral"; the quality of his love *requires* the lady's aloofness. But, since pity is also a requisite of gentility, her aloofness or pitilessness must appear in the *Rose* as non-noble, as *vilain*, and her "unwillingness to yield" must be "represented allegorically as a peasant with a club." This in turn suggests that (from a masculine perspective) a woman's resistance to a man is some kind of rebellion against social norms: her power to withhold herself "is an affront to the male-female hierarchy, which is expressed symbolically as an affront to the social hierarchy," perhaps as a way of releasing anxiety about the potentially humiliating role imposed on the male in this convention of courtship.[35] In NLW 5017D there remains a cudgel to imply Refusal's sub-aristocratic

---

appears to us ambiguous. Some courtly figures adopt it in an illuminated fourteenth century Swiss lyric manuscript: see *Die grosse Heidelberger "Manessische" Liederhandschrift*, ed. Ulrich Müller (Goppingen: Kümmerle, 1971). But, for examples of peasants wearing it, see the early fourteenth century Queen Mary's Psalter (BL, MS Royal 2 B VII, e.g., fol. 77v) and the sower in the October scene of the early fifteenth century Très Riches Heures of Jean de Berry (Chantilly, Musée Condé MS 651284, fol. 10v).

[32] Dangiers'/Refusal's cudgel is actually described in the text as *un baston d'espine* (3141; "a thorn club," Horgan 48). The model with large rounded club on his shoulder possibly connects with illustrations of the "fool" in Psalms (Vulgate) 13 and 52; see McMunn, "Iconography of Dangier," 89.

[33] E.g., Florence, Bibl. Mediceo-Laurenziana MS Acq e Doni 153, fol. 37v (Peruzzi, *Codice Laurenziano*, plate XIII); BL, MS Royal 20 A. XVII, fol. 125r; Bodl., MS Douce 371, fol. 20r; Morgan, MS M 132, fol. 109v, MS M 324, fol. 23v, and MS M 245, fol. 22v (Robbins, trans., facing page 63).

[34] McMunn, "Iconography of Dangier," 87.

[35] Felicity Riddy, "Engendering Pity in the *Franklin's Tale*," in *Feminist Readings in Middle English Literature*, ed. Ruth Evans and Lesley Johnson (London: Routledge, 1994), 54–71 (here 58–59).

behavior, but one can see from Riddy's analysis how key strands of the social design of the poem are disturbed when Refusal's status is as visually elusive as this.

Here then is an example of what we have termed accidental interpretative possibilities in a miniature. The picture can prompt us to reflect that, although cast as *vilain* in the Lover's mind, from another point of view Dangiers is a facet of the mind of the woman he desires: from her point of view, and from the Lover's, too, if he would only see it, refusal is legitimate social behavior.[36] That Dangiers can be on the side of *cortoisie* is interestingly demonstrated late in the poem when the Lover tries to pluck the rose after Bel Acueil/Responsiveness (following the Old Woman's tutorial) offers him "anything of mine" (14765). Dangiers springs up and rebukes the Lover for interpreting that polite offer basely (*vilenement*, 14833). In Guillaume's part also, although cast as a lout by the Lover, Dangiers in his own estimate eschews peasant behavior: he would consider it *grant vilenie* (3305) to refuse the entreaties which the ladies Openness and Pity make on the Lover's behalf.

A final point about Plate 1 is that while the picture does its best to encapsulate the action of the *Rose*, it can communicate this only to a reader who knows the story. The uninitiated might justly read here something contradictory to the poem — that the lord of that tower (even God, perhaps) has dispatched a bailiff to arouse from slothful slumber a man in the lap of luxury who ought to be tending the rose-plant. However, the evolution of the poem's *incipit* illustration diminished such ambiguity by increasingly adopting the *ad verbum* principle; that is, by restricting the narrative span of the miniature to the immediately ensuing stages of the narrative. Instead of leaping ahead to the antagonism of Dangiers (3000 lines into the poem), frontispieces began to confine forward projection to the more immediate events; the Dreamer getting up, dressing and washing, and walking out through the meadows beside a river to the point where he meets Oiseuse/Ease at the door in the garden wall. During the fourteenth century this progress from bed to garden was increasingly represented in one of two alternative ways: either in a compartmental design, devoting each of (usually) four compartments within one overall frame to particular segments of the progression; or in a multiscenic left-to-right narrative showing the narrator several times within a single miniature, first inside his room, then outside, then at the wall.[37]

---

[36] For insights into such equivocations in the function of Dangiers/Refusal, see Kay, *The* Romance of the Rose, 109–10.

[37] Compartmental: Bodl., MS Selden Supra 57, fol. 1r; Morgan, MS M 324, fol. 1r; Princeton, University Library MS Garrett 126, fol. 1r; BN, MS fr. 1565, fol. 1r, and MS fr. 24388, fol. 1r (and see Walters, "A Parisian Manuscript"). Multiscenic: CUL, MS Gg. IV. 6c, fol. 1r; BL, MS Add. 31840, fol. 3r; BN, MS fr. 19156, fol. 1r. The term "multiscenic" is adopted from Weitzmann by Braeger, "Illustrations in New College 266," 279–80 and n. 12. Kuhn illustrates both types, which he categorizes as Groups V and VI.

CHAPTER TWO

The *incipit* pictures in NLW 5011E (Plate 47) and 5014D (Plate 48) fall into the compartmental and multiscenic modes respectively, but they further limit the range of the visual introduction they offer, for we see only the Dreamer asleep, then dressed and washing. Let us study each before reflecting on them together.

The artist of 5011E produces twinned scenes of extraordinary simplicity and power. In some ways they seem rudimentary. As we have mentioned, the Dreamer's bed is a strangely slab-like structure on which no bedclothes are defined, though the hump of the bolster is firmly indicated. Above the bed an awning juts out, its folds drawing out the bolster's sharp upward diagonal until it is suddenly interrupted by a downward thrust of material, which drops the viewer into empty space above the totally level landscape of something like an unripe cornfield. There is no rosebush. The focus is absolutely on the bed and the Dreamer: but by contrast with the empty terrain and the abstract bed, he is delicately modeled. One hand cradles the cheek of his heavy-lidded head, which is well wrapped in a hood; his legs are slightly splayed in the oblivion of sleep. Only a hint of flesh disturbs the *grisaille* monochrome shading, which observantly picks out the loose structure of his ample gown. The bed is clearly outside and exposed, and the sleeper seems not to be in night attire, but we shall defer consideration of that until later.

In the right compartment the landscape has not changed — to that extent the picture might as well be multiscenic — but color has brought the Dreamer to life. He is dressed in a long robe not dissimilar to his "night" clothing; only it is a luxurious pink and is gathered in quite high on the waist, hanging from there in long neat folds. His hood in matching material fits snugly over his shoulders. He concentrates on washing his hands, with a sentimentally melancholic air. His hair, unexpectedly tinged blue, bunches symmetrically out either side of a small black cap with a central bobble. It is the cap of an intellectual, covering the tonsured part of the head of the Dreamer—who, as we have said, is also Guillaume, a writer, and hence in the medieval mind a *clericus*. (Such a cap is elsewhere worn by a figure depicting Jean de Meun, at the start of his continuation, as university lecturer or *Magister*.[38]) The washstand or ornamental fountain at which he stands is a de-

---

[38] Vatican MS Urb. lat. fol. 26r (König, *Die Liebe*, 33). Similar caps are worn by figures such as Theophrastus in Bodl., MS e Mus. 65, fol. 66r, and the dreamer/author in figure 2 from *Le Songe du Verger*, BL, MS Royal 19 C. IV, fol. 1v (color reproduction in Avril, *Manuscript Painting*, plate 31). The cap remains a uniform of intellectual authority during the fifteenth century: hence it is worn by Vincent of Beauvais in a *Speculum historiale* (c. 1480), BL, MS Royal 14.E.I (pt. 1), fol. 3r (reproduced in Michelle P. Brown, *Understanding Illuminated Manuscripts* [London: The J. Paul Getty Museum and the British Library, 1994], 114), and by the Warden and Fellows of New College in a drawing ca. 1461–65 in Oxford, New College MS 288, fol. 3v (Christopher de Hamel, *A History of Illuminated*

lightfully dainty Gothic edifice rising from a plinth to an ecclesiastical pinnacle beneath which a practical tap supplies water to its basin. Again nothing else enters the frame but greeny-yellow stalky vegetation leading back to a dark green horizon. There is nothing to focus on but the wistful figure washing his hands. Why?

Before commenting on that, we shall turn to NLW 5014D in Plate 48. The contrast is like chalk and cheese. The central ingredients are the same — Dreamer in bed, Dreamer standing to wash hands — but the impression is vastly different. Now, a single domestic interior is divided in two by a central pillar in blue-green marble: it supports gold-painted arches which are held at the edge of the picture by flanking marble columns. Carved in relief above the central pillar is a solemn monkish or prophet-like figure standing frontally, with hands together in prayer. Although a wealthy fifteenth-century gentleman might cultivate morally-toned décor of this kind, it is perhaps nevertheless one of the rare occasions when one might genuinely speak of a "visual gloss" on the poem. The somber religious figure carved there represents an austerity and rectitude which the Lover will put behind him and which will also be severely challenged by the likes of the Old Woman in the poem.

Beneath is an elaborate interior whose windows are draught-proofed with hanging tapestries. The sleeping area on the left shows a deep bed with red canopy, side-curtains, and matching bedcover. The Dreamer, in the now familiar cheek-on-hand posture, is apparently naked apart from his cap. His hair is a slightly straggly version of the bunched style noted in the previous plate and visible again when the Dreamer stands with neat coiffure under his distinctive brown hat on the right in this one. Nothing else straggles here. The room is tidy (complete with its handsome chair, placed next to the bed in a familiar late-medieval arrangement) but hushed, static, somehow still. The unadorned blackness of the robe in which the Dreamer has dressed — in conformity with fifteenth-century color trends — contributes to the sense of stillness. Such stillness devitalizes even the trickle of water seen splashing on the man's hands from the flagon upturned by his young servant over a small handbasin. The gaze of the two participants is concentrated downwards. Or is the standing Dreamer perhaps shown half-asleep, as if mesmerized? Perhaps the miniaturist has sensed something of the archness of Guillaume's opening — a "sleep" in which the first thing that happens is that the dreamer thinks he "wakes up" (but remains of course asleep) to begin a seemingly normal day.

Manuscripts, 2nd ed. [London: Phaidon, 1994], figure 118). See further the Commentary on "Changing the Author," below.

CHAPTER TWO

As we saw earlier, Kuhn approved of the continuous visual narrative method found here, which had a certain vogue in fifteenth-century *Rose* manuscripts especially: it got rid of the "nonsense" of pictures where beds and gardens and towers jostled together.[39] But if in this miniature and in NLW 5011E (Plate 47) the introductory narrative plan is pared down to its most easily assimilable contiguous preliminaries, there seems a risk of a "nonsense" of another sort arising because the act of washing the hands has achieved a prominence which many readers of the text would consider to be out of all proportion. The narrator tells us that he arose, dressed "and washed my hands" before roaming out, lacing up his sleeves. Have the illuminators discovered some mystery in the half-line about washing, *et mes mains lavé* (90)? One might at a pinch argue that such representations focus on the prosaic business of handwashing because it offers an opportunity to anticipate, in a semi-ritual act, something of the poem's concern with transparent or reflective water (the river in which the Dreamer goes on to wash his face, the spring of Narcissus which is both mirror and clear water). The basin in Plate 48 could be said to be mirror-like: the structure in Plate 47 could be interpreted as a spring that has been plumbed in.

While visual anticipations of such a kind cannot be ruled out, we are inclined to consider them wishful thinking. The illuminators are painting *ad verbum*. Dressing and washing are what come next after sleeping in the poem's opening, so that is what they paint, though in the present miniatures they elect to elide the act of dressing. In some of the "compartmentalized" *incipit* miniatures, it had been the other way round, the second compartment showing the Dreamer pulling on hose or boots, though usually with a tall washbasin close by to include a hint of washing. The selection of washing over dressing perhaps sustains a greater level of dignity, which could be one reason for not depicting him dressing. On the whole we suggest that this is not an interpretative choice. It is precisely an instance of the rule enunciated by Lawton, that an episode illustrated may have no particular significance in itself: but "significance is conferred upon it by the structure of the work which places it at the beginning."[40] One would have to labor hard to invest the washing with, say, a ritual significance (as of baptism) appropriate to the *rite de passage* which is detected in the later narrative by critics such as Poirion.

There remains the frontispiece in NLW 5013D (Plate 2), an image of deceptive simplicity which confirms that the least elaborate option for an introductory picture, categorized by Kuhn as Group IV and restricted to Dreamer and rosebush, still offered creative scope near the end of the fourteenth century. The de-

---

[39] Kuhn, "Illustration des *Rosenromans*," 33, in a passage which Fleming criticized for its "inflated regard for pictorial movement," *Study in Allegory*, 40.

[40] Lawton, "Illustration of Late Medieval Secular Texts," 15.

sign of the present miniature is not unlike that of a London manuscript of c. 1380 (BL MS Yates Thompson 21, fol. 3r) which also shows Dreamer, bed-awning, abstract background, and roses sprouting from a solid stem beyond the foot of the bed. But Plate 2 deploys the rosebush so as to raise deliberate questions about the location of the bed.

In NLW 5011E (Plate 47), as we saw, the bed with its curtain appurtenances stands isolated in a long field. There is no rosebush. Some later medieval literary dreams occur when the dreamer is asleep outside. For instance the fictional connoisseur of dreams, the "Chaucer" who narrates *The Prologue to the Legend of Good Women*, even has a bed of some sort made up in the garden (perhaps in emulation of *Rose* pictures).[41] It is not unlikely that the artist in Plate 47 means us to think of a bed literally plonked down in the meadow: after all, the Dreamer here seems fully clothed, and lies *on* the bed rather than beneath any sheets, so we may well wonder whether bed (and bed curtains, too) have somehow migrated out of doors. The dramatic juxtaposition of bed and landscape is a means of reinforcing the *idea* of dreaming, and of dreaming about landscape. This artist has chosen a powerfully minimalist reinforcement, with not even a rosebush in sight. The spur probably nevertheless comes from designs such as that in NLW 5013 (Plate 2) which include the rose and which embody ambiguous suggestions that the bed is both inside and outside.[42]

Kuhn, applying naturalistic criteria, saw an exterior location as potentially more natural wherever the rosebush was represented as realistically planted.[43] Here, the palpable chunky stem of the bush rises from a green and vaguely fertile area at the end of the bed. Its pink flowers spread up and across the matching pink contoured folds of the bedcover in a now familiar way. At the left, beneath the striking scarlet of the curtain suspended from the frame, the Dreamer is propped up half facing us. His distinctive, long, mature-looking face lolls against pillow and shoulder, though his right elbow takes some weight in a slightly tensed way which suggests wakefulness as much as sleep. On this left side of the frame, he may be said to be in a bedroom, and we might read the deep blue background with its triple gold criss-cross lines as an abstract interior backcloth. But reading from the other direction, the rosebush tendrils do not merely spread against the geometric background: they interweave behind and in front of the gold lines. When this subtle *trompe*

---

[41] "G" text, lines 97–99: "And in a lytel herber that I have . . . I bad men shulde me my couche make."

[42] There were, however, other models for the bed-in-landscape, such as the representation of Eve, Adam, and progeny in a Jean de Limbourg Genesis illustration: Meiss, *The Limbourgs and their Contemporaries*, plate 285.

[43] As in BN, MS fr. 803, and also MS fr. 1576 and Chantilly, Musée Condé, MS 911; Kuhn, "Illustration des *Rosenromans*," 31–32.

l'oeil effect (not easily visible in reproduction) is noticed, it turns the gold grid into a trellis and the blue into a night sky. Boundaries are blurred. This is bedroom as well as garden: the man is slipping into his dream, and the rose is both in the foreground and attached to the background.

The notion of step-by-step evolution in these *incipit* pictures is hard to sustain. The model so subtly used by the NLW 5013 artist was essentially already in existence at the end of the thirteenth century.[44] Nevertheless, what is interesting at the end of the fourteenth is that the impact of the roses seems lessened. Attention concentrates on the Dreamer, whose torso is so sharply picked out. His own inner concentration and his physically detailed features, including that naked and somewhat androgynous chest, dominate our initial responses. Much more than in earlier productions such as NLW 5017D, the Dreamer exists as a challenging center of consciousness, and it is in this respect that certain analogies with literary development suggest themselves: for the narrator/dreamer figure attained an enhanced and more demanding consciousness precisely in the poetry of Machaut, Chaucer, and others in the later fourteenth century, who extended the possibilities in this figure from the teasingly half-developed point at which Guillaume and Jean had left him. To that extent the frontispieces offer absorbing testimony to the creative literary influence of the *Romance of the Rose*. The rose itself did not matter so much to the later poets, but the first-person narrator certainly did. In their own poetry they made a big investment in the presence and the psyche of the narrator. Plate 2 shows how the concept of the dreaming narrator really mattered to the illustrator of that period, as well.[45]

III. The Images on the Wall

With the exception of the opening scene of the Dreamer in bed, no part of the *Rose* is more often illustrated than the sequence of caricatures — usually referred to as "the vices" — whose images the Dreamer beholds on the exterior of the wall which encloses the square Garden of Pleasure. The poetry constructs them primarily in the mind's eye as "images" that are "painted." Although it is not absolutely clear whether the images, or just accompanying inscriptions, are also carved (*entaillié*, 132), the reader who thinks initially of flat wall-paintings needs to note that medieval bas-relief carvings on buildings were usually colorfully paint-

---

[44] Kuhn, "Illustration des *Rosenromans*," 27, citing Dijon, Bibl. mun. MS 526.
[45] Kathleen Scott has commented interestingly on the primacy of "author or main actor" in late medieval English illumination: "Design, Decoration and Illustration," 47.

ed,[46] and that where the illuminators present an impression of the images all together, as occurs sometimes at the start of the poem, they frequently register the medium of carving.[47] "Viewed" sequentially by the poem's narrator and reader, the series inevitably challenged illuminators and might even have been the spur which made the *Rose* such a favorite text for illustration. The vices seemed particularly apt for serial re-representation beside the text. Rubricators generally (as in the Aberystwyth manuscripts) identify each miniature in the resultant gallery of figures either with the personification's name alone (NLW 5013D and 5016D), or with the name followed by *pourtraite* (5017D).

Three general features of the sequence might be kept in mind while it is studied. The first is that the narrator's caustic attitude to the concepts portrayed here, enhanced by their apparent exclusion from the garden of eros (implying that they are antithetical to it), and encouraged by their intermittent overlap with conventional sins such as Envy and Avarice, leads to a visual presentation in terms of relentless ugliness. Exaggerated noses and grotesque scowls abound. This is a "pictorial ugliness ... reserved for the morally ugly" in medieval perception, as Rosemond Tuve points out: "Haine, Vilenie, Envie, familiar members of the usual sin-series" characteristically display "distorted, even deformed, unnatural ugliness."[48] Simultaneously, given the equation of courtliness with physical beauty in medieval culture, the ugliness is a means of socially demonizing the concepts personified on the wall.[49] Socially and aesthetically as well as ethically they constitute that which is "beyond the pale," not only in the transferred sense of that expression (they are "beyond acceptance") but in the literal sense from which it derives — "outside the fence or boundary."

The second general feature is simply that all Guillaume's "vices" are female. Since that was the norm in conventional vices/virtues discourse it may hold no significance beyond the imponderables of inherited grammatical gender which are

---

[46] The vocabulary may be summarised as follows: ... *portret dehors et entaillié / a maintes riches escritures* (132–33); *pointe/pointure* (134, 163, 169, 279, 292); *portreite* (132, 163, 235, 339, 441); *ymage* (134, 144, 152, 156, 164, 189, 195, 463, *ymage escrite* 407. Fleming asserts that the figures are "sculpted and painted," *Study in Allegory*, 33; but Ménard seems to conclude that for Guillaume it is a matter of paintings: "Représentations des vices," 178.

[47] Among frontispieces apparently presenting the "portraits" as relief carvings in niches are: BL, MS 31840, fol. 3r; Tournai, Bibl. Munic. MS C. I, fol. 1r; Morgan, MS M 324, fol. 1r; BL, MS Egerton 1069, fol. 1r. But sometimes the nature of the medium presupposed by the miniaturist is indeterminate (e.g., CUL, MS Gg. IV.6c, fol. 1r). Some late manuscripts such as Bodl., MS Douce 195 render individual vices as statuettes in niches.

[48] Tuve, *Allegorical Imagery*, 191–92.

[49] On the rhetoric of ugliness which expresses the antithesis of courtliness, see David Burnley, *Courtliness and Literature in Medieval England* (Harlow, England: Addison Wesley Longman, 1998), 46–50.

assumed to be operative in that discourse. Hence, for example, the English *Gawain*-poet personifies Poverty as feminine, along with other Virtues named after the Beatitudes.[50] Yet, a rival tradition for Poverty (a condition which in Guillaume's scheme is a "vice") could bring to mind the utter poverty of Job in his misfortune, and gender it masculine. With the conventions available to them illustrators were therefore not always disposed to agree with Guillaume's gendering, and this is potentially an interesting point if the feminine gendering of all these unattractive figures insinuates a layer of misogyny into the poem, complementing perhaps the implications of Guillaume's decision to assign masculinity to the Rose's most welcoming feature, Bel Acueil.

A third general feature of these vilified female "vices" is that the illuminators habitually present them in a homely form of headdress whereby both neck and head are swathed in a crude linen veil wound round (and often knotted at the side of) the head, so as to frame the face. The fashion for the female *couvrechief*, of which an elaborate one is sported by Chaucer's Wife of Bath,[51] was widespread in the later Middle Ages. Aristocratic versions of it had delicately crimped edges whereas less ornamental versions seem to have been characteristic of lower social ranks.[52] It is risky to generalize on such a point since one can, for example, find Mary Magdalene represented (c. 1300) in a relatively plain coverchief as she kneels to Christ in the garden of Gethsemane, and she is not typically imagined as socially inferior.[53] Nor is she associated in medieval culture with any lack of youthful beauty though that, too, is another possible signification of the full-blown coverchief or kerchief. The theory was that only young, unmarried girls went about bareheaded, with their hair loose. Other women covered their head, "and with increasing age more and more of it."[54] A beautiful young married woman might

---

[50] "Dame Pouert, Dame Pitee, Dame Penaunce the thrydde," etc., *Patience*, line 31: in *Poems of the Pearl Manuscript*, ed. Malcolm Andrew and Ronald Waldron (London: Edward Arnold, 1978).

[51] "Hir coverchiefs ful fyne weren of ground; / I dorste swere they weyeden ten pound / That on a Sonday weren upon hir heed," *The General Prologue to the Canterbury Tales* (I. 453–55).

[52] Coverchiefs are discussed in Newton, *Fashion*, 62 and 87, with illustrations of the frilled linen in figures 28 and 35. The possibility that the *Rose* coverchiefs might signify non-courtliness could be confirmed by their appearance among peasant women in BL, MS Add. 42130 (1330s/40s), fols. 158r, 172v, 166v (respectively Backhouse, *Luttrell Psalter*, frontispiece, plate 25, plate 28); but the social status of a woman in similar coverchief enticing a man to bed in Bodl., MS Douce 6, fol. 160v (Michael Camille, *Image on the Edge: The Margins of Medieval Art* [London: Reaktion Books, 1992], 123) is unclear.

[53] The Ramsey Psalter, Morgan, MS 302, fol. 3v (Marks and Morgan, *The Golden Age of English Manuscript Painting*, plate 16).

[54] Scott, *Late Gothic Europe*, 82.

wear an elegant yet revealing veil, as does Lady Bertilak in the poem *Sir Gawain and the Green Knight* when she is first introduced; but Lady Bertilak is pointedly contrasted with an aged companion whose head and neck are altogether muffled as though, in the hostile perspective adopted for the description, this of itself — however ornamental the material — made her an emblem of female unattractiveness.[55] Kuhn took age as a determinant of the full kerchief, and this can be supported from the fact that when it comes to presenting the comic stereotype of the Old Woman, an illustrator of the plays of Terence gives her the wrap-around kerchief.[56] In the *Rose* manuscripts it is only women such as Jealousy or Scandal (figure 10) and the Old Woman (figure 11), impediments to the Lover's quest, who otherwise wear the coverchiefs typical of the "vices."[57]

The illuminators' representations of the figures on the wall therefore include a marked dimension of social and aesthetic critique. This critique would support the notion that the love-garden is projected to be socially and aesthetically exclusive; that is, as is often supposed, that the "vices" — from Abuse to Avarice, from Poverty to Senility — are relegated to outside the love-deity's precinct because it is imagined that a cultured love cannot rightly incorporate them. This reading is actually encouraged by Jean de Meun in his continuation, where the character Genius refers back to the garden of Guillaume's narrative and to the "ten ugly little images" depicted outside it (20,273–74). By contrast, declares Genius, depicted outside the eternal Park of Love one would find hell, vices, the whole of temporal creation: "you would see all these things *excluded from* the fair park" (20,301–2, Horgan 313, our emphasis).

Counter-readings of the meaning of this exclusion in the poem can be envis-

---

[55] The passage refers to lady Bertilak's "Kerchofes ... wyth mony cler perlez," and "Hir brest and hir bryght throte, bare displayed." But "That other wyth a gorger watz gered ouer the swyre, / Chymbled ouer hir blake chyn with chalk-quyte vayles, / Hir frount folden in sylk" so as to enclose all but a section of her face from mouth to eyebrows: ed. Andrew and Waldron in *Poems of the Pearl Manuscript*, lines 954–63. Newton refers to the *gorget* as a type of veil "worn round the necks of mature women in the north of Europe": *Fashion*, 88. While the coverchief and the gorget might be separable (129), one piece of material could serve both functions as in many *Rose* illuminations and as in a fourteenth-century painting (Avignon, Petit Palais) of the elderly Elizabeth, reproduced in Duby, *History of Private Life*, 2:246.

[56] Kuhn, "Illustration des *Rosenromans*," 15: and cf. Syra, the old woman in *Hecyra*; Paris, Bibl. de l'Arsenal MS 664, fol. 210r, reproduced in Marcel Thomas, *The Golden Age: Manuscript Painting at the Time of Jean, Duc de Berry* (London: Chatto and Windus, 1979), plate 19.

[57] See Morgan, MS M 132, fols. 32v, 91v, etc.; and MS M 324, fols. 25v, 85v. There is marked contrast between Jalousie (with kerchief) and a female Bel Acueil/Responsiveness (without) in Bodl., MS e Mus. 65, fol. 26r.

aged: for example, that what a new recruit to the love-garden will experience within it is adolescent fantasy futilely attempting to define itself against, or turn its back on, the constituents of life imaged on the wall like low social rank, old age, and misery; or, that all who enter this Love's domain dedicated to beautiful youth and courtesy actually take with them what the encompassing images bespeak: they will need hoarded wealth with which to show courtly generosity, will find envy within the garden, will reduce themselves to hypocrisy if not poverty in the amorous quest, and must meanwhile grow old.[58] The text will disclose, for instance, that from one point of view the Lover will be a *felon* (2916) in wanting to pluck (steal) the rose. The Lover does not recognize that these constituents "lurk inside him," as Joan Ferrante suggests, "and that his pursuit of love will bring them out."[59] Such counter-readings are neither programmatically encouraged nor discouraged by the illustrators so far as we can see, but they remain tentatively possible, and one should be on the alert for their potential actuation.

Haïne/Hatred (Plates 3, 4, 5)

The "vice" series begins with the antithesis of love in Guillaume's brief sketch of Hatred, which mentions this figure's angry, provocative, sullen disposition. Although the text supplies specific visual prompts in her "snub nose" and manic appearance ("hideously wrapped in a towel"), illuminators typically respond to the former but ignore the latter.[60] They invoke a pre-existent iconography of aggression as they respond to the name itself in the rubric or (it might sometimes be) to an instruction to paint a woman "wild with fury," *forcenee* as line 146 puts it.

A measure of the slackness which can affect placement of miniatures and which should caution us not to hold overambitious expectations about their textual integration is that although the rubric *de haine* in NLW 5016D (Plate 4) follows the statement "whose name I read above her head" (154, Horgan 5), the "name" this line refers to should not be Haine's but that of the *next* personification called Violence (*apellee . . . felonnie*, third line below the miniature). The scribe's difficulty in defining the break-point for a miniature between one description and another leads to potential confusion about the referent of line 154.

---

[58] As Genius also retrospectively observes, everything in Guillaume's garden is subject to death (20,324).

[59] Joan Ferrante, *Woman as Image in Medieval Literature from the Twelfth Century to Dante* (New York: Columbia University Press, 1975), 111; cf. Fleming, *Study in Allegory*, 32.

[60] The referent for *entortillie / Hideusement d'une toaille* (150–51) is ambiguous. Dahlberg and Horgan translate that "she" was wrapped in the towel; but Ménard interprets that "the head" is so wrapped: "Représentations des vices," 180. Her headgear is not usually hideous in miniatures.

CHAPTER TWO

The three Aberystwyth examples subscribe to widespread convention by seating Hatred and several of her fellow figures on benches or chests or stone slab seats — it is hard to distinguish which form of seat is which, though when a chest is for valuables, it will sport a lock. This convention will seem the less surprising if it is recalled that while chairs were relatively scarce, chests or more often benches — like the one on which a visiting friar sits in the house of a villager in *The Summoner's Tale* (III.1773–75) — were the universal medieval furniture. Where figures of all sorts are depicted sitting frontally in medieval art of the thirteenth and fourteenth centuries, they sit on benches.

In NLW 5016D (Plate 4), where the merest hint of an indoor scene is provided by the arches in the upper corners, the reader encounters a woman in a decorous lavender-pink dress, the standard female attire in this manuscript, in fact. Her neck and head are swathed, like those of other "vices" in the series, in a coverchief knotted to one side, so neither her head nor her body is "hideously wrapped." The chief articulations of "hatred" are in the arched back and leftward twist of her body, in her raised arms, and above all in her clenching fists.[61] Her fixed sideways stare would qualify as a hint of malice, perhaps, were it not that it is shared by several other figures in the manuscript. Such a stare can acquire a more dynamic point if it is fixed upon some *object* of hatred, a variant which is sometimes found elsewhere.[62]

NLW 5013D's Hatred (Plate 5) scowls beneath jutting eyebrows and (just visibly) bares her teeth. She, too, wears normative female attire and sits on a bench or slab. Again, the impulse to hate is primarily configured through the visual rhetoric of gesture. Here the clenching fists are purposefully braced against the inside of the thighs in a wrathful version of a gesture of aggression associated in medieval religious art with dangerous figures such as Herod. The hand or fist on thigh is a feature of Haine elsewhere,[63] but can also be found combined with other assertive gestures.[64] In NLW 5017D (Plate 3) she matches the sideways posture found in 5016D, but the 5017D artist has been content to assign her a broad and rela-

---

[61] François Garnier, *Le Langage de l'image au Moyen Âge: Signification et symbolique* (Paris: Le Léopard d'Or: 1982), 161–64.

[62] E.g., in Paris, Bibl. Ste-Geneviève MS 1126, fol. 2r (Garnier, *Langage de l'image*, figure 159), where an elegant woman offering advice gives Hatred something to react against. In BL, MS Royal 19 B XIII, fol. 5v, Hatred reacts angrily to a young man (*or* the dreamer confronts her?).

[63] Morgan, MS M 132, fol. 2r; Bodl., MS Douce 332, fol. 1v, and MS e Mus 65, fol. 2r; Paris, Bibl. Ste-Geneviève MS 1126, fol. 2r: and see Garnier, *Langage de l'image*, 185, 189, "main appuyée sur sa hanche/sa cuisse/son genou; assurance, fermeté, détermination."

[64] E.g., one hand raised to point, Bodl., MS Selden Supra 57, fol. 2r.

tively unmalicious "speaking" gesture (open palm extended) with her left hand, echoed in a minor key with her right.[65] She is flanked by two trees, as are three of the other images in this manuscript's sequence. No particular rationale for this can be deduced. In 5013D (Plate 5), however, the trees flanking Haine are consistent with a location on a vegetative green ground in front of abstract patterned backgrounds which is common to all the images (including even Hypocrisy at the altar): this artist's intention perhaps is to sustain the spring meadow context in which the dreamer beholds these images.

Felonie/Violence (Plate 6)

Felonie is a problem for illuminators because Guillaume mentions her almost in passing, before hastening on to Vilanie. In some manuscripts (like NLW 5016D) both figures are ignored. In others the solution is an economy plan, representing one figure but not the other, as adopted in NLW 5017D.

If Felonie is presented, her undeclared significance has to be projected. The evidence of the illustrations is that the noun was understood as it would have been at law, to indicate major — especially violent — crime.[66] Thus in British Library MS Yates Thompson 21 where Felonie and Vilanie are juxtaposed, the former is represented seated frontally, brandishing a stick. NLW 5013D (Plate 6) may at first seem merely a naturalistic extension of that threat. Here a curly-haired youth in a short blue tunic hastens barefoot away from a heavier, hooded male figure dressed in orange-brown and wearing hose and shoes. He brandishes a sharply-cut cudgel over his right shoulder.

The clue to such projection of Felonie as intent to cause "grievous bodily harm" probably comes from schematic pictures in manuscripts of a widely disseminated account of vices and virtues known as *Le somme le roi*. Representations of Equité in these manuscripts (see figure 1) contrast an emblematic depiction of a crowned woman who symbolizes equity with a scene labeled "Felonnie" in which Cain, sometimes represented as a hooded laborer, commits the first murder by

---

[65] These relatively muted gestures occur also in the standing Hayne of BL, MS Royal B. XIII, fol. 5v.

[66] For an indicative use in English, see the reference to murder as *felonye* in *Man of Law's Tale*, ll. 643. Broadly, a felony was an action committed against the king's peace, though according to John Alford the concept "was not used with great precision in the Middle Ages": *Piers Plowman: A Glossary of Legal Diction* (Cambridge: D. S. Brewer, 1988), 58.

striking down Abel, a curly-haired youth, with a spade.[67] The Aberystwyth artist may have introduced the club as a weapon by association with a second projection of Felonie in the same *Somme* pictures, where men fighting with cudgels are separated by Moses the lawgiver.

However, aside from demonstrating that artists faced with an undescribed personification might have recourse to whatever model visual tradition supplied for the relevant concept, this miniature prompts two further thoughts. One is that by accident or design the artist has produced this Felonie as a sort of Dangiers figure: it is Dangiers, after all, who memorably wields a club in the poem to frighten the Lover away from the Rose (3755ff.). There are close parallels to the Felonie/Violence of Plate 6 in miniatures of Dangiers threatening the Lover at line 14,797, notably the relevant illustration in a New York manuscript which, we have suggested, is closely linked with NLW 5013D (see figure 12).[68] In a way, the Aberystwyth artist has discovered a clever way to superimpose Dangiers upon Felonie, or Felonie upon Dangiers.

But the second point is that whatever identity is attributed to the man wielding the stick, the image in Plate 6 breaks the gender continuity that is undisturbed in Guillaume, whereby the "vices" are female. This is interesting and prompts explanation. Maybe, even though there existed a well-known burlesque visual image of female violence in the conventional model of the wife beating her husband with a distaff, inhibitions could arise when it was a question of showing a woman engaging in outright physical attack. In the early fifteenth century it seemed to Christine de Pizan that major criminal acts (Felonie, in other words) were not characteristic of women.[69] The received exemplar of *felonie* (Cain) was masculine. The *Roman de la Rose* itself will later assert that from one point of view it is the male Lover who is *felon* (2916) in wanting to pluck (i.e., violently steal) the rose. The most blatant instance of *felonie* in the narrative will be the Jealous Husband's abuse of his wife (Plate 40): illuminators most often represent him beating her with a cudgel — further reinforcement of the gendering of felonie as masculine. So, factors conspire to produce in Plate 6 an illustration which *defies* Guillaume's gendering of the image on the wall, but does so in a way that happens to be in line with the poem's later gendering of felonious behavior (especially that of Dangiers) as masculine.

---

[67] Abel is again curly-haired in the "Equité" page in Cambridge, Fitzwilliam Mus. MS 192 (Tuve, *Allegorical Imagery*, figure 18). Cain strikes down Abel with mattock or spade in Bible pictures reproduced in Branner, *Manuscript Painting in Paris*, figures 26b, 26c, 395.

[68] Morgan, MS M 132, fol. 109v.

[69] See Alcuin Blamires, *The Case for Women in Medieval Culture* (Oxford: Clarendon Press, 1997), 143–44.

CHAPTER TWO

Vilanie/Abuse (Plates 7, 8)

"Abuse" is our translation for the personification whom Guillaume sums up as "a woman incapable of honoring others as she ought to." In medieval culture the *vilain* was a peasant-like person of grossly undisciplined (*outrageuse*, 161) and immoral behavior. The emphasis is directed in the present case especially towards *defamatory* behavior, for she is described as a "scandalmonger" (*mesdisans*, 162, Horgan 5). Although the hint that "vilanie" is betrayed through speech can be matched elsewhere in medieval literature, there is a certain misogynous predictability in Guillaume's presentation of her as a perversion of speech. However, while illuminators had a plentiful repertoire of gestures signifying sorts of speech such as conversation, command, or preaching, they could scarcely encode loutish talk as such: they needed *outrageuse* action. Hence the common alternatives for this personification — a woman disgracefully kicking a servant, or a woman using her body "indecently."

NLW 5017D (Plate 8) gives us an almost comically gymnastic version of the abusive kick. A seated lady whose head is swathed in a kerchief jerks up her right foot at a young squire's hand even as he holds it up to offer her a goblet (his other hand holds a jug with more supplies). The artist has orchestrated the abrasive signals through the lady's sharp, angular gaze, through her drastic pointing action, and especially through the failure of decorum as her skirt rides up her legs.[70] Vilanie in NLW 5013D (Plate 7) replicates much of this. The physics of the image are more feasible because it allows the woman to lean back to balance the energy of her kick, but it caricatures the ugliness in her face, and it again draws attention to the exposed ankle and calf.

Since visual sources for the *Rose* "vices" are rare, scholars have been somewhat obsessed by the implications of a possible source for this image in a similar image carved just before 1210 in Notre Dame cathedral at Paris.[71] The carving has been interpreted by art historians as *Malignitas*, or Hard-heartedness or Ingratitude, but a more recent suggestion is that one can argue backwards from the subsequent

---

[70] These features are also apparent in a version of the scene confusingly labelled "Felonie" in Bodl., MS Selden Supra 57, fol. 2r. Vilanie in Bodl., MS e Mus 65, fol. 2v repeats them but is smudged; ÖNB, MS 2592 (Kuhn, "Illustration des *Rosenromans*," plate II) lacks the exposed leg. The kicking model occurs frequently: cf. Morgan, MS M 132, fol. 2v, and MS M 324, fol. 2r; CUL, MS Gg IV. 6c, fol. 4r. Exposed legs as an attribute of Venus are discussed by Friedman, "L'iconographie de Vénus," 66–67.

[71] The Paris medallion and an analogous one in Amiens cathedral are reproduced in Robertson, *Preface to Chaucer*, figures 56 and 70, and discussed on page 198.

occurrence in *Rose* iconography to interpret it as Vilanie.[72] What this debate seems to overlook is that Ingratitude and Vilanie were more or less synonymous in moral analysis. The *vilenye* that is a sub-species of Pride "is a vice that clerkes clepen ingratitudo, that is unkyndenesse," according to one influential moral handbook, and it is manifest in someone who "yeldeth . . . evele for good."[73]

Getting beyond the source debate, discussion might more fruitfully concentrate on the resonance of the configuration in the poem. For one thing, the youth in both the Aberystwyth miniatures is not a menial servant. This reflects the fact that, in practice, highborn youths were usually sent away to be brought up as pages in aristocratic households, learning the etiquette of *cortoisie*. As we remarked earlier, in NLW 5013D (Plate 7) the youth is dressed in the high fashion of the end of the fourteenth century. In the longer perspective of the poem this figure puts one in mind of the aspirations of the poem's Lover, "serving" a potentially imperious lady. His action is as representative of *cortoisie* as the lady's is of the reverse. (In one *Rose* manuscript the female personification of Cortoisie in the garden is actually painted in a pose similar to that of the squire, offering a goblet to a youth who graciously bends to accept it.)[74] If the Felonie image prompts us to prefigure the recalcitrance of the Rose as masculine, this image prefigures it as feminine and, in a way, provides a hint of the kind of emotive coercion by which the entire poem will seek to ostracize the "discourtesy" of rejecting a young man's attentions.

The "kicking" model incorporates as sub-theme an "immodest" exposure of female limbs which, in some manuscripts, is separately developed to define the Abuse illustration. That is, they show a woman who pulls her skirt right up to reveal thigh and buttock,[75] or who is even seen in the act of going to toilet. (Allegations of a like "indecency" were used to buttress the exclusion of women from public roles. A certain Caphurnia who "bared her bum" in court proceedings was reputed to have caused by that *oultrage* the ejection of all women from pleading at law.)[76] The reader of the *Roman de la Rose* will eventually have cause to question

---

[72] Ménard, "Représentations des vices," 188–89. For the earlier view see Kuhn, "Illustration des *Rosenromans*," 51–53, and Dahlberg, trans., 360, n. to lines 156–68.

[73] From a Middle English translation of the thirteenth century *Somme le roi: The Book of Vices and Virtues*, ed. W. Nelson Francis, EETS OS 217 (London: Oxford University Press, 1942), 13.

[74] Bodl., MS e Mus 65 (c.1390), fol. 10v.

[75] A classic example is Bodl., MS Douce 332, fol. 1v (Tuve, *Allegorical Imagery*, figure 62); other examples are listed in Ménard, "Représentations des vices," 184.

[76] See *Woman Defamed and Woman Defended*, ed. Alcuin Blamires (Oxford: Clarendon Press, 1992), 183–84; *oultrage* is the description applied in the account of "Calphurnia" given by Jean Le Fèvre, *Les Lamentations de Matheolus*, ed. A. G. Van Hamel (Paris: Bouillon, 1892/1905), Bk. II. 183–200.

and even mentally correct all this gendering of Abuse as feminine. It becomes increasingly clear in the poem that *vilanie* in the courtly love context primarily signifies thoughtless masculine sexual aggression. For instance, Bel Acueil/Responsiveness considers the Lover to be *vilains* (2899) when he first asks to have the rose; also, the Old Woman later tries to reassure Responsiveness that the Lover has never committed *outrages*, and that he will not be so dishonorable (*vilains*) as to make untoward demands (12,611–16, Horgan 195). The reassurance is empty. Despite the Lover's ostensible commitment to a behavioral code in which *vilanie* is the ultimate transgression (2074a–j, Horgan 32), the Lover will deflower the Rose when her Responsiveness has been rendered totally compliant: Responsiveness nevertheless utters a weak protest that this behavior is indecent (*trop outrageus*, 21,709). Readers of *The Wife of Bath's Tale* will likewise recall that *vileynye* is a subject on which a rapist knight has to be pointedly chastened.

Covoitise/Greed (Plates 9, 10, 11)

Guillaume produces twinned descriptions of Covoitise/Greed and Avarice "seated side by side" (Horgan 5–6). The broad distinction is that the first is the amassing principle, lust for possession; the second is the principle of miserliness, inability to use the hoard.[77] The separate identities tend to be lost in manuscript miniatures, which disclose the pull of an archetype of materialism: a figure obsessed with the contents of a treasure chest — even though this item is not specifically mentioned in either description.

The poem defines Greed through emphases on heaped treasure, theft, fraud, and disinheritance, and through the grotesque emblematic detail of "clawlike hooked" hands. Hands quite prominently hover over or grasp treasure in all three Aberystwyth illustrations without reaching hooked proportions. In NLW 5017D (Plate 9) Greed is a woman, dressed no differently from the other "vices," who sits on a bench as close as possible to an open chest. The open-palm gesture of her right hand towards the contents (unless it is an invitation to viewers to aim at wealth like hers) seems to declare a proprietorial claim over the gold objects, towards which she stares fixedly; the claim is confirmed by the way the fingers of her left hand hover over the coin collection at her end of the chest. In NLW 5013D (Plate 11) a coarse-featured woman standing at the end of a chest bends forward, reaching in to grasp a silver plate with one hand and a gold goblet with the other. That it is not realistic to try to get at the contents of such a chest from

---

[77] The distinction is articulated later in the poem by Amis/Friend (9545–48).

the end rather than the front is a technicality: the paradoxical objective of these miniatures is to display the contents to the reader.

Greed in NLW 5016D (Plate 10) is not very different. She stands at one end of a chest which is stacked with gold coins, each sporting a cross, and grasps a goblet with her right hand while the left holds a purse, full to the brim with coins. A sign of her wealth is that instead of a bench she possesses a horseshoe chair from which she has just risen. Above, as in NLW 5017D (Plate 9), clothes hang on a horizontal pole — a detail to which we shall return: but for now something else should be noted, namely that Greed does not wear the kerchief in Plate 10. Should we be content with a simple explanation for this? Perhaps the absence of headdress, allowing both neck and modish hairstyle (on which we shall comment later) to be highly visible, merely attests the status proper to an aristocratic young woman who owns such wealth.[78]

However, a more absorbing possibility suggests itself once we notice that, with her neatly braided-up hairstyle, she is most closely echoed in this manuscript in the figures of Oiseuse/Ease (folios 5v and 7r) and Venus (folio 129v).[79] Without pressing the observation too hard, we might speculate further why for this artist the woman who projects Greed is distinct from the other vices, and somehow assimilates herself to the courtly female figures who will promote the Lover's quest. The point could be twofold. In one way her conspicuously revealed hair contributes a sense of allure, proper to the understanding of Greed as an enticement; for Guillaume states that she "entices" people to take rather than give (170–71). Secondly, and perhaps more strikingly, she implicitly brings to the front of the poem an asset-stripping mentality which will intermittently be imputed to beautiful much-courted women in the poem and will be positively urged as feminine policy by the Old Woman. The present miniature perhaps instinctively associates amassed wealth with a woman who, unlike the other "vices" in this manuscript, is presented as potential love-object; yet if so, the instinctive equation of love-object with acquisitiveness is precisely one that is to become a problematic emphasis in the poem: "nearly all women," alleges Amis/Friend "take greedily" (*sunt . . . covoiteuses de prendre*), leaving destitute those who love them (8251–56, Horgan 127). Here therefore is a suggestive lesson in what narrative illustrators can do. Consciously or unconsciously, their techniques run visual parallels past us so as to produce reflection on deep structures within the poem.

---

[78] Covoitise is also bareheaded in Morgan, MS M 324, fol. 2v. Other "vices" who sometimes lack the kerchief are Tritesce (because she tears her hair) or Povrete (because ill-provided with clothes: cf. plate 27).

[79] See plates 29, 31, 44.

CHAPTER TWO

Auarice/Avarice (Plates 11, 12, 13)

The illuminators disclose that they are not responding scrupulously to the visual details supplied by Guillaume, for they do not generally show Avarice as dirty or emaciated, and never as discolored — "green as a chive." In the Aberystwyth manuscripts she is not even "poorly dressed" (as she is supposed to be) in a worn and patched old tunic.[80] In NLW 5016D (Plate 13) there is only the return to the knotted coverchief to differentiate her clothing from Greed's. In the other two manuscripts, there is no differentiation in clothing.

The sign chiefly chosen to express avarice pictorially is her purse,[81] which according to Guillaume she holds tightly tied up, reluctant to extract anything from it. NLW 5017D and 5013D (Plates 12, 11) both register the closed neck of the purse, the latter miniature more expressively projecting its owner's obsession with it in that she holds it with both hands, one keeping the neck tight and the other cradling its weight like a baby against her waist.[82] In NLW 5016D too (Plate 13) the purse is central, but while the treasure chest is now aptly shown closed tight, the purse is open. Although this might register Guillaume's wry remark that the removal of a coin from it would have been a slow business, it is more likely that the 5016D artist has a preconceived and indiscriminate idea of the need for an open purse to signify wealth both in Avarice and in Greed. Similarly the 5013D artist has a preconceived and indiscriminate idea that the chest should be open in either case. And again, in a different permutation, the 5016D and 5017D artists incorporate an emphatic detail of Guillaume's Avarice in their Greed miniatures as well, for they attribute clothes hung on a horizontal clothes pole to both vices.

The clothes pole is worth a moment's attention. Clothes poles were part of the scanty fittings of a medieval chamber. They are sometimes mentioned in medieval romance, mainly because when heroes are in a tight spot they find them useful as impromptu weapons.[83] Strictly the pole in the *Rose* sequence should be confined

---

[80] Avarice has patched clothes in, for example: BL, MS Add. 31840, fol. 4v, and MS Royal 20 A. XVII, fol. 3v; BN, MS fr. 378, fol. 13v (Dahlberg, trans., figure 5); Bodl., MS Douce 332, fol. 2v; Morgan, MS M 245, fol. 2v.

[81] The symbol is even multiplied in Bodl., MS Douce 332, fol. 2v by the presence around Avarice of five pot-shaped objects stuffed with coins on the floor — apparently monster purses. However, variants are found, such as weighing gold in scales, BL, MS Egerton 2022, fol. 6r.

[82] Avarice often holds a purse in her lap: e.g., BL, MS Stowe 947, fol. 2v; Morgan, MS M 132, fol. 3r, and MS M 324, fol. 2v; Bodl., MS e Mus 65, fol. 2v, and MS Douce 332, fol. 2v. In ÖNB, MS 2592, fol. 2v, she is using both hands to hold, or tie, the drawstrings of a purse in her lap.

[83] *Guigemar* 593–600, in Marie de France, *Lais*, ed. A. Ewert (Oxford: Blackwell, 1978); and *The Lais of Marie de France*, trans. Glyn S. Burgess and Keith Busby (Harmondsworth: Penguin, 1986), 51.

to Avarice. In the text it serves to demonstrate her miserliness because on it hang only two sorry items: a mantle, lined not with fur but with ragged black lambswool, and a nondescript tunic. In rare cases the black lambswool appears in the miniature,[84] but in many examples the clothes pictured are either colorful or even (as in NLW 5016D and 5017D, Plates 13, 12) fur-lined, in outright defiance of the text. Where fur-lined clothes on a pole have also crossed over into the Greed miniature (as in NLW 5017D folio 2r, Plate 9) that is apt enough, since she might fittingly be construed to have an appetite for expensive clothes. But in the case of nice clothes attributed to Avarice one must assume that illuminators have wrongly imported them as characteristic accompaniments of the pole. Later in the poem the Jealous Husband is imagined criticizing his wife's extravagant clothes, nothing but an encumbrance to himself and an illusion to others, the "dresses and miniver furs" which are "put on a pole to hang all night" (8843–45, Horgan 136). Furs on a clothes pole evidently have a quasi-proverbial status. But the interesting thing is that those Avarice miniatures which disobey Guillaume's text and give Avarice (as a woman) a stock of fine clothes, are actually confirming the misogynous stereotype alleging women's dressiness, as voiced by the Jealous Husband.[85] The omission of "patches" from Avarice's own attire together with the presence of rich fabrics in her room therefore firm up the trend we noticed in the previous miniature, associating women (though not in this instance an aristocratic woman) with expense and money. The illuminators, prone to query misogynous nuance in some quarters — by gendering Felonie masculine — are found to exacerbate it in others.

Envie/Envy (Plates 14, 15, 16)

The keynotes of Guillaume's Envy are rather abstract and consist in her loathing of the achievements of others, her spiteful delight in others' misfortunes (such as the ruin of a great family), and her defamatory practices; she is said to squint obliquely at everything, one eye closed in disdain. (Evidently there was overlap with the concept of *jalousie*, for the Friend later characterizes Jealousy as a fierce, tormented woman "who is always enraged by the joy of others" [7373–74, Horgan

---

[84] For instance, BN, MS fr. 380, fol. 2v; Bodl., MS Douce 332, fol. 2v; ÖNB, MS 2592, fol. 2v. Ménard observes that Guillaume's point could be affected by the vagaries of fashion: hence black lambswool acquired more positive connotations early in the fifteenth century: "Représentations des vices," 181.

[85] The stereotype is familiar from its exploitation in Chaucer's *Shipman's Tale*: "The sely housbonde, algate he moot paye, / He moot us clothe, and he moot us arraye" (VII. 11–12).

113].) There seems to have been no paramount cue for illuminators here. They quite often painted her alone in various postures of malicious "squinting" disdain. The NLW 5017D artist has reduced her to an icon of melancholy (Plate 14), adopting the gesture of leaning the cheek on the palm of one hand which ubiquitously signified melancholic reflection in the Middle Ages.[86] She sits frontally but with face sideways, her other arm drooping slackly across her lap, and is more a figure of pathos than the creature seething with malice in the text. Although versions of Envy in a comparable posture occur elsewhere,[87] *Rose* artists betray uncertainty about the gestures appropriate to this personification when presenting her in isolation.[88]

The most consistent means of expanding this illustration was to give Envy something to show ill will about — usually, a pair of lovers at the other end of the picture space — thus providing "an exemplification of envious conduct, as opposed to abstract Envy."[89] NLW 5016D (Plate 15) epitomizes that tradition. Envy in a pale violet dress sits, both her hands gesturing across in some kind of remonstration at a couple embracing on the right. There a fresh-faced youth is dressed in a fashionably short knee-length tunic in pink; his hood has a fashionably long "liripipe" extension hanging behind his back to a matching length. He wears dapper black shoes and the artist has emphasized his athletic calves to the point of distraction. Made to stand on the lowest section of the miniature frame, he appears shorter than his partner, at whom he looks upward and into her eyes, as she gazes back downward into his while they embrace. His right hand is on her upper arm, but equivocally close to her breast. She wears a dress whose color pointedly echoes Envy's, and the fact that her hair is unbraided visually corroborates the sensuality of the moment.

Other artists articulate this image with minor variations (for instance, more decorum, a recognition by the couple that they are watched, more sexual hand-contact, or a more abandoned embrace).[90] The only textual warrant for it is

---

[86] Identified as *douleur* by Garnier, *Langage de l'image*, 181–84: sometimes used for Envie elsewhere, e.g., Morgan, MS M 324, fol. 3r. "All sorts of grief, misery, depression, pain, and remorse were expressed by the pose," as James A. Rushing Jr. observes, *Images of Adventure: Ywain in the Visual Arts* (Philadelphia: University of Pennsylvania Press, 1995), 61.

[87] E.g., Bodl., MS e Mus 65, fol. 6r.

[88] See various arm gestures in Bodl., MS Selden Supra 57, fol. 3r, and Brussels, Bibl. Roy. MS 9576, fol. 3r (both seated); and in Bodl., MS Douce 371, fol. 2v (standing).

[89] Fleming, *Study in Allegory*, 33. See BN, MS fr. 1561, fol. 2v, MS fr. 1564, fol. 2r, and MS fr. 1565, fol. 3r; also Ménard, "Représentations des vices," 183; Robertson, *Preface to Chaucer*, 207–8; and Kuhn, "Illustration des *Rosenromans*," 55.

[90] See respectively BN, MS fr. 378, fol. 13v (Dahlberg, trans., figure 6); ÖNB, MS 2592, fol. 3r (Kuhn, "Illustration des *Rosenromans*," plate II); BL, MS Royal 19 B. XIII,

glimpsed in Guillaume's closing comment that Envy "melted with rage when she saw anyone who was worthy or good or fair, or whom men loved or praised [... *amez ou loez de genz*]" (287–90, Horgan 7). The mere hint that she cannot bear to see anyone "loved" has been thoroughly sexualized by the illustrators, and this confirms their interest (which we have already begun to trace) in assuming more explicit links between the "vice" sequence and the poem's notorious amorous action than Guillaume himself seems to present.

The Aberystwyth example compounds reasons for Envy's sexual jealousy: the other woman wears "her" own dress, has nice blonde hair, she is tall, she has a lover, her lover has magnificent calves and is a person of fashion, and the relativities of height declare the lady to be sovereign over him.[91] And of course sexual *jalousie* will be a thread in the poem: blatantly, in the case of the Jealous Husband; and enigmatically, in the case of the Jealousy who will seek to prevent the seduction of the Rose. It is far-fetched, in our view, to go further than this and claim that Envie in such a configuration signifies the "voyeuristic" clerkly author gazing at Lover and Rose, or enacting "the ambivalent subjectivity of the older author ... watching his younger self."[92]

In NLW 5013D (Plate 16) Envy reacts to something different. Beak-nosed and snarling toothily in conformity with other vices in the manuscript, she leans back in a horseshoe chair (repeating the chair of Avarice on the manuscript's facing page), supporting her face with the "melancholy" gesture already discussed. There is an impression that she is recoiling from the figure who stands before her. He has a neat pointed beard, wears a long blue robe, and holds a book in one hand while making a pointing gesture with his other. The beard and book denote wisdom. It is not immediately clear whether his attitude bespeaks accusation, exhortation, or just advice,[93] nor whether the upward-pointing gesture of Envy's right hand signifies her attempt to sustain authority against him.[94]

The text/illustration relation here is quizzical. The viewer is bound to speculate that this might be Envy resenting a "worthy" man: but the effect is interestingly complicated by a counter-suggestion that the worthy man is castigating Envy. In fact, there is a case for describing the miniature as the Narrator/Dreamer's encounter with Envie. A closely matching configuration in a Morgan manu-

---

fol. 6v; and Paris, Bibl. Ste-Geneviève MS 1126, fol. 3r (Garnier, *Langage de l'Image*, figure 162).

[91] Camille comments on a "subservient-size relationship" created on an enamel box where a man stretches up to caress his lady, because she stands on a plinth: *Gothic Idol*, 299.

[92] Nichols, "Ekphrasis, Iconoclasm, and Desire," 156.

[93] A horizontally pointed index finger indicates "assertion of ideas" or "advice" according to Garnier, *Langage de l'image*, 168–70.

[94] Cf. Garnier, *Language de l'image*, 169 figure A, and comment, 167.

script has been reckoned to show Envy "in the company of the *Rose* poet himself, Guillaume de Lorris. Portrayed as a tonsured clerk holding a book, Guillaume points to Envy."[95] As Nichols suggests, this would indicate something distinctive about this particular portrait since "none of the others is privileged by the presence of the author" (153) — as though Envie is such a repulsive phenomenon that it (she) has to be specially reprimanded by the writer.

Yet the very fact that this would be a major deviation from the norm of the poem's "vices" iconography should make us think twice. The "presence of the author" (or of the Dreamer) may be questioned here and in the few other parallels that exist.[96] We suggest, rather, that the key to this variant of Envie lies in the meaning of the verb *envier*. Douglas Kelly has said of the personifications in the *Rose* that they "act out their semantic potential."[97] The configuration in this miniature acts out the semantic potential of Old French *envier* to mean "to compete with/contend with." In the early fifteenth century Louis of Orléans adopted the device of a knotty stick with the words *Je l'envie*, "I challenge him," to indicate his opposition to John the Fearless, Duke of Burgundy.[98] Plate 16 imagines *envie* in terms of the vice's angry disputation with a learned man. It is no coincidence that her opponent replicates the figure of a "debating churchman" in a manuscript of *Le Songe du verger* roughly contemporary with NLW 5013D. The frontispiece to the *Songe* in that manuscript (figure 2) shows the writer as dreamer lying beside a spring, while a theologian and a knight debate the relative claims of spiritual and secular power.[99] The parallel between the theologian figure in the *Songe* miniature and the clerical figure in Plate 16 indicates that the *Rose* artist is expressing the *contentiousness* of Envy, who confronts and is confronted by an academic disputant.

Tritesce/Misery (Plates 17, 18, 19)

Gaunt and yellow-complexioned, Guillaume's personification of Misery is driven

---

[95] Nichols, "Ekphrasis, Iconoclasm, and Desire," 153, referring to Morgan, MS M 132, fol. 3v, reproduced by Nichols on page 164.

[96] Draguignan, Bibl. mun. MS 17, fol. 3r (fourteenth century); Valencia, Bibl. Univ. MS 387, fol. 3v; and BN, MS fr. 12596, fol. 4r (fifteenth century). We are indebted to Meradith McMunn for information on variant Envy miniatures.

[97] Kelly, *Internal Difference*, 140.

[98] Scott, *Late Gothic Europe*, 96. The use of Middle English *envien* in its sense "contend, vie with" is found also in Chaucer.

[99] BL, MS Royal 19 C. IV, fol. 1v (color reproduction in Avril, *Manuscript Painting at the Court of France*, plate 31): in both manuscripts, the white fur-lined hood with floppy white lapels is probably an academic hood.

by such convulsions of grief that she has scratched her face, torn her dress, and tugged her hair into straggling confusion. In this it is the visual rhetoric of dishevelment that many illustrators attempt. They show a woman with a wretched face in the act of pulling her hair down each side of her neck.[100] In many cases the effect of this Mary Magdalene-like abandonment to grief is intensified by the fact that her dress is falling (or being pulled) open.

All three NLW artists have opted for an alternative model. Electing to keep her hair tidily out of the way in the standard coverchief, they have concentrated on a dejected hang of the head and (in two instances) on another visual signal for intense grief, half hinted in Guillaume's remark that Misery "beat her hands together (*ses poinz ensemble hurtoit*)" (328, Horgan 7). This converges with the medieval iconography denoting the emotional misery of mourners or those condemned to hell, though more accurately in such cases it is less a question of the hands beating each other than of one hand grasping the other wrist.[101] This is the gesture of Tritesce in NLW 5016D (Plate 18). In 5017D (Plate 17) her fingers interlock in a more contorted gesture reminiscent of pictures of the Virgin and St John in the throes of grief beneath the cross.[102] The NLW 5013D illuminator reverts to the iconography of melancholy (arguably less appropriate to the vehemence of Misery's state), showing her cheek supported by one hand, while the other hand touches a fold of her dress in her lap (Plate 19).[103] None of the Aberystwyth artists acknowledges the notion of a torn dress.

Misery (perhaps the simplest of these "vices") will turn up like the others inside the garden from which she ostensibly faces away. Guillaume's section of the poem concludes with the Lover reduced to desolation, "given over to grief and

---

[100] Bodl., MS Selden Supra 57, fol. 3r, and MS e Mus 65, fol. 6v; ÖNB, MS 2592, fol. 3v (Kuhn, "Illustration des *Rosenromans*," plate II); BL, MS Add. 31840, fol. 5r, MS Egerton 2022, fol. 6v, MS Royal 19 B. XIII, fol. 7r, MS Royal 20 A. XVII, fol. 4v, and MS Yates Thompson 21, fol. 5r; Morgan, MS M 324, fol. 3v.

[101] Garnier, *Langage de l'image*, 198, 200–1. Garnier also discusses one image of Tritesce (Paris, Bibl. Ste-Geneviève MS 1126, fol. 3v) in which she is slumped forward with crossed forearms, a sign of powerlessness: 128, 179, and plate 158. For more discussion of gestures of grief see Moshe Barasch, *Gestures of Despair in Medieval and Early Renaissance Art* (New York: New York University Press, 1971).

[102] The Gorleston Psalter, BL, MS Add. 49622, fol. 7r (Marks and Morgan, *Golden Age of English Manuscript Painting*, plate 20): cf. Tritesce in BN, MS fr. 378, fol. 14r (Dahlberg, trans., figure 7). Onlookers in *Rose* illustrations of Lucretia's suicide also twist hands or fingers together, e.g., Morgan, MS M 324, fol. 59r (see figure 7). For the use of the gesture in a fifteenth-century manuscript to illustrate "Damon mourning the loss of his mistress" see Meiss, *The Limbourgs and their Contemporaries*, plates 241, 244.

[103] Again, 5013D closely matches its counterpart in Morgan, MS M 132, fol. 4r.

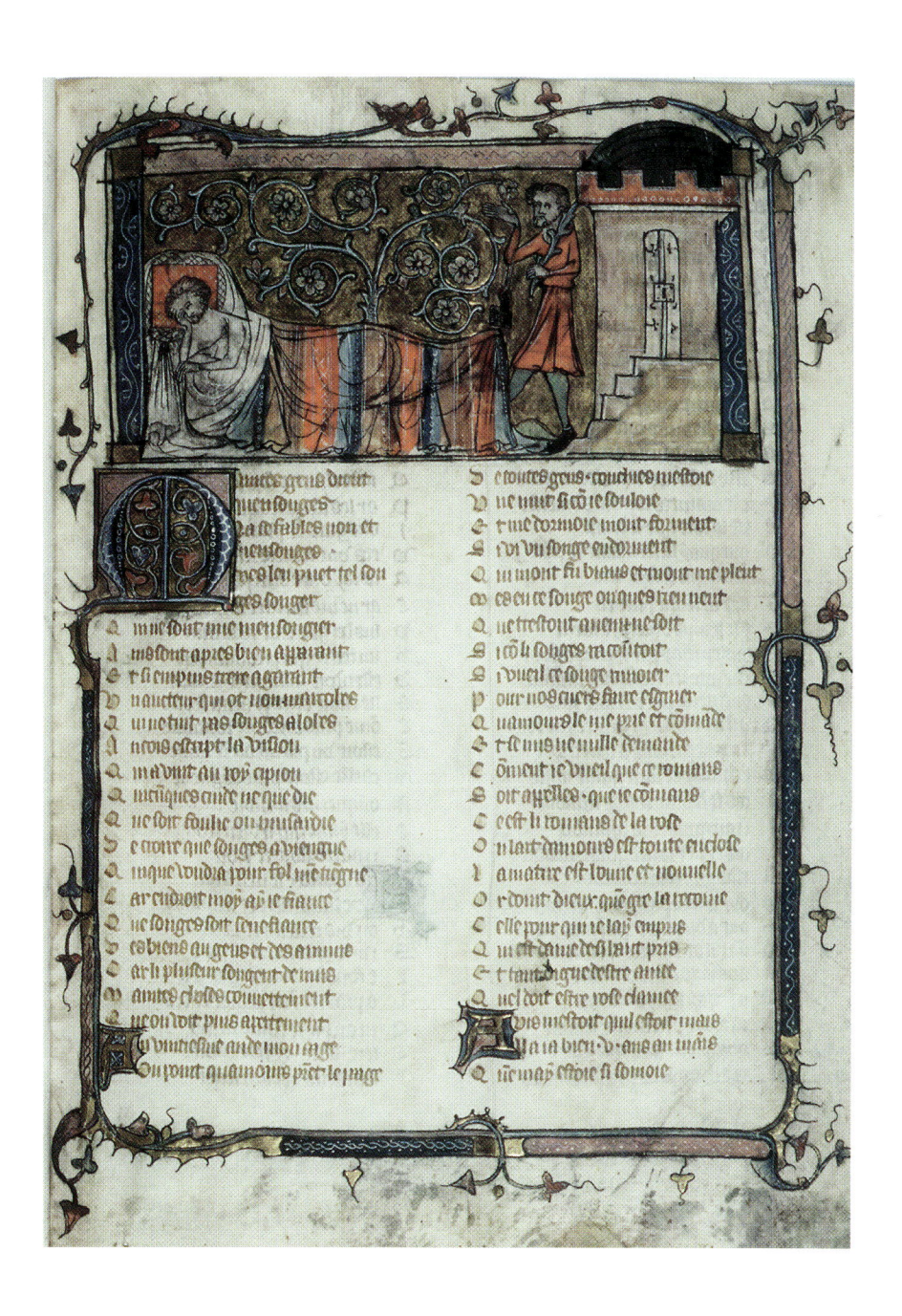

Plate 1: Frontispiece; Aberystwyth, NLW MS 5017D, fol. 1r (c. 1330–50).
By permission of the National Library of Wales.

Plate 2: Frontispiece; Aberystwyth, NLW MS 5013D, fol. 1r (c. 1380–1400). By permission of the National Library of Wales.

Plate 3: Haïne; Aberystwyth, NLW MS 5017D, fol. 2r (c. 1330–50).
By permission of the National Library of Wales.

Plate 4: Haïne; Aberystwyth, NLW MS 5016D, fol. 3r (c. 1365–75).
By permission of the National Library of Wales.

Plate 5: Haïne; Aberystwyth, NLW MS 5013D, fol. 2r (c. 1380–1400).
By permission of the National Library of Wales.

Plate 6: Felonie; Aberystwyth, NLW MS 5013D, fol. 2r (c. 1380–1400).
By permission of the National Library of Wales.

Plate 7: Vilanie; Aberystwyth, NLW MS 5013D, fol. 2r (c. 1380–1400).
By permission of the National Library of Wales.

Plate 8: Vilanie; Aberystwyth, NLW MS 5017D, fol. 2r (c. 1330–50).
By permission of the National Library of Wales.

Plate 9: Covoitise; Aberystwyth, NLW MS 5017D, fol. 2r (c. 1330–50).
By permission of the National Library of Wales.

Plate 10: Covoitise; Aberystwyth, NLW MS 5016D, fol. 3r (c. 1365–75).
By permission of the National Library of Wales.

Plate 11: Covoitise and Avarice;
Aberystwyth, NLW MS 5013D, fol. 2v (c. 1380–1400).
By permission of the National Library of Wales.

Plate 12: Avarice; Aberystwyth, NLW MS 5017D, fol. 2v (c. 1330–50).
By permission of the National Library of Wales.

Plate 13: Avarice; Aberystwyth, NLW MS 5016D, fol. 3v (c. 1365–75).
By permission of the National Library of Wales.

Plate 14: Envie; Aberystwyth, NLW MS 5017D, fol. 2v (c. 1330–50).
By permission of the National Library of Wales.

Plate 15: Envie; Aberystwyth, NLW MS 5016D, fol. 3v (c. 1365–75).
By permission of the National Library of Wales.

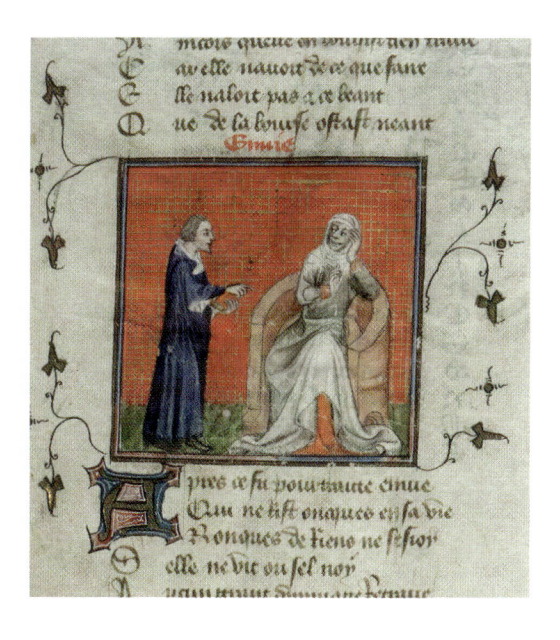

Plate 16: Envie; Aberystwyth, NLW MS 5013D, fol. 3r (c. 1380–1400).
By permission of the National Library of Wales.

Plate 17: Tritesce; Aberystwyth, NLW MS 5017D, fol. 3r (c. 1330–50).
By permission of the National Library of Wales.

Plate 18: Tritesce; Aberystwyth, NLW MS 5016D, fol. 4r (c. 1365–75).
By permission of the National Library of Wales.

Plate 19: Tritesce; Aberystwyth, NLW MS 5013D, fol. 3v (c. 1380–1400).
By permission of the National Library of Wales.

Plate 20: Vielleice; Aberystwyth, NLW MS 5017D, fol. 3v (c. 1330–50).
By permission of the National Library of Wales.

Plate 21: Vielleice; Aberystwyth, NLW MS 5016D, fol. 4v (c. 1365–75).
By permission of the National Library of Wales.

Plate 22: Vielleice; Aberystwyth, NLW MS 5013D, fol. 4r (c. 1380–1400).
By permission of the National Library of Wales.

Plate 23: Papelardie; Aberystwyth, NLW MS 5017D, fol. 4r (c. 1330–50).
By permission of the National Library of Wales.

Plate 24: Papelardie; Aberystwyth, NLW MS 5016D, fol. 5r (c. 1365–75).
By permission of the National Library of Wales.

Plate 25: Papelardie; Aberystwyth, NLW MS 5013D, fol. 4v (c. 1380–1400).
By permission of the National Library of Wales.

Plate 26: Povreté; Aberystwyth, NLW MS 5017D, fol. 4r (c. 1330–50).
By permission of the National Library of Wales.

Plate 27: Povreté; Aberystwyth, NLW MS 5016D, fol. 5r (c. 1365–75).
By permission of the National Library of Wales.

Plate 28: Povreté; Aberystwyth, NLW MS 5013D, fol. 4v (c. 1380–1400).
By permission of the National Library of Wales.

Plate 29: The Lover encounters Oiseuse;
Aberystwyth, NLW MS 5016D, fol. 5v (c. 1365–75).
By permission of the National Library of Wales.

Plate 30: The Lover in the garden with birds;
Aberystwyth, NLW MS 5016D, fol. 6v (c. 1365–75).
By permission of the National Library of Wales.

Plate 31: Oiseuse leads the Lover to the garden gate;
Aberystwyth, NLW MS 5016D, fol. 7r (c. 1365–75).
By permission of the National Library of Wales.

Plate 32: The *carole*; Aberystwyth, NLW MS 5017D, fol. 6v (c. 1330–50).
By permission of the National Library of Wales.

Plate 33: Deduiz (or the Lover) walks among trees;
Aberystwyth, NLW MS 5016D, fol. 8r (c. 1365–75).
By permission of the National Library of Wales.

Plate 34: Narcissus gazes at the spring;
Aberystwyth, NLW MS 5016D, fol. 11v (c. 1365–75).
By permission of the National Library of Wales.

Plate 35: The God of Love shoots an arrow at the Lover;
Aberystwyth, NLW MS 5016D, fol. 13r (c. 1365–75).
By permission of the National Library of Wales.

Plate 37: The God of Love locks the Lover's heart;
Aberystwyth, NLW MS 5016D, fol. 15r (c. 1365–75).
By permission of the National Library of Wales.

Plate 36: The Lover's homage; the God of Love locks his heart;
Aberystwyth, NLW MS 5016D, fol. 15r (c. 1365–75).
By permission of the National Library of Wales.

Plate 38: Bel Acueil reprimands the Lover;
Aberystwyth, NLW MS 5016D, fol. 20v (c. 1365–75).
By permission of the National Library of Wales.

Plate 39: Reason addresses the Lover;
Aberystwyth, NLW MS 5016D, fol. 21r (c. 1365–75).
By permission of the National Library of Wales.

Plate 40: The Jalous beats his wife (misplaced);
Aberystwyth, NLW MS 5016D, fol. 26v (c. 1365–75).
By permission of the National Library of Wales.

Plate 41: Author writing;
Aberystwyth, NLW MS 5016D, fol. 28r (c. 1365–75).
By permission of the National Library of Wales.

Plate 42: Friend advises the Lover;
Aberystwyth, NLW MS 5016D, fol. 47r (c. 1365–75).
By permission of the National Library of Wales.

Plate 43: The Lover meets Richece and her partner;
Aberystwyth, NLW MS 5016D, fol. 64r (c. 1365–75).
By permission of the National Library of Wales.

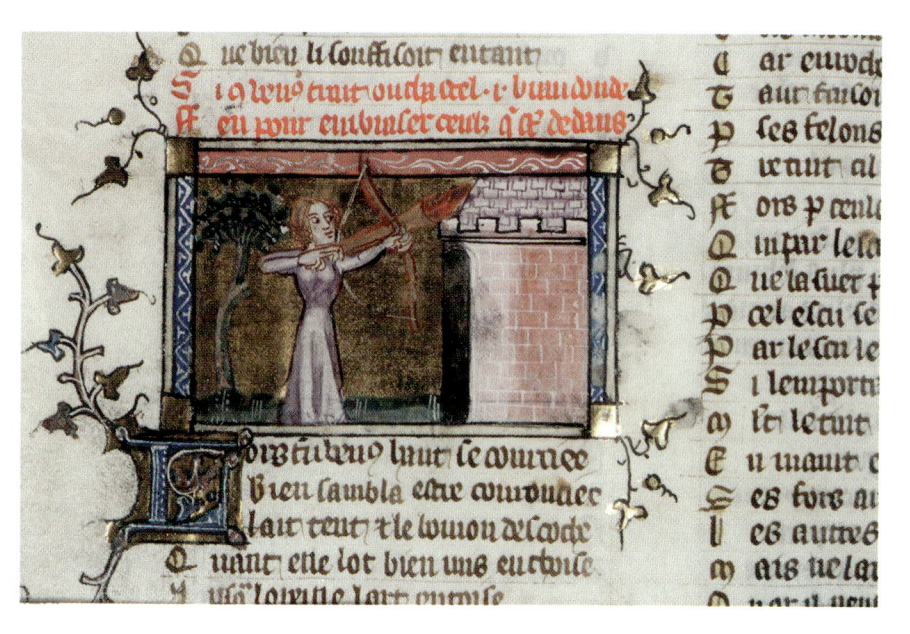

Plate 44: Venus aims at the castle;
Aberystwyth, NLW MS 5016D, fol. 129v (c. 1365–75).
By permission of the National Library of Wales.

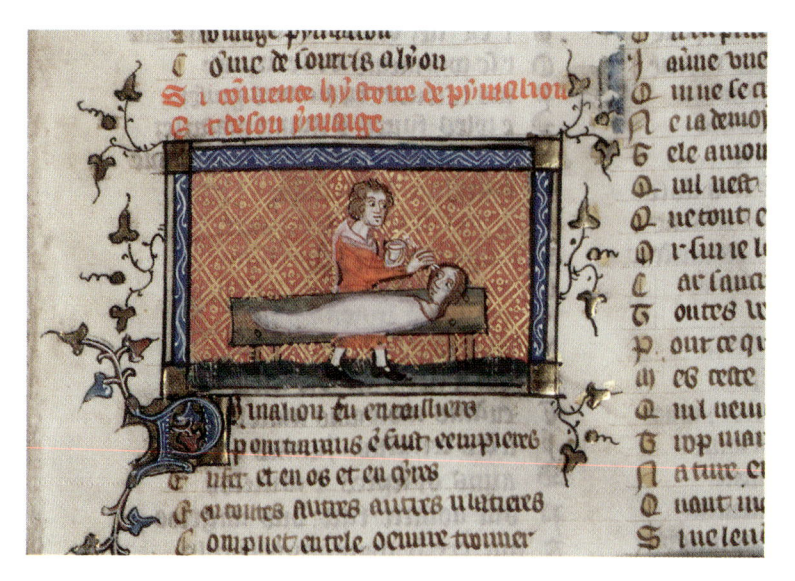

Plate 45: Pygmalion sculpts a female form;
Aberystwyth, NLW MS 5016D, fol. 130r (c. 1365–75).
By permission of the National Library of Wales.

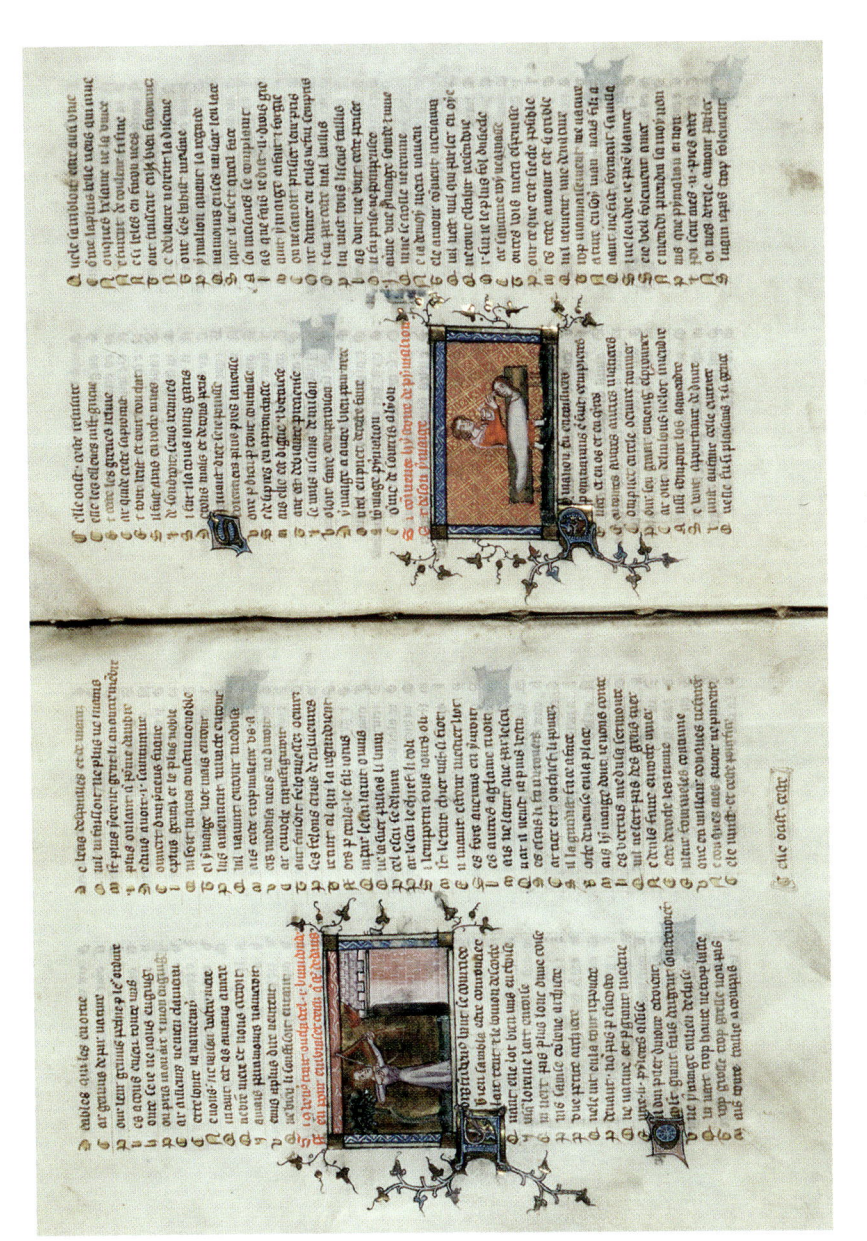

Plate 46: Venus and Pygmalion (whole opening);
Aberystwyth, NLW MS 5016D, fols 129v–130r (c. 1365–75).
By permission of the National Library of Wales.

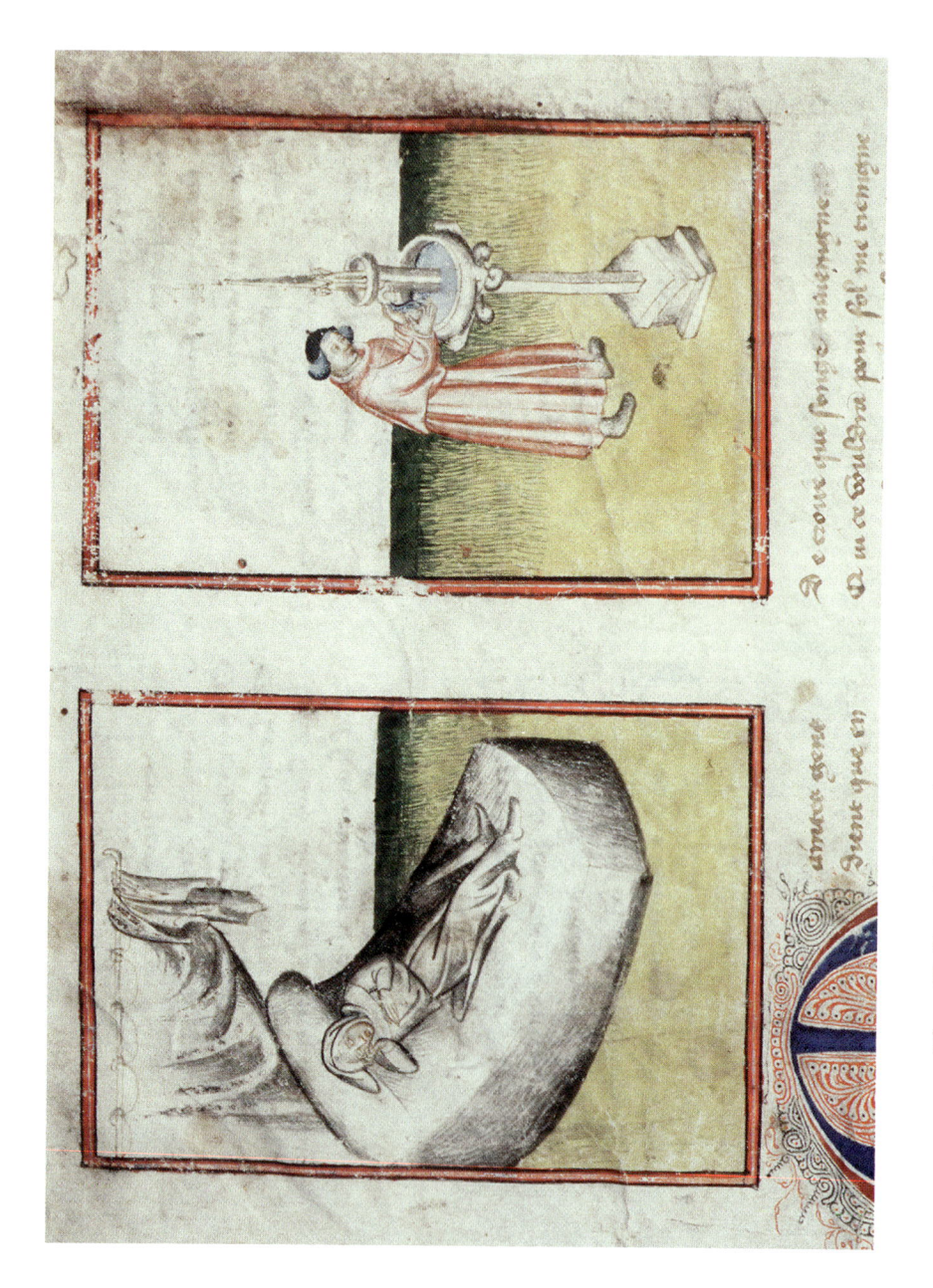

Plate 47: Frontispiece; Aberystwyth, NLW MS 5011E, fol. 1r (c. 1420–30). By permission of the National Library of Wales.

Plate 48: Frontispiece; Aberystwyth, NLW MS 5014D, fol. 1r (c. 1480–1500).
By permission of the National Library of Wales.

Ains que diller me peuusse
En mon lieu encor demourasse
Par huit jolineto nulle
A fleur du beau rosier sueilly
I mis en la rose vermeille
Dorant sic souez ie me sueille

Cy fine le romant de la Rose
ou lart damors est tout enclose
Deo gracias

Plate 49: *Explicit* with scribal sketch of a rose;
Aberystwyth, NLW MS 5014D, fol. 146r (c. 1480–1500).
By permission of the National Library of Wales.

torment" (*a duel et a poine*, 3921, Horgan 60) when his quest for the Rose is blocked.

Vielleice/Senility (Plates 20, 21, 22)

The Senility image opens up possibilities for illuminators even though they do not emulate Guillaume's density of detail. What he calls her "bleached" head and hairy ears are often ruled out visually by the retention of the perennial coverchief, and one can hardly expect the miniatures to express the poetry's sense of *process* (the slow rot of Time which has taken away Vielleice's prime). Nevertheless NLW 5016D (Plate 21) catches Guillaume's suggestion of the elderly person's need for warmth: depicting her body "covered in a fur-lined cloak" (398–400, Horgan 8), and not only carefully showing the fur lining but also having her arriving on her crutches in front of a roaring fire, whose elegant green chimney breast above produces a puff of smoke through an aperture rising impishly through the top of the miniature's frame. Her left hand is cleverly balanced on top of the crutch so that she can open her palm to the heat. (The fireplace motif is not uncommon in other manuscripts.[104] One prompt for it in visual tradition would have been illustrations for the month of February where someone would be seen warming or dressing beside a roaring fire.) The woman's face in NLW 5016D is not ravaged with age. Suggestions of physical decrepitude are more marked in NLW 5017D (Plate 20), where Senility's face betrays considerable pain and her hunched back catches Guillaume's observations on the dwindling physical stature of the very old. This manuscript along with NLW 5013D (Plate 22) imagines Senility outdoors amongst representative trees, which is perhaps another way of enhancing vulnerability, away from domestic comfort.[105] But on the other hand the 5013D manuscript's illuminator is so committed to painting figures tall that his ugly, toothless woman seems elevated rather than shrunken in stature.

The image of Senility forces upon our attention the erosive power of time. Her halting infirmity casts a shadow over the easy amblings of the Lover and the light steps of the dancers which are illustrated soon afterwards, and in some illuminated manuscripts Jean de Meun's creation, the Old Woman, will be found to echo Senility's gracelessness, though not her crutches. If in the narrative there is no sign that the Lover registers the lesson on Time, the visual dimension helps make it unavoidable for the reader.

---

[104] E.g., Bodl., MS Douce 332, fol. 4r; BL, MS Royal 19 B. XIII, fol. 7v.

[105] In Morgan, MS M 245, fol. 4r, Senility hobbles past a house whose door is shut tight.

CHAPTER TWO

Papelardie/Hypocrisy (Plates 23, 24, 25)

Papelardie was a newish word for false piety when Guillaume used it,[106] but a model of religious hypocrisy was available to him and to the poems' illuminators in the thirteenth century, namely the figure of the Publican (hypocrite) who in the *Somme le roi* composition on Humility was juxtaposed with the repentant sinner. Papelardie sometimes replicates the backward-turning theatricality of the Publican figure in the "Hypocrisy" panel of these *Somme* manuscripts.[107]

The most consistent pictorial convention for Papelardie in the *Rose* was to comply with Guillaume's stipulation of a figure clothed like a nun and holding a psalter (419–21), but to supply in addition an altar at which she could make her "sham prayers" (Horgan 8). NLW 5017D and 5013D differ little in producing this model. The 5017 artist (Plate 23) gives a strong sense of the woman's parade of commitment to her psalter, which she holds open with much intensity. Also notable is the grandiose swirl of her nun's veil and its incongruous orange-red coloring. There is a strategic hint of red on her lips. The altar vestments and the chalice surmounting it are commonplace for this illustration. They reappear in NLW 5013D (Plate 25) in which, despite the unfortunate damage to the picture, can still be seen the rosary dangling from one wrist, a detail which amplifies the text's mention of feigned prayers. Although the nun/psalter/altar configuration is frequent,[108] Hypocrisy may alternatively stand in isolation reading her psalter, with or without such extra ostentations of piety as a flagellation whip.[109]

Papelardie appears kneeling again in NLW 5016D (Plate 24), veiled, with flame-red dress revealed beneath the cooler tones of her open habit. Holding herself very upright, she grips her psalter and, with the rigid sideways glare that is characteristic of this manuscript's facial expression, she concentrates on a white-clad altar surmounted by an elegant gold cross. Paradoxically the effect of her own concentration is to concentrate our attention upon her; a trick not unsuggestive of theatrical piety. Yet it is only knowledge of the text which justifies such a suspicion. The whole point about "hypocrisy" is that it looks like the real thing.

---

[106] Ménard, "Représentations des vices," 186.

[107] *Rose* examples such as BN, MS 378, fol. 14r, (Dahlberg, trans., figure 9); and *Somme le roi* examples such as BL, MS Add. 54180, fol. 97v, and BN, MS fr. 1895, fol. 77r (Kuhn, "Illustration des *Rosenromans*," figure 39).

[108] See BL, MS Royal 19 B. XIII, fol. 8r; Bodl., MS Selden Supra 57, fol. 4r, MS Douce 332, fol. 4v, and MS e Mus 65, fol. 8v; Morgan, MS M 132, fol. 5r and MS M 324, fol. 4v. In ÖNB, MS 2592, fol. 4r, Hypocrisy kneels (minus psalter) to a crucifix on an altar. In BN, MS 380, fol. 4r she "brandishes her book in two hands and beholds the heavens in a spectacular posture": Ménard, "Représentations des vices," 182 n. 17.

[109] BL, MS Royal 20 A. XVII, fol. 5v.

Here, she looks genuinely devout. To the extent that Guillaume undermines her in the ensuing description, he is undermining an image of female piety. The difference between Plate 23 (NLW 5017) and Plate 24 (NLW 5016) is the difference between a *jeu d'esprit* mocking the idea of ostentatious devotion and a version of devotion which might not be out of place in a Book of Hours. Illustrators who avoid caricature here run a very real risk of blanket insinuation that female piety is generically a sham.

Although readers may wonder for a moment whether the trenchant concept of Hypocrisy has strayed into the *Rose* by mistake, it is no excrescence to the poem. In the description the Lover asserts that the gate of "Paradise" was forbidden to her and her kind (432–33) — and this only shortly before he begins his own efforts to find a gate into a paradisal garden. The banishment of Hypocrisy, that is, feigned devotion, prepares us for the love-deity's insistence on unstinting fealty within the garden: but, for all the narrator's hostility, falsity will eventually insinuate itself into his quest in the form of Fraud (Faus Semblant) and the pseudo-nun (who might as well be Papelardie) who accompanies him. In terms of Jean's continuation, therefore, Hypocrisy could have made a fittingly provocative climax to the "vice" series. Guillaume has other ideas, however, and concludes it with Poverty.

Povreté/Poverty (Plates 26, 27, 28)

Cowering apart in a corner, according to Guillaume, is the despised figure of Poverty. She shivers in the cold, more or less "naked as a worm,"[110] or at least dressed in nothing better than an old patched sack.

The first thing to note about the Aberystwyth manuscripts is that the "corner" (*coignet*) is interpreted as a mound or hillock. Although elsewhere sometimes Poverty is depicted in something like a cavity or bivouac *within* a mound,[111] the location atop or astride a mound predominates. There is surely little doubt that this occurs through the lure of an available visual model in the destitution of Job on his dunghill.[112] The dung-like quality imported to Poverty's mound is sometimes clear;[113] though more often illustrators render it as a grassy knoll (NLW 5016D, 5017D, Plates 27, 26) or a bare but indistinct protuberance. But the rela-

---

[110] Dahlberg's trans. for *nue come vers* (443), rendered by Horgan as "stark naked" (9).
[111] E.g., Bodl., MS Selden Supra 57, fol. 4v; ÖNB, MS 2592, fol. 4v (Kuhn, "Illustration des *Rosenromans*," plate III).
[112] *Sedens in sterquilinio*, as the Vulgate version has it (Job 2:8). Cf. Branner, *Manuscript Painting in Paris*, plate VI and figures 221, 235, 236, 330, 406.
[113] E.g., BL, MS Royal 19 B. XIII, fol. 8r.

tive consistency of approach is slightly misleading. More than most of the other *Rose* "vices," Poverty miniatures diversify during the fourteenth century: the figure can be found begging alms, being preached at by a monk, warming hands at a fire, eating frugally, or wandering as a vagabond.[114]

Poverty's exposure to cold is usually rendered through patched, holed, torn, or inadequate clothes which leave knees or shoulders, and especially feet (bare or in broken shoes) prey to the elements. In Plate 27 the NLW 5016D miniaturist has limited this effect by dressing Poverty in a robe that is quite full (though systematically patched) and exposing only the neck. This Poverty is a woman with hair that is mildly unkempt — by the standard of braided coiffures seen elsewhere in the manuscript — whose gesticulating hands somewhat vaguely signal her distress. The flanking trees hinting at her social alienation are quite conventional.[115] They reappear in NLW 5017D (Plate 26). But here it is immediately apparent that Poverty, her front and arms more dramatically exposed,[116] has been supplied with a melodramatic gesture appropriate to misery (overlapping in fact with the *Rose* iconography of Tritesce); for she tugs at the ends of her hair. This is in contrast with the personification's more resignedly dejected posture in most manuscripts with head on hand or even with arms folded.[117]

The ample lower folds of Poverty's orange robe in NLW 5017D do not illustrate her deprivation: that is articulated in NLW 5013D (Plate 28) in a more standard way through a "skimpy" and "sack-like" garment (again, hanging open below the neck) from which bare legs and feet protrude in an ungainly frontal posture. Here Guillaume's suggestion that the poor are "shamed and despised" (*honteuse et despite*, 455, Horgan 9) emerges from the hang of the head and expressionless eyes. Her (his?) hair sticks up in wild disorder. Here on a barren heap cut off from foreground vegetation she (or he?) sits in a solitary world of utter depression and destitution, though the artist has not altogether reduced the figure to emaciation, as is the case in a strikingly parallel Bodleian miniature.[118]

The representation of Poverty often seems curiously androgynous. Little or no

---

[114] Ménard, "Représentations des vices," 185.

[115] Cf. BN, MS fr. 378, fol. 14v (Dahlberg, trans., figure 10); Morgan, Library MS M 324, fol. 4v; Bodl., MS Selden Supra 57, fol. 4v.

[116] Cf. Bodl., MS Selden Supra 57, fol. 4v, and MS e Mus 65, fol. 9r.

[117] Head on hand: BN, MS fr. 378, fol. 14r; Bodl., MS Selden Supra 57, fol. 4v; and Morgan, MS M 324, fol. 4v; arms folded, ÖNB, MS 2592, fol. 4v (Kuhn, "Illustration des *Rosenromans*," plate III).

[118] Bodl., MS e Mus 65, fol. 9r closely parallels 5013D's pose and gestures, but with skinnier arms and ribs visible at the chest: a very similar model is adhered to also in Morgan, MS M 132, fol. 5r.

bust appears if the garment hangs open.[119] The straggly hair is unisex. Where bare feet are displayed, they look large and masculine. Not much remains to mark gender except lack of a beard — and in NLW 5013 even that sign is unclear because the jaw is shadowed as if by stubble. Although the pull of the Job model is a relevant factor, what remains interesting is that in so far as a viewer infers that Poverty might be male, this connects with the traffic of wealth from male to female which we found implied in Greed and Avarice earlier. Whether intentionally or not, a masculinized Poverty is a way of anticipating the notion put about later in the poem — that men in love risk becoming victims of asset-stripping women, "for women nowadays are such demented creatures that they run after nothing but purses," as the Lover's Friend alleges (8317–22, Horgan 128): a grudge reinforced by a Vatican manuscript which presents at that point a woman snatching a purse away from a youth's fingers.[120] It is as though the pictorial convention for Poverty displays already such a victim — a victim of the strategies urged on mistresses by the Old Woman (La Vielle) in Jean de Meun's continuation: "sell [your heart] very dearly and always to the highest bidder" (13,011–12, Horgan 201). La Vielle even imagines a deliberate campaign to ruin her own former admirers:

> I would so pluck them and rob them, right and left, that I would make them dine on worms and lie stark naked on dung-hills. . . . I would leave them with nothing worth a bean . . . I would reduce them all to poverty. (12,880–93, Horgan 199)

This, not the admirably stoic Poverty eulogized by some speakers in the poem, is the Poverty imaged on the garden wall. In a poem supremely and sometimes cynically conscious of interconnections between generosity and desire, it is no coincidence that the series of concepts anathematized by Guillaume culminates with poverty, and no coincidence that some illustrators hinted that destitution might be a threat primarily to males.

---

[119] Fleming notes that Poverty is sometimes male: *Study in Allegory*, 46. The androgynous effect in NLW 5013D can be confirmed by contrast with examples such as CUL, MS Gg IV.6c, fol. 6v, in which the open robe definitely reveals female breasts; also by contrast with the allied figure Tritesce, whose breasts are visible in the same CUL MS and in Bodl., MS e Mus 65, fol. 6v.

[120] Vatican, MS Urb. lat., fol. 51v (König, *Die Liebe*, 37).

Chapter Two

IV. The Garden

The Garden Doorkeeper (Plate 29)

In manuscripts with picture cycles extending beyond the Vices, few illustrations are more regularly provided, or have provoked more comment, than that which shows the Dreamer meeting Oiseuse/Ease at a doorway into the garden, which he desperately wishes to enter. Some manuscripts, including one at Aberystwyth, even double the scene to show both the meeting and the moment when the Dreamer is allowed to enter.[121] Most often there is one picture to cover both actions. Dramatically, visual interest centers on processes of welcoming and penetration figured in the invitation to pass through the barrier of the wall into a wooded space beyond. Iconographically, interest centers on the accoutrements of Ease herself.

Although illuminators do not always provide a locus, most situate Ease within or just outside a small aperture or doorway in a substantial stone structure (usually crenellated, from *bataillié*, 131). She may stand in the Dreamer's way, motion him towards the doorway, or open or unlock the door for him.[122] At her most forceful, she is represented grasping his wrist to draw him in[123] — an action reproduced in NLW 5016D in a second miniature assigned to this episode (Plate 31). The artists freely take the liberty of bringing her outside the doorway and wall, as Suzanne Lewis has noted, hence reinforcing her role as porter — a quasi-St Peter at the gate of this particular "paradise."[124]

In NLW 5016D folio 5v (entitled "How he [the Dreamer] found Oiseuse"), Ease is encountered brandishing both the mirror which Guillaume says she "held in her hand" (555) and the comb whose use is described as her entire day's preoccupation (566–68). As we saw in Chapter One, there has been a tendency to label the whole as emblematic of lust (*luxuria*), whereas it is more rational to identify here a primary iconography of the cultivation of beauty which only ease or *otium* can afford, as Ovid had insisted. Ease therefore controls access to the garden of pleasure because dedication to pleasure entails (in Sarah Kay's apt phrase) "conspic-

---

[121] E.g., BL MS Royal 20 A. XVII, fols 7r and 7v (at lines 580 and 629).

[122] The first in Vatican, MS Urb. lat. 376, fol. 4v (König, *Die Liebe*, 25); Bodl., MS e Mus 65, fol. 7r; BN, MS fr. 25526, fol. 6r (Lewis, "Images of Opening," figure 8); and Morgan, MS M 132, fol. 6r: the second in BL, MS Royal 20 A. XVII, fol. 7r (the door is shut), and MS Stowe 947, fol. 5v: the third in Bodl., MS Selden Supra 57, fol. 5r, MS Douce 332, fol. 7r (Lewis, "Images of Opening," figure 9), and priv. coll., formerly Astor MS A. 12, fol. 8r (Lewis, "Images of Opening," figure 7).

[123] BL, MS Yates Thompson 21, fol. 6v; CUL, MS Gg. IV. 6c, fol. 7v.

[124] Lewis, "Images of Opening," 218.

uous consumption of time."[125] She carries with her the formal implements by which through leisure she enhances beauty and attraction, including the attraction of the elegant braids of her own hair. In close-up, the chief feature of the hairstyle is that strands of hair are bunched to curve from the top of her head to chin length, being neatly plaited and rounded off at that level. It is a hairstyle old-fashioned by the probable date of this manuscript, for it is characteristic of the mid-fourteenth century — a restrained forerunner of what became in many regions a dramatic framing of women's faces within geometric side-plaits known as *cornettes* (see figure 6).[126] We have already seen the 5016D illuminator assign Ease's coiffure to Covoitise/Greed (Plate 10).

Illustrators were too wedded to their own conventions for visual beauty to pay too much attention to precise textual details of appearance and dress: so Ease in Plate 29 has neither the gold-embroidered chaplet nor the white gloves nor the green dress found in her description. In her pale blue open-necked dress, body-tight at bust and waist, she is caught up in contemplation of her image in the mirror. John Berger argues that the "real function" of a mirror in the hands of a woman in visual representations of this kind is "to make the woman connive in treating herself as, first and foremost, a sight." No doubt this image of Oiseuse does bespeak the fetishization of the female body as visual object, a fetishization which has been detected in the narrative concentration on her person at this point.[127] But does the Dreamer arriving in his natty red-hooded pink robe gaze at her, or at the mirror? Standing out against the large background masses of this illustration — the gold leaf, the expanse of pinkish masonry — the mirror itself commands attention. The Dreamer's conventional gestures of communication direct us, and him, towards it. The question for the viewer is therefore not so much

---

[125] Kay, *The Romance of the Rose*, 39.

[126] See Newton, *Fashion in the Age of the Black Prince*, 96–8 and 103. For analogues to the 5016D style see various women in Peruzzi, *Codice Laurenziano*, plates III, XXI, XXIII; Franchise in BL, MS Stowe 947 (mid-fourteenth century), fol. 110r; Nature in Morgan, MS M 324 (mid-fourteenth century), fol. 106v; and the woman in bed in BL, MS Add. 42133 (2nd half fourteenth century), fol. 105v. The more developed fashion is already seen in England in the 1330s (e.g., Backhouse, *Luttrell Psalter*, figure 12), but the same manuscript also shows (figure 59) a less developed hairstyle very close to that in NLW 5016D. For examples of the developed style in the 1350s and 1370s, see the Machaut manuscript in Avril, *Manuscript Painting at the Court of France*, plates 23–25; and Hedeman, *Royal Image*, esp. figure 70.

[127] A. C. Spearing, *The Medieval Poet as Voyeur: Looking and Listening in Medieval Love-Narratives* (Cambridge: Cambridge University Press, 1993), 201; and John Berger, *Ways of Seeing* (London: BBC, 1972), 51.

CHAPTER TWO

"Will the Lover enter here?" or even "Why does Oiseuse hold a mirror?" as "What will be the significance of her mirror for the Lover?"[128]

The Garden: A Problem of Sequence (Plates 30, 31, 33)

The picture program in NLW 5016D is not comfortably synchronized with the text and rubrics on folios 5v, 6v, and 7r. The Lover's first scene with Ease (Plate 29), rubricated "Comment il trouva oyseuse," is placed at a point in the narrative (line 495, rather earlier for this scene than usual) where, tantalized by birdsong within, he searches along the outside of the garden wall for an entrance.[129] Oiseuse miniatures are more frequently allocated to the verses where she is first described (523–25) or to line 580 where she gives her name. But the next picture slot in the Aberystwyth manuscript is at the *end* of her speech ("Quant Oiseuse m'ot ce conté," 617), where the Lover declares his intention to enter Pleasure's garden and goes on to enthuse over the gathering of songbirds found within. The illustration on folio 6v (Plate 30) seems to allude to that sequel (641ff., the Lover's description of all the songbirds inside the wall) — ignoring the rubric above the frame which states that the miniature shows "How he tells Oiseuse about his situation."[130]

Worse, both rubricator and artist find themselves inserting apparently out of sequence a *subsequent* illustration (Plate 31) showing the Lover being ushered into the very garden in which the viewer has already seen him walking in the miniature at line 617. This misplaced miniature occurs at a point in the text (725) normally reserved for a picture of Pleasure's dance.[131] But the artist has followed the rubric above this picture space, which demands an illustration of "how she [Oiseuse] opened the garden door for him," a rubric which best befits the text at 629–30.[132] While confusions of sequence and subject are not uncommon in il-

---

[128] The mirror has a similar centrality in Morgan, MS M 324, fol. 5v (Fleming, *Study in Allegory*, figure 17); Bodl., MS e Mus 65, fol. 7r; and BN, MS fr. 25526, fol. 6r (Lewis, "Images of Opening," figure 8).

[129] "Quant j'oï les oisiaus chanter" (495). Former Astor MS A.12, fol. 7v, presents the defensively enclosed garden topped by birds here, but without the Lover: Lewis, "Images of Opening," figure 7.

[130] "Comment il deuise a oyseuse son estat," which is at best an inaccurate description of Amant's declaration earlier, in lines 619–28.

[131] "Cestez genz don je vos parole / s'estoient pris a la querole" (725–26).

[132] "Comment elle li ouuri luis du iardin": cf. "Lors entrai . . . par l'uis que Oiseuse overt m'ot" (629–30).

luminated manuscripts,[133] it is interesting to speculate what might have happened here.

There is a tension among three factors: the narrative implications of the locations at which the scribe has left spaces; the rubricator's attempt to prescribe a whole triptych of Oiseuse scenes;[134] and the illustrator's more conventional (but chronologically confusing) provision of two Oiseuse scenes bracketing a garden scene. Perhaps the illustrator's exemplar — or memory of one — differed from the rubricator's. Perhaps both of them were struggling to adapt an exemplar with more miniatures than the present manuscript could allow. Or perhaps the illustrator made the best of a bad job by locating a representation of the Lover wandering among the garden birds (Plate 30) beneath the rubric "Comment il deuise a oyseuse son estat" because his illustration could makes sense of the rubric if it were understood to signify "how the Lover tells the birds [*oisiaus*, rather than *oyseuse*] about his situation." To compound the confusion, there is a further garden miniature on folio 8r (Plate 33), with a rubric "How the Lover describes the birds," which is out of place there but which would suit the present miniature (Plate 30).

There is one further option about the image in Plate 30. Oiseuse has just alluded to Pleasure's enjoyment within the garden, "listening to the song of the nightingales" and other birds (605–8). In the parting speech the Lover makes to Oiseuse just after the miniature, he picks up what she has said and alludes to the attraction of joining Pleasure and company within (621–23). It is therefore conceivable that the illustration is actually intended to depict Deduiz/Pleasure, not the Lover, perambulating amid the trees and birds. In that case chronology is rescued and the Lover does not roam the garden before he enters it, though his entrance itself is nevertheless inserted curiously late in the text. The fact that no significant attempt is made to distinguish Pleasure visually from the Lover would not rule out the suggestion. On balance, however, we conclude that Plate 30 is out of sequence and represents the Lover, not Pleasure, in the garden.

Lover, Garden, and Songbirds (Plate 30)

The Lover has passed through the narrow black entrance of the gate-tower seen in the previous miniature (a little more of its conical red-tiled roof is now visible).

---

[133] For instance, in Morgan, MS M 324, fol. 140v beneath a rubric describing "how Venus set fire to the castle," the illuminator has unmistakably shown not Venus but the God of Love shooting the firebrand at the edifice.

[134] The evidence suggests that the scribe was not the rubricator, as indeed do differences in the writing.

Chapter Two

He walks behind the wall, which is laid out as if octagonally — a strategy adopted by some illuminators to compromise with the fact that it is meant to be square.[135] The songbirds which so attract the Lover and Pleasure are sometimes incorporated atop trees visible above the wall in illustrations of his encounter with Ease. Here, four birds are distinguished, more by color than by shape or size. They perch on variants of the manuscript's standard type of tree, defined by its sinuous two-tone (gold-green) trunk, leading up to double fan-shaped layers of foliage designed as alternate bands of light and dark green, the latter flecked so as to suggest either fruit or gaps between the leaves. A visual anthology of trees in medieval art would be extremely interesting. A moment's comparison shows that those of this manuscript are quite distinct from what might be called the "cabbage-leaf" trees of NLW 5017D (see Tritesce, Viellece, Plates 17, 20) and from the later "broccoli" trees of NLW 5013D folio 2r (Haïne, Plate 5). As observed above, the distinctive trees in NLW 5016D help to identify the artist as an imitator of a distinguished French illuminator of the 1350s.

The Lover wears an orange robe with a lavender hood, a color scheme for him which alternates in the manuscript with that exemplified in Plates 29 and 39, folios 5v and 21r. His head, exaggeratedly erect, expresses the impact of the garden upon him, as do his active hand gestures. "The Lover," as Hult reminds us, "is also a poet, whose essential function is to sing — a fact which explains his frequent metaphorical association with birds."[136] But it is difficult to know whether this picture reinforces a metaphorical nuance in the birdsong.

Oiseuse/Ease Admits the Lover into the Garden (Plate 31)

We are back outside the garden wall. Behind the crenellations is seen this time not the outline of trees but a riot of leaves. The foreground shows a simple action whose large size is suggestive of its dramatic importance: the moment when the Lover enters the garden enclosure. It is the first of many narrative penetrations, as has been noted, which anticipate the sexual invasion at the poem's conclusion.[137]

Are we to perceive a hint of coercion in the scene? That would be unwarranted by the text, since the Lover merely states "I entered the garden by the door

---

[135] "Hauz fu li murs et toz quarez" 462; cf. former Astor A. 12, fol. 7v (Lewis, "Images of Opening," figure 7); BL, MS Yates Thompson 21, fol. 6v; Bodl., MS Selden Supra 57, fol. 1r; Tournai, Bibl. Munic. MS C.I, fol. 1r (Kuhn, "Illustration des *Rosenromans*," figure 7).

[136] David Hult, "The Allegorical Fountain: Narcissus in the *Roman de la Rose*," *Romanic Review* 72 (1981): 125–48 (here 135).

[137] Lewis, "Images of Opening," 218.

CHAPTER TWO

that [Ease] had opened for me" (Horgan 11).[138] Those artists who (as in this manuscript) show Ease leading the Lover in by the wrist really replace the autonomy of the Dreamer in the text with a clear suggestion that he is drawn in under the spell of a seductive woman. The wrist-hold gesture is disconcertingly forceful in some manuscripts.[139] Iconographically, the gesture is ambiguous in medieval art because it denotes that the one person is taking the other either into possession (especially a man taking possession of a woman), or into protection.[140]

Moshe Barasch has shown how the gesture can incorporate these ideas both of taking possession and leading into safety or paradise, in the iconography of Christ's rescue of Adam from Limbo, and of the Ascension of Christ.[141] An important analogous case (see figure 3), where the significance is benign, is St. Peter's reception of Duke Jean de Berry into paradise in an early fifteenth-century Book of Hours.[142] In the present case, a suggestion that benign reception shades into sexual capture surfaces because the artist has deployed his limited repertoire of the fixed stare between the two figures in such a way as to suggest a kind of hypnotic chemistry between them. Ease's determination is further enhanced by her controlled movement, whereas her partner not only sways slightly forwards under her pressure, but is being brought in from the picture frame, over which protrude his shoes (a type of black sandal seen before only in the youth of the Envy miniature, Plate 15). This hint of seduction, if intended, would amount to a proactive visual interpretation of Ease's role. To be sure, in the text Ease is described as a sex object — one who would "excite the desire of the featherbrained" (532). Has the miniaturist responded by turning her into a siren-figure, luring naive Youth into a dangerous Bower of Bliss?

---

[138] "Lors entrai . . . par l'uis que Oiseuse overt m'ot" (629–30).

[139] E.g., CUL, MS Gg. IV 6c, fol. 7v. Its survival into the fifteenth century is attested by Bel Acueil's use of it to draw the Lover to the roseplot in Bodl., MS Douce 195, fol. 105v, an illustration reproduced on the jacket of the Horgan translation.

[140] See Garnier's category, "Tenue du poignet d'Autrui," *Langage de l'image*, 199–205, esp. 203 A, B, E, and 205 A, C, E; and his reproduction of the seizure of Helen by Paris (107), from the *Grandes Chroniques de France* (c. 1275), Paris, Bibl. Ste-Geneviève MS 782, fol. 2v.

[141] Moshe Barasch, *Giotto and the Language of Gesture* (Cambridge: Cambridge University Press, 1987), Chap. 8, "Grasping the Wrist," 128–44.

[142] *Grandes heures*, completed 1409, BN, MS Lat. 919, fol. 96r; see Thomas, *Golden Age*, plate 20. Droitture welcomes a lady into the City of Ladies with the same gesture (c. 1405) in Brussels, Bibl. Roy. MS 9393, fol. 35v (Meiss, *The Limbourgs and their Contemporaries*, plate 40).

Chapter Two

Deduiz/Pleasure in the Garden (Plate 33)

Again there is a problem of identification. In the narrative the Lover is now watching a courtly dance in the garden, led by Deduiz/Pleasure and his partner, Joy. The lines that follow the illustration in Plate 32 tell us that on Joy's other side is the God of Love (863–64, Horgan 15). By convention a miniature usually refers to ensuing, not preceding, text; but it is inconceivable that an illustrator would present Love here without his emblems of bow and arrows. Comparison with other manuscripts indicates that whether or not the space might have been intended for the God of Love, the figure actually presented in it signifies Pleasure. He is usually represented slightly earlier, at line 799. Most often he is among several others dancing the *carole*: but he is sometimes depicted alone, wandering among trees, as in the case of the early manuscript reproduced by Dahlberg.[143]

The keynotes of Guillaume's Pleasure are that he is handsome, elegant, charming, with the "shapely limbs" (812) and agility of youth (817). Whether to emphasize youth or handsome calves or both, the miniaturist has assigned him a knee-length tunic. If one can deduce anything from the deployment of the shortened male attire in the manuscript, it is that it is felt to befit modish or wealthy youths ("demoisiaus"), including the God of Love and Narcissus, but not the Lover himself, who generally wears a longer robe. However, it is above all the shapely limbs or "paire of legges and of feet so clene and faire," as the Wife of Bath would have put it (*Wife of Bath's Prologue*, 597–98), that declare Pleasure to be a fashionable young blade; other features such as his reddish hood and blonde hair are routine for this illustrator's male figures. If the manuscript were yet more modishly ambitious, the hood would sport an extravagantly long tail, and there would be an ornamented low-slung belt around his thighs. As it is, the selection and isolation of this image communicates, somewhat against the grain of Guillaume's persistent sexualization of his female characters, a fetishized *male* body as visual object. The manuscript thereby contrives a kind of counter-emphasis in such an illustration, to which we shall return a little later.

The rationale for this model of Pleasure as opposed to the dancing one must be that (as Ease has informed the Lover) Pleasure is the *owner* of the garden, who indeed had the trees brought here (588–92). That information triumphs over the local narrative detail about his place in the dance, with which he is associated in the part of the poem to which Plate 33 belongs. Instead, Pleasure takes the air in his garden, relaxes among his trees. It is probably an unconscious irony that in a poem devoted to sexual desire, "Pleasure" should be illustrated in solitary activity.

---

[143] BN, MS fr. 378, fol. 15v (Dahlberg, trans., figure 12). See also CUL, MS Gg. IV. 6c, fol. 9r.

CHAPTER TWO

The rubricator and the illuminator certainly do not seem to agree with each other, for this miniature cannot be showing us, as the rubric wants it to, "Comment lamant deuisoit les oysiaus" ("How the Lover describes the birds"). The rubric would befit the earlier miniature in Plate 30. A medieval reader of the manuscript, seeing no birds, would have been puzzled: yet it is well to remind ourselves that such a reader had seen "the Lover" among the trees once, and would not be able to defy the rubricator's identification as confidently as — with hindsight — we can.

The Carole (NLW 5017D: Plate 32)

Like the majority of manuscripts but unlike NLW 5016D (whose sequence we shall temporarily interrupt here), NLW 5017D acknowledges visually the fact that the Lover's discovery of Pleasure is also the discovery of a *carole* danced and sung by Pleasure and his companions (712–28). The Lover is at first a voyeur, marveling at the spectacle of all these fine people — at a lady (Joy) who sings, at the supple movements of the musicians, women who juggle tambourines and catch them on one finger, and at two girls dancing an erotic routine within the circle.

The miniature of the dance is inserted in MS 5017D at line 776, a moment when one of the company, Courtesy, invites the Lover to join in. Usually it is the concept of the dance as it is beheld, not the Lover joining it, which illustrators present. In Plate 32 there is a classic disposition of elements in this illustration: musicians to one side, and a line of dancers holding hands in a semicircular formation. The configuration admits of a narrative reading, in that the woman in blue who is conspicuous in the center could be Cortoisie, drawing the Lover (the male figure at the left who looks back as if mesmerized by the music) into the dance. On the other hand, in a more cautious reading the same man would be Deduiz/Pleasure, leading the dance, a commanding and ostentatious figure straddling the frame in a fashionable three-quarter length orange tunic with plunging sleeves cut away at the elbow. But there is no great impetus to differentiate most of the dancers, and the women all wear similar long floppy dresses[144] with but a hint of ornament at the hem around the neck.

Seven dancers are included: five, six, or thereabouts is standard in the fourteenth century. The text speaks of their "executing many fine steps and turns" (743–44) on the fresh grass, and artists do attempt all sorts of variations, from the elegantly demure step to the swaying body, jutting hip and (occasionally) cocked-

---

[144] Cf. BL, MS Stowe 947, fol. 7r (fourteenth century) and Florence, Mediceo-Laurenziana MS Acq. e Doni 153, fol. 12v (early fourteenth century; Peruzzi, *Codice Laurenziano*, frontispiece).

CHAPTER TWO

up leg. The NLW 5017D illustration has convincing lateral movement despite its tense facial expressions. It is interesting for its view of one dancer entirely from the back, which implies a circle facing outward (though the medieval *carole* characteristically faces inward as demonstrated by the Laurenziano manuscript).[145] Energy is imparted to the dance especially by the upraised instruments. A variety of trumpets, crumhorns, bagpipes, and stringed instruments is found in *carole* miniatures: here the instruments are executed in silver-gray and jauntily pierce the frame above. Whether he is in the illustration or not, the Lover's own excitement is communicated by such an image. What a pity, then, that this is the last miniature in NLW 5017D. For illustration of the narrative from this point on among the Aberystwyth manuscripts we have to rely on MS 5016D.

At the Spring of Narcissus (NLW 5016D; Plate 34)

Few episodes in the poem, and few illustrations to the text, have provoked more comment than those concerning the Lover's encounter — once he leaves Pleasure's company — with the *fontaine* ("spring") of Narcissus. According to the narrative, he arrives in a secluded spot at a spring gushing from a "marble stone" (1430, Horgan 23) beneath a pine tree. An inscription on the marble states that this is the very place where Narcissus died in futile love of his own reflection in the water. The Lover, at first scared, rashly decides that the past cannot affect his own experience, and proceeds to gaze there too. The spring contains a "perilous mirror" (1569) of love which he now shares with Narcissus. It is formed by crystal(s) at the bottom of the water: the crystal reflects not only himself but also half the garden, and within that, rosebushes, and within them (as his eyes penetrate the reflection further) one rosebud in particular, "chosen" now as the object of his quest.

Since this momentous episode is quite long, illuminated manuscripts sometimes multiply illustrations, even to the extent of providing three.[146] The main options seem to be: a youth approaching the spring; a youth gazing into the spring and seeing his reflection; a youth gazing at the spring with roses represented nearby. The pine tree is optional (in 5016D the artist deploys three conventional trees); Echo sometimes appears, pining for Narcissus; and another allusion to the Narcis-

---

[145] See Peruzzi, *Codice Laurenziano*, frontispiece; Morgan, MS M 132, fol. 7v (in a circle around a tree); and the *carole* miniature from the *Remède de Fortune* in BN, MS fr. 1586, fol. 51r (Avril, *Manuscript Painting at the Court of France*, plate 24). For the back view, cf. BL, MS Royal 20 A XVII, fol. 9r, and MS Add. 31840, fol. 11r (Fleming, *Study in Allegory*, figures 21 and 20).

[146] E.g., BL, MS Royal 20 A XVII, fols 14r, 14v, 15v.

sus story features if a horse is present — the horse upon which he has been returning from a hunt until this moment of pausing to drink at the spring.

Illustrators are divided over the necessity of including a "marble stone" at the source of the spring. They may represent the spring arising within a small rudimentary square edge, which grows increasingly elaborate as the tradition develops, until it becomes a Gothic font-like edifice. But there is a preference in the earlier manuscripts for a simple circular water source (inaccurately termed "a formless splotch" by Fleming), the water tapering neatly away from it in the shape of a "Q" across or down the picture space.[147] In NLW 5016D the blonde-haired youth, wearing the manuscript's variant short form of tunic in orange with a light pink tailed hood, is reclining sideways on a verdant bank beside just such a balloon-like spring. While his legs relax idly into the corner of the frame (a witty effect), his arms balance his twisting torso against the ground, one each side of the spring. A moment's consideration explains why this is so, even though the posture entails cranking his left elbow somewhat awkwardly around the water source. It is not just that the youth is getting as close as he can to his reflection: the visual suggestion is of a vain attempt to *embrace* that reflection.[148]

The reflection itself is painted very clearly within the white balloon-shaped source, upon which an abstract sign of fluidity is lightly imposed in the form of blue semicircular ripples. The fact that the water abruptly tapers away into obscurity emphasizes the analogy which the other evidence promotes, namely the mirror-like nature of this spring upon which everything converges at the center of the illustration. Guillaume's allegorical mode finds an apt visual complement in such a configuration. The solution is not unique, for there are other manuscripts which forcibly construct the spring into a mirror, notably a Lausanne example in which the youth seems in the act of half-lifting the square pool-edge, as though it were a mirror frame.[149] Some also express the youth's futile desire for his reflection by showing him stretching hands out to the very surface of the water as if to grasp the facial image seen there.[150] Yet since, as Lewis has pointed out, "the only way to preserve the illusion is to look but not to touch the image,"[151]

---

[147] Fleming, *Study in Allegory*, 93. The "Q-shaped" structure was traditional for representing a spring in the fourteenth century: cf. Alexander, *Medieval Illuminators*, figure 189.

[148] This is a more convincing example of the suggestion of self-embrace than found in, e.g., Morgan, MS M 324, fol. 11v, or in BL, MS Royal 20 A. XVII, fol. 14v where it has been noted by Lewis, "Images of Opening," 222. Elsewhere, theatrical or almost suffocating encircling gestures are sometimes made by Narcissus as he crouches over the well.

[149] Lausanne, Bibl. Cantonale et Universitaire MS 454, fol. 6r (Hicks, "Donner à voir," figure 1).

[150] E.g., CUL, MS Gg. IV. 6c, fol. 14r; BL, MS Royal 19 B. XIII, fol. 14v.

[151] Lewis, "Images of Opening," 225.

CHAPTER TWO

an encircling embrace is perhaps the most powerful way of expressing desire while sustaining the futile stasis that comes of loving an unattainable object.

The NLW 5016D picture is located where a "Narcissus" miniature is almost obligatory, between the two lines which first name that ill-fated youth: line 1436 stating that Narcissus died here, and 1437 that he "was a young man whom Love caught . . ." (Horgan 23: *Narcisus fu uns demoisiaus / qui Amors tint . . .*). Yet although the rubric here claims the image as his ("How Narcissus died above the spring"), this manuscript, along with others which assign only one picture to the whole episode, thereby potentially allows Narcissus to stand for the Lover, his alter ego, as well. The Lover in the next miniature in this manuscript wears the same colors and the same shoes: nothing but the length of his robe differentiates him from "Narcissus." Manuscripts with more than one illustration for the spring tend to confirm the symbiosis between Narcissus and the Lover by rendering them identically. Thus in a manuscript in London, Narcissus beholds his reflection at line 1476, but the Lover who beholds roses growing from the spring one folio later is almost identical: and in a Cambridge manuscript, successive illustrations replicate almost every detail except that in the second image the youth's eyes appear closed, and a rose climbs behind the spring.[152]

We cannot be sure how far Narcissus in the NLW 5016D rendition signifies also the Lover. The impact of this beautiful image is above all to assert the intense concentration of the male gaze and — in the clarity and precision of the identical reflected face — to assert the utter reflexivity (hence homo-eroticism) of this experience of desire. The picture, no less than the text, tantalizes us with a question which vexes readers, for as Susan Stakel observes, "Guillaume never responds to the question implicit in the fountain: to what extent is Amant loving himself under the guise of dedication to a woman?"[153]

The Arrow of Desire (Plate 35)

Although the next illustration is contrastingly dynamic, in a sense it reasserts the homo-eroticism of Narcissus. The God of Love, who has emerged from the dance and stalked the Lover (lines 1679ff., beneath the miniature), ritualizes the moment of the Lover's selection of a love-object by shooting him through the eye into the heart. In representing the God, the illustrator makes extravagant efforts to combine the semiotics of authority with the semiotics of handsomeness. Amors dominates, even outgrows, the picture space, his large orange wings arching around his

---

[152] BL, MS Royal 20 A. XVII, fols. 14v, 15v; CUL, MS Gg. IV. 6c, fols. 30r, 14r.

[153] Stakel, *False Roses*, 110. The question is absorbingly explored by Hult, "The Allegorical Fountain."

CHAPTER TWO

crowned head and his sumptuous regal fur-lined mantle spreading open from shoulders to the ground, the white fur dramatically highlighting the shapeliness of limb disclosed by his tight-fitting lavender pleated tunic with matching hose. As elsewhere in the manuscript, the male leg struts forth in uncompromising black outline. There is no sign of the impossibly baroque robe which Guillaume has asked us to visualize as Amors's attire, made of flowers and decorated with animals.[154] The intention, rather, is to construct visually the element of power in one who "rules over lovers ... making lords into servants" (866–67, Horgan 15).[155] The same intention explains the hint of a beard on the God's jaw.

The tautness of body implicit in the release of the arrow appears in the God's tensed arms and fingers and in other details of posture right down to those strategically planted feet, conspicuous in striped or thonged shoes. (These are a frequent sign of status or fashion in fourteenth-century art. Gallants wore exotically patterned versions of them, to judge from Chaucer's hint that Absolon in *The Miller's Tale* has a veritable cathedral window of tracery "corven on his shoes."[156]) The Lover here, by contrast, is a feeble ungainly figure of meaner stature, edging away with hands aloft in consternation and head anxiously turned back at the threat of the arrow.

The left-right configuration is commonplace. Other illustrators sometimes relish creating postures of shock for the Lover, even to the extent of depicting him reacting with splayed legs and arms akimbo as he is horribly transfixed right through the chest with an enormous weapon.[157] Such effects make awkwardly palpable the enigmatic nature of the Lover's wound, however — a "wound" from a ballistically implausible arrow which in the text is said to enter his eye before lodging in the heart (from which he proceeds to extract the shaft). In practice illuminators have to opt for one target or the other, and do so in roughly equal numbers.

NLW 5016D follows the eye-target model. It shows moment of entry but no damage and hence confirms that the eye itself is the channel, not site, of the wound. It has been suggested that such images are motivated by "not literalism alone ... but a desire to focus the reader's attention on the centrality of *vision* in

---

[154] 874–94: and he should wear a garland, not a crown (895–901).

[155] On the regality of Amors in medieval art see Erwin Panofsky, "Blind Cupid," in idem, *Studies in Iconology* (New York: Harper and Row, 1962), 95–128 (esp. 101–3, 114).

[156] *The Miller's Tale*, I. 3318: and see *Livre du sacre de Charles V*, London, BL, MS Tiberius B. VIII. fol. 48v (De Winter, *Bibliothèque de Philippe le Hardi*, figure 4), and shoes worn by the Lover in BL, MS Add. 42133, fol. 14v and in ÖNB, MS 2592, fols. 13v, 15r, etc. (Kuhn, "Illustration des *Rosenromans*," plates VI–VII).

[157] E.g., BL, MS Royal 20 A XVII, fol. 16r, and Amiens, Bibl. municipale MS 437, fol. 14v.

the discourse,"[158] a possibility that becomes particularly interesting in the context of the preceding miniature's insistence on reflexive masculine gaze. Now, again, male eyes male, investing the impact of love with a homo-erotic quality emphasized by the fact that Amors's sexualized body with its fetishized legs is displayed as much to the Lover as to the book's reader.[159] Yet the display is also interesting because it confirms a current in this — as in many other — illustrated versions of the *Rose* which, as we hinted earlier, may offset the apparent domination of Guillaume's poem by a masculine subjectivity. Where Spearing has emphasized that the Lover's entrance into the dream-garden is "an encounter with sexuality, defined as perceived by a young male,"[160] Plate 35 insists that the male body can be fetishized and (literally) opened up for the viewer's gaze no less than the female body. Although the viewer within the picture is male, the viewer *of* the picture might be of either sex, and it may therefore prompt us to speculate whether miniaturists found themselves presenting the male body as a sexual object both to highlight a homo-erotic implication in Guillaume's text and perhaps to engage a female public more radically than Guillaume.

However, an alternative view of an image such as this is that it reinforces a strategy in the narrative which renders woman invisible. In the text the woman at this point is elided to a rose: the rose is the "real" object of the Lover's attention when Amors shoots him. In NLW 5016D even the rose is elided, as if in anticipation of Ferrante's observations that courtly love is "a game that men play for their own satisfaction" and that Amors has to be masculine because "the lover cannot face the Venus in himself."[161] If this view is in some way substantiated by Plate 35, it is nevertheless corrected within the visual architecture of the book's illumination as a whole, since the ostensibly male source of desire in this inaugural episode will be formally complemented by a closing image of Venus, using a bow with equal panache to fire off her own weapon of desire.

Homage to Love (Plate 36)

The next miniature comes after an account of the Lover's mock-heroic determination to stagger forward towards the rose despite, or rather because of, a hail of psychological arrows from his adversary, a saga which ceases when the God com-

---

[158] Lewis, "Images of Opening," 227; our emphasis.

[159] Although the male leg is often prominent in fourteenth-century *Rose* illustrations (Kuhn, "Illustration des *Rosenromans*," 15, mentions the "extravagant calves" in ÖNB, MS 2592), NLW 5016D is particularly conspicuous in this regard.

[160] Spearing, *Medieval Poet as Voyeur*, 204.

[161] Ferrante, *Woman as Image*, 111 and n. 16.

mands him to surrender as "vassal" rather than trying to resist,[162] and bids him become his liege (i.e., solemnly commit himself to love) by means of a ritual kiss. "Thereupon I joined my hands and became his liegeman," the Lover relates in the lines which follow the miniature, "and you may be sure that I was very proud when his mouth kissed mine" (1953–55, Horgan 30).[163]

Some manuscripts insert a prior picture of Love seizing his victim (line 1879), but the image showing how the Lover "does homage," as the Aberystwyth rubric puts it, is especially common. The text makes quite clear that the homage includes a kiss which is a mark of special favor not allowable to any *vilain*, because the God construes the Lover to be free from *vilanie* or dishonorable behavior.

Homage is found enacted in medieval art both in terms of the kiss Guillaume has in mind (the *osculum foedale*, of which a powerful example between Mark and Tristram, both standing, is found on a thirteenth-century tile at Chertsey[164]), and in terms of the *immixtio manuum* ritual where the kneeling vassal holds out joined hands — as in prayer — which are to be clasped between the hands of the liegelord. The latter was more common visually, and was also of momentous significance where disputes about tenure of fiefdoms were concerned, as they were between the French and English kings during the Hundred Years' War.[165] The kiss is perhaps the more interesting form of homage, since although it consummates (so to speak) the feudal pledge and enacts its reciprocity, women were excluded from it on grounds of modesty.[166] This would explain why romanticized medieval seals represent knights kneeling with joined hands in amorous vassalage

---

[162] The significance of *dangiers* is clarified by its use here as a common noun: the Lover is not to "resist arrest," as it were (*Ne fai pas dangier de toi rendre*, 1884).

[163] The capital "A" of "Atant deuin[s] ses ho[n]s" has erroneously become a "U" in the manuscript.

[164] London, British Museum: reproduced and discussed in Camille, "Gothic Signs," 161.

[165] See Hedeman, *Royal Image*, 116–21 and figures 82–83; also the fourteenth-century *Sachsenspiegel* illustration reproduced in E. H. Gombrich, "Ritualized Gesture and Expression in Art," in idem, *The Image and the Eye: Further Studies in the Psychology of Pictorial Representation* (Oxford: Phaidon, 1982), 63–77 (here 64 and figure 41); and the drawing of a lost original of the Duke of Bourbon rendering homage to the King of France, in Avril, *Manuscript Painting at the Court of France*, 27, figure XII, and in Charles Sterling, *La peinture médiévale à Paris, 1300–1500* (Paris: Bibliothèque des Arts, 1987), 209–17 and figures 123–25.

[166] Camille, "Gothic Signs," 161; Jacques Le Goff, "The Symbolic Ritual of Vassalage," in idem, *Time, Work and Culture in the Middle Ages*, trans. Arthur Goldhammer (Chicago: University of Chicago Press, 1980), 256.

to ladies, but without the *osculum foedale*.[167] Technically, the kiss which passes between Love and the Lover could not therefore have been represented as passing between a man and a woman.

Some *Rose* illuminators resorted to the *immixtio manuum* on its own; some represented the kiss alone; some, like the NLW 5016D artist, risked contortion and attempted both at once.[168] The difficulty of having the two men close enough for the kiss is that the full hand clasp becomes hard to convey, though it can be managed, as the Vienna manuscript proves. The Aberystwyth illustration retains the crucial hand gesture of the supplicant, one which constitutes (as Rushing has confirmed) "a very old gesture of submission, originally associated with the ceremony of enfeoffment, but also signifying the submission of the lover to his lady."[169]

What remains distinctive about the Aberystwyth miniature and underlines its development of the homo-erotic theme we have been tracing is its color coordination. Whereas the preceding illustration aimed at a striking contrast between Amors and the Lover, the present illustration insists on likeness: the God's size and mantle have become more ordinary, and he now wears a long robe not significantly different from the Lover's as well as coming down to his vassal's plainer level of footwear. The twinned trees bracket them together in their intimacy. Though he is still crowned, the God's wings conjoin him visually with his new retainer whose shoulder his arm gently and protectively encircles. The gentle embrace is reminiscent of the serenity of certain Visitation scenes.[170] If there is residual anxiety on the part of the Lover in his upturned glance (as if tentative about the kiss?), the situation nevertheless exudes reassurance and mutuality. It reverses the preceding trauma.

Securing the Lover's Heart (Plate 37)

In a *jeu d'esprit* of sentiment the Lover suggests, and the God of Love agrees, that

---

[167] Alwin Schultz, *Das Höfische Leben zur Zeit der Minnesinger*, 2 vols. (1889, repr. Osnabrück: Zeller, 1965), 1:649–50 and figures 173–75.

[168] *Immixtio*: BN, MS fr. 378, fol. 18v (Dahlberg, trans., figure 16); Morgan, MS M 132, fol. 17r: *osculum*: CUL, MS Gg. IV. 6c, fol. 16v; Bodl., MS Selden Supra 57, fol. 15r and MS e Mus 65, fol. 15v; Morgan, MS M 245, fol. 15r: both: ÖNB, MS 2592, fol. 15v; BL, MS Add. 42133, fol. 14v; Morgan, MS M 324, fol. 14v.

[169] Rushing, *Images of Adventure*, 63 (see also 74), commenting on Yvain kneeling to Laudine with "folded hands" in a Rodenegg mural; for a bibliography on the gesture see Rushing, 87 n. 95.

[170] Especially the Harley Hours, BL, MS Harl. 928, fol. 4r, reproduced in Donovan, *de Brailes Hours*, figure 92.

the Lover's heart should be "locked" to confirm its absolute loyalty to Love. Producing what the narrative calls a "little key of purest gold," Amors proceeds to "touch [the Lover's] side" with it (1998–99 and 2006, Horgan 31).

The narration of this episode seems to us to offer considerable sexual innuendo. Amors says of his key, extracted from his purse (*aumouniere*), that "[his] jewels are under it," giving it great power (2002–5). Is there not a teasing suggestion of testicles empowering the phallus, and of the implement's touching Amant's "side" as a euphemism for sexual activity? Purses, being frequently slung between the legs from the belt, certainly lent themselves to wordplay. During Jean de Meun's more explicitly bawdy continuation, the "purse" becomes a metaphor for the phallus in Genius's harangue to Love's followers on the subject of procreation.[171] It is therefore interesting to find illustrations of the present episode where Amors holds the purse at his crotch while raising a key whose erect shaft the Lover's hand formally caresses;[172] or where the Lover reacts to the touch of Amors's key upon his body by grasping the hilt of a phallic dagger which stands prominently at his own crotch.[173]

Whereas in the text the Lover is "gently" secured for Amours by voluntarily becoming his sexual or material property, the poem's illustrations sometimes communicate the locking action rather differently in terms of threat. Although they may appropriately invoke in the Lover standard gestures of acceptance, such as palms held upwards and outwards,[174] they alternatively envisage the God's application of the usually massive key to the Lover's body as an attacking maneuver: it sometimes generates corresponding gestures of anxiety or shock in the recipient.[175]

In the NLW 5016D image there are certainly intimations — even if subdued — of aggression and (in the Lover's arched back) recoil. A contrast with the emphatic reassurance of the preceding miniature is forced on the viewer, because the two pictures are in the left and right columns respectively of the same page. Amors, gathering the folds of his mantle around his waist, is now again a more forbidding figure who is reopening the physical and emotional gulf between himself and the Lover, narrowed during the "homage" but seen in his first appearance two folios earlier. In fact the trio of images of Love and the Lover, succeeding

---

[171] Genius curses those who offend Nature sexually: may they "lose the purse and testicles that are the signs of their manhood" (19637–38, Horgan 303).

[172] Vatican, MS Urb. lat. 376, fol. 14v (but König sees this as a formal legalistic gesture, the swearing of an oath: *Die Liebe*, 30).

[173] ÖNB, MS 2592, fol. 15v (Kuhn, "Illustration des *Rosenromans*," plate V).

[174] BL, MS Add. 42133, fol. 15r (Lewis, "Images of Opening," figure 24), Morgan, MS M 324, fol. 15r: cf. Garnier, *Langage de l'image*, 176–77. In Bodl., MS e Mus. 65, fol. 16r, Amors's hand remains protectively around the Lover's shoulder.

[175] ÖNB, MS 2592, fol. 15v.

each other in quick succession in the manuscript, invites response as to a mini-sequence. They focus visually what illustrators cannot represent from the God of Love's long ensuing speech about the torments and consolations of love: that love is an oscillation between experiences that are emotionally endangering, then welcoming, then again alienating. There is no way that the heart-locking can be portrayed to avoid altogether a predatory impression.

Therefore, although Plate 37 can be read as a contribution to an unfolding textual and visual discourse on gates, keys, openings and penetrations, its immediate context is a visual discourse on individual experience of love characterized by balletic variation in the relations of Love and Lover. From outright attack to acceptance and welcoming proximity, and then again to an unnerving hint of domination — the trio of illustrations constructs eros as an unpredictable site of pleasure and pain. It is no coincidence that there has been detected in Guillaume's episodes of shooting, homage, and locking a threefold repetition of the concept of submission: "a single, engulfing experience ('falling in love') is being diffused through a series of lyric stanza-like moments, each realized as a kind of tableau."[176] NLW 5016D shows how the narrative "tableaux" translate effortlessly into painted tableaux. At the same time these images paint the authority of a male love-deity firmly into the book, and thereby encourage the viewer to reflect further on questions about homo-eroticism in masculine desire, first mooted in the Narcissus illustration.

The Limits of Bel Acueil/Responsiveness (Plate 38)

Left on his own by Amors, the Lover timidly contemplates a hedge which prevents access to the roseplot, but finds an unexpected ally in the male personage of Responsiveness (Bel Acueil or "Fair Welcoming"), a handsome and courteous young man who comes forth and guides him through a gap to bring him tantalizingly close to the desired rose. Located just before the Lover's remark that Responsiveness "did me a great service when I saw the rose-bud from so close" (2807–8, Horgan 54), the next miniature showing a young woman remonstrating with the Lover does not immediately make sense. Instead of showing the Lover being welcomed, it anticipates instead, by eighty-five lines, the *repulse* which the Lover subsequently provokes from his new friend Responsiveness; moreover, it confusingly represents that friend as female rather than male.

Guillaume's decision to adopt a masculine name for the "welcoming" impulse, *bel acueil*, which we have chosen to call the "responsiveness" of the love-object,

---

[176] Kay, *The Romance of the Rose*, 55.

CHAPTER TWO

is one of the poem's notorious features. If the grammatical gender of *acueil* in some sense leaves Guillaume with no choice, that has not prevented critics from pondering the consequence of such gendering in the poem, namely a strong insinuation that what most urges a woman to socialize affectionately with a man is something masculine in herself, or, to change the emphasis, that the quality in a woman which most attracts a man is actually a masculine quality. There is more ammunition in this gendering for the allegation that courtly love is narcissistic, fundamentally a game that men play among themselves. The rose is replaced by a masculine personage replicating the Lover. Does this mean that we should follow Simon Gaunt in drawing out "the homo-erotic impulse that seems to lie behind Amant's attraction to Bel Acueil"?[177]

The provocative nature of Guillaume's choice certainly shows through in the reactions of illustrators: for they simply cannot decide whether to let Responsiveness be a male as the text dictates, or (as it were) to dive through the allegory and present him as a beautiful woman, as if he is himself the female love-object — or in Suzanne Lewis's words "takes the place of the rose as figure for the immaterial Lady."[178]

The sense of puzzlement is manifest in manuscripts which present Responsiveness as both male *and* female in quick succession. Thus, Pierpont Morgan Library MS M 324, folio 20v identifies the character as a youth sporting a neat beard and a red tunic who draws the Lover towards a rosebush with one hand and picks him a leaf with the other. On the facing page is an image of the Rose's thuggish minder, Refusal, leaping up to chastise Responsiveness for over-responsiveness. Responsiveness is now transformed into a tall young woman with blonde hair.[179] (She remains female in subsequent miniatures, even against the grain of accompanying text which has Venus addressing her as "Fair Sir.")

It has been argued that such "sexual metamorphosis" actually demonstrates a

---

[177] Simon Gaunt, "Bel Acueil and the Improper Allegory of the *Romance of the Rose*," *New Medieval Literatures* 2 (1998): 65–93 (an exciting essay, whose arguments we should have liked to have had more time to absorb into the present discussion).

[178] Lewis, "Images of Opening," 229. For further discussion of the gendering question, see Fleming, *Study in Allegory*, 43–46; Tuve, *Allegorical Imagery*, 22; Kelly, *Internal Difference*, 107–10; and Huot, *The Romance of the Rose and its Medieval Readers*, 190–91, pointing out that one *scribe* also genders Bel Acueil female at the point when he or she is instructed by the Old Woman.

[179] Lewis notes that Bel Acueil is depicted in both genders on the same page in Malibu, Getty Mus. MS 83. MR. 177 (Ludwig XV.7), fol. 19r: "Images of Opening," 229–30. Gaunt gives interesting statistics about the gendering of Bel Acueil in "Bel Acueil and the Improper Allegory," 75, n. 19, in the course of a stimulating review of the textual and visual evidence (74–84).

sensitivity to the "idea" of Bel Acueil as "elusive and mercurial sexual response ... today one thing, tomorrow another."[180] Perhaps some illustrators deliberately draw attention to the problematics of the role of Responsiveness by muddling "his" gender. Most illustrated manuscripts make a decision one way or the other and stick to it. The majority represent the gender given in the text. A significant minority, however, persist in making Responsiveness a young woman, and consequently they do not so much problematise Bel Acueil's gender as they *correct* it; whether because they are resistant to homo-erotic overtones in Bel Acueil's role,[181] or because they are convinced that receptivity and vulnerability are feminine traits, or because they sense in Responsiveness the one figure who might "stand in for" the woman of whose psyche he is but a fragment, is not clear. One Vatican manuscript takes such tendencies to their limit. It is not just that Bel Acueil is there presented as a young woman. When the Lover first spies in the fountain's mirror a profusion of roses, the Vatican illustrator juxtaposes the fountain's abundance of roses with a line of six girls. Moreover, the wound which is the Lover's first perception of love is interpreted for the viewer by visually identifying the amatory arrow as a woman at whom he gazes.[182]

Without approaching that level of interventionism, NLW 5016D adheres to the tradition of illustration that "translates" the gender of Bel Acueil/Responsiveness.[183] The Lover, in the ankle-length lavender robe with matching hood seen just before in his dealings with Amors, halts in mid-approach. No rosebush is in sight to supply a dramatic "prop" for the present crisis, but the raised index finger of the woman speaking with him makes it clear that she is assuming authority over him. Clearly this represents the moment when Responsiveness becomes angry at the extent of the Lover's designs on the rose ("it is unworthy of you to ask it!" Horgan 45).

The illustration "translates" the allegory, simplifies it so that the retraction of the Rose's responsiveness is represented as an admonition given to the Lover by a tall woman with long blonde hair (not braided up) in a flowing red dress. Of course the red dress is itself redolent of that warmth defined in her name, which has lulled the Lover into his precipitous request. But now, in this one image which has to encapsulate a complex action, we see the limits of Responsiveness. It is indeed a miniature which risks a contradiction of Bel Acueil's identity. Responsiveness is found to be unresponsive: becomes, so to speak, Mal Acueil. Many

---

[180] Fleming, *Study in Allegory*, 45–46.
[181] 180. As Gaunt suggests, "Bel Acueil and the Improper Allegory," 75.
[182] Vatican, MS Urb. lat. 376, fols 19r (female Bel Acueil), 12r (six women and roses), and 13r (arrow as sight of one woman); König, *Die Liebe*, 31 and 28–29 respectively.
[183] Cf. Bodl., MS e Mus 65, fol. 22r, etc., and Morgan, MS M 324, fol. 24v., etc.

manuscripts more logically present not Bel Acueil's demurral but its sequel: the eruption of Dangiers/Refusal who comes to stiffen resistance against the Lover and order him out of the enclosure, causing Responsiveness to flee also. In the Aberystwyth manuscript it is as though Responsiveness *becomes* Refusal, an interesting but allegorically muddled idea.

Confrontation with Reason (Plate 39)

The Lover is recriminating with himself alone in his misery, when a lady named Reason comes down from a tower and accosts him. (In other words, he reasons with himself, communes with his own reasonable self, as one manuscript possibly implies by making her male.[184]) Physically she is described by Guillaume as a sort of golden mean; and she has God-given perfection and authority, signaled also by her crown. The tower presumably encodes not only her far-sightedness — occupying a "high vantage-point" (*haute engarde*, 2957, Horgan 46) — and her Godlikeness, but also her protective capacity. Like Truth in the opening of Langland's *Piers Plowman* who occupies a "toure on a toft," she dwells, in effect, in a verse from the Book of Proverbs: "The name of the Lord is a strong tower."[185] Reason immediately criticizes the youthful *folie* of the Lover's situation, picking out Oiseuse/Ease as chief culprit for introducing him to it. She demands that he should get control of his heart.

Of Reason's attributes in Guillaume, the 5016D illustration presents only the tower, and even this is not distinguishable from the crenellated structures used already in the manuscript for the entrance through the garden wall. (These crenellated semicircular tower and wall structures with conical tiled roofs optionally visible, and entrances defined as black round-topped apertures, can be paralleled in other mid-fourteenth-century manuscripts, such as an illuminated Paris *Yvain*.[186]) Moreover, Reason has no crown, nor does anything about her dress distinguish her from the woman representing Ease seen earlier in this book. Many (though by no means all) other illuminated manuscripts supply Reason with a crown — she is specifically "a queen who speaks to a clerk" according to the instruction left for the illumination in one manuscript[187] — and make more effort to indicate that she descends to meet the Lover. Is the Aberystwyth manuscript

---

[184] Vatican, MS Urb. lat. 376, fol. 20r (König, *Die Liebe*, 32).

[185] See William Langland, *The Vision of Piers Plowman, a Critical Edition of the B-Text*, ed. A. V. C. Schmidt (London: Dent, 1978), Prologue 14 and I.173–75; and Prov. 18:10.

[186] Rushing, *Images of Adventure*, 162, and figures 4–2, 4–3, 4–4, 4–8, 4–9.

[187] "Une roine qui parle a un clerc," in BN, MS fr. 25523, fol. 37r; Fleming, *Study in Allegory*, 113.

obliviously recycling visual formulae (wall; doorway; standard beautiful woman), or is something more suggestive going on?

Actually the alternatives in that question beg to be collapsed. That is, what probably originates as visual formula has the effect of provoking absorbing comparisons, in two ways. First, the reader is bound to view Reason as an alternative to, or substitute for, Responsiveness, who happens to have been represented confronting the Lover on the facing verso. The symbolic red attire of Responsiveness now gives way to Reason's cooler color, while Reason nevertheless matches Responsiveness in wearing her hair long, hanging behind neck and shoulders. But if this implies that Reason in some sense counterpoints Responsiveness and that, rather than being an austerely regal figure, she is a rival for the Lover's attentions (a role she in fact later adopts in Jean's part of the poem), the nature of the "tower" produces a second visual cross-reference. We are instantly reminded of the garden doorway shown in folios 5v, 6v, and 7r. Negotiating with the Lover outside a doorway, Reason reconfigures the role of Ease and the question of entering the garden. (Interestingly, while Reason's hairstyle complements that of Responsiveness, her dress color complements that of Ease.) And this retrospect is clever because, whether fortuitously or (less likely) by knowing something about the text, the illustrator has thereby reinforced precisely what Reason asserts with threefold emphasis as she speaks to the Lover, namely, that in light of his present trouble he should reconsider the advisability of having been introduced to the garden by Ease.

While the miniature invites such comparison with those involving Responsiveness and Ease — and thereby helps construct the Lover, in Fleming's phrase, as a sort of "Hercules at the crossroads" influenced by competing counselors[188] — it does *not* invite us to a moral or hierarchical judgement. In the text Reason lectures the Lover on the dangerous (*perilleuse*, 2990) character of Ease. The illuminator, having dispensed with Reason's crown and providing no other hierarchical or religious attributes, has humanized her. Her valence is neutral, except in so far as she is not in scarlet. The miniature neither signals that Reason is "the great Lady of the *Roman*" (in Fleming's phrase) nor urges us that the Lover is "increasingly stupid in his rejection of good counsel for bad."[189]

Intervention of Jealousy (Plate 40)

The Lover rejects Reason and resorts to Friend, who advises mollification of

---

[188] Fleming, *Study in Allegory*, 52.
[189] Fleming, *Study in Allegory*, 45, 52.

Refusal. In a busy part of the allegory, there is much to-ing and fro-ing as Franchise/Openness and Pity are introduced to subdue Dangiers/Refusal, though it takes the intervention of female sexual desire in the shape of Venus to rekindle Responsiveness and allow the rose to be kissed. But this causes retaliation in a chain reaction started by Male Bouche/Scandal, who prompts Jealousy, who blames Responsiveness, then Modesty and Timidity (Honte and Poor), for failing to support Chastity: so Modesty and Timidity hasten to rouse Refusal from where he has fallen asleep.

Illuminated manuscripts vary in the proportion of attention they give to these maneuvers. The intervention of Venus is quite often depicted, and the re-awakening of Refusal would appear to have been thought especially pivotal, or perhaps particularly interesting visually. Since both illustrations are absent in NLW 5016D we have included examples from other manuscripts (figures 4 and 5).

As for Jealousy herself, she can appear in various postures of rebuke, but is most consistently presented in relation to line 3779 or thereafter, where the narrative consciously gathers itself to describe graphically how she carries out her earlier threat (3606) to have a wall and *forterece* built to imprison both roses and Responsiveness. NLW 5016D allocates a miniature at this point ("Now it is time for me to tell you about what Jealousy was doing," ... *la contenance Jalousie*, 3779–80, Horgan 58): but in place of the expected picture of the construction of a tower (as in figure 6) there is a representation of a man beating a woman. A reader new to the poem could be forgiven for wondering whether this is the Lover attacking Jealousy, or whether it is Jealousy threatening Responsiveness. Familiarity with *Rose* iconography would suggest that the configuration represents instead the Jealous Husband (the *Jalous*) of Jean de Meun's part of the poem, not the female Jealousy of Guillaume's part. What is the significance of this switch?

Of course one has to reckon with the possibility of expediency (bringing forward a second jealousy image to cope with the absence of a model for the first), or of sheer error (muddling one image of jealousy with another). One clue to the potential for error is that there is an overlap between the rubric the NLW artist has to follow at 3779 ("Comment ialousie se *contient*") and the words used by the Jealous Husband ("Qui me *tient* ...?", "Who will stop me from breaking your bones ... with this pestle or this spit?" 9328–30, Horgan 143) immediately before the conventional location (9331) for the present wife-beating image. The NLW miniaturist has certainly observed the letter of that exclamation in identifying the Jealous Husband's weapon as a pestle,[190] but could have jumped from the later

---

[190] Many manuscripts depict the weapon as a stick or club. Variants such as a distaff can be found, as in Morgan, MS M 324, fol. 63r.

context to the earlier through the *tenir/contenir* association, buttressed by the reference to Jalousie's *contenaunce* at line 3780.

Whatever the reason, the placement of the illustration at this point has the effect of collapsing the hybrid poem's distinction between two sorts of "jealousy": the violent, domineering possessiveness of the *Jalous*, and the more ambiguous watchfulness over chastity which *Jalousie* seems to project.[191] For the reader of this manuscript the physical enclosure of the Rose and of its/her Responsiveness recounted by Guillaume is hence made tantamount to violence against a woman: jealousy can *only* signify control of the woman's sexuality by a male relative; it cannot be her own sexual self-control. Probably by mistake, this amounts to an unusual interpretation of Guillaume's text.

Viewed simply as a misplaced Jealous Husband miniature, the illustration decisively articulates standard elements of that model. Leaning forward to wrench the woman's hair and drag her, half upright, with one hand (9332–35), the man threatens a blow with his weapon in the other hand. Illuminators often concentrate on the weight of the suffering woman's body, her lower half trailing on the ground, her torso yanked upwards and sometimes along the ground.[192] In Plate 40 a different emotive effect is achieved by envisaging the violence as perpetrated even while the woman begs or prays for mercy. This emphatic petitioning posture in the miniature is really a significant modification to the text because, although there is a passing reference to her "excuses," the reader's primary impression is (as Heather Arden reminds us) that "the jealous husband's wife never gets the chance to speak, to present her side."[193] Friend's main emphasis is on her screams and the abuse which she hurls back at her husband.

The *Romance of the Rose* is, as we have seen, often thought an implicitly misogynous work. Would the present miniature support the contention? The effect is rather ambivalent. If such an image by its very existence sanctions medieval society's apparent belief that women may on occasion be beaten,[194] it is difficult

---

[191] Brook, "Jalousie and Jealousy in Jean de Meun's *Rose*," describes jealousy in the poem as "part interior impulse and part exterior guardian," 69.

[192] See BN, MS fr. 380, fol. 62v; Morgan, MS M 132, fol. 66r, and MS M 324, fol. 63r.

[193] Heather Arden, "Women as Readers, Women as Text in the *Roman de la Rose*," in *Women, the Book, and the Worldly*, ed. Lesley Smith and Jane H. M. Taylor (Cambridge: D. S. Brewer, 1995), 111–17 (here 114).

[194] Although men had authority over wives in marriage and wife-beating was often considered a right (Duby, *History of Private Life*, 2:260), it was nevertheless punishable: see Paul Hair, *Before the Bawdy Court* (London: Elek, 1972), 44, case no. 33, against Thomas Louchard in 1300. Counter-images of husband-beating in medieval art (by wives, with distaffs) are usually interpreted as facetious practice in the "world upside-down" tradition confirming, not reversing, male authority. In one example (BL, MS Add. 42130, fol. 60r:

to imagine that Plate 40 would elicit no sympathy for the plight of abused women. On the other hand, the woman's pleading rather than defiant role could be held to contribute to an ideologically defined ideal of feminine quiescence which refuses to challenge patriarchy by returning violence for violence.

One further point may be noted. The Jealous Husband echoes the artist's stereotype for the Lover in most respects: in length of robe, hood, style of shoes, hair, youthfulness. Ostensibly that could support Fleming's provocative notion that Jean de Meun means to align the *Jalous*, who would brutally possess his wife, with the Lover, who ultimately means to pluck and possess the Rose.[195] But this is precisely a case where the accidental nature of visual evidence needs to be treated with caution. The miniature enables us to raise the possibility of that likeness. But, unless the text really encourages it, the possibility needs to be suppressed again by recognizing that the illuminator's stock male figures inevitably overlap. The fact that the man in Plate 40 wears dullish gray, rather than an orange or lavender color, is probably meant to be sufficient to differentiate him from preceding figures.

V. The Continuation

Changing the Author (Plate 41)

As David Hult has emphasized, the ubiquitous insertion of an author portrait at line 4029 of the *Rose* is actually an intrusion into the unbroken meditations of the Lover.[196] Its rationale is the statement retrospectively made by the God of Love later on at the midpoint of the combined poem (10,465–648), that this line constitutes the start of the continuation by Jean de Meun. Although Jean declined to signal a change of author in the text at the junction of Guillaume's work with his own, rubricators and scribes nevertheless signaled it there for all they were worth. The rubric preceding Plate 41 states "Here Guillaume de Lorris finishes and Jehan de Meun begins." Arguably this might prepare a reader to imagine either Guillaume, or Jean, or both, but there are some grounds for reading the accompanying miniature as a notional representation of Jean "beginning." First, author portraits characteristically appear at the start of a text; and second, the sheet on which the writer works is blank.

Backhouse, *Luttrell Psalter*, figure 59) the man crouches and prays, not unlike the woman in NLW 5016D.

[195] Fleming, *Study in Allegory*, 157.

[196] Hult, *Self-Fulfilling Prophecies*, 14 and 74–89. Hult's interesting discussion of author portraits has been consolidated by Walters in "A Parisian Manuscript," and in "Author Portraits and Textual Demarcation in Manuscripts of the *Romance of the Rose*," in Brownlee and Huot (eds.), *Rethinking the Rose*, 359–73.

Chapter Two

We should not get too carried away by the capacity of such an image to underline the change of authorship. There is another sense in which an illuminated manuscript characteristically evades, even defies, all the multifarious signals in the ensuing narrative communicating the altered personality of the text. The really clever way to complement that alteration would be to *change the artist* at or after this point. (It is a ploy which Dahlberg is able to effect somewhat drastically in his translation by switching to reproductions from a different and later manuscript to illustrate Jean's part of the poem.) In practice, of course, except where a frontispiece miniature was separately assigned to some up-market artist, one illuminator often worked on all the miniatures from beginning to end. The consequence in NLW 5016D and elsewhere is to reinforce continuity more than discontinuity. The divergent temperaments of Guillaume and Jean, so elaborately addressed by modern critics, are as nothing to the miniaturists. Having dutifully shown the Changing of the Bard, they pursue their craft in subsequent pictures as though nothing actually has changed. An illuminated *Rose* asserts the unity of the poem more than an unilluminated one.

In Plate 41, against a salmon ground triangulated with a pattern of double gold lines, a man sits side-saddle (as it were) on a bench seat. There is either a footrest or a cushion matching the bench in the foreground. It is worth emphasizing that this author is not presented as a cleric. He is neither tonsured nor wearing a clerical cap, though these constituted medieval visual stereotypes for authorship, as is demonstrated by many other illustrations at this point.[197] Instead, he has the same abundance of youthful locks as the God of Love and the Lover, and wears a pink tight-sleeved robe and hood not distinct from the Lover's, all of which accords with the fact that there has hitherto been no demarcation between the poem's dreamer, narrator, and Lover. In deference to the circumstances of writing (an indoors occupation but often a cold one), there is a hint of ceiling architecture in the picture's upper corners, and the writer works in a long blue gown which keeps draughts off his feet.

Presumably because the illustrator wants to display the act of writing as frontally as possible, he or she has arranged the author figure in a contorted relation to the writing-lectern itself,[198] which sprouts whimsically from beyond and behind one end of the bench and lunges forward towards his turned face so that it seems as mobile a participant in the scene as the writer. Centered on the nearly vertical surface thus presented is something like a flat sheet, blank except for a grid of ruled lines prepared for writing. The square sheet acknowledges the fact that

---

[197] See the discussion of the NLW 5011E frontispiece, above.

[198] By contrast with comparable miniatures viewing writer/lectern in profile, e.g., CUL, MS Gg. IV. 6c, fol. 30r.

scribes wrote on the separate leaves of unbound quires; the representation of a single- rather than double-page space is probably visual shorthand for the open bifolium one might expect to see. The writer is holding down the sheet with his left hand, while wielding the quill in his right with an open-fingered hold which, though not very practical-looking, can be paralleled elsewhere.[199]

Some versions of the *Rose* author portrait go to more lengths to imply the moment of the text's transference from Guillaume to Jean (juxtaposing two writers, for instance, one ending and one beginning; or presenting a figure who does not write but reads, as though Jean were absorbing his predecessor's poem). In a way NLW 5016D is more interesting because it offers not a conventional cleric or *auctor* but an enigma: a personage somewhat too dapper and curly to shoulder the "overwhelming cult" that "developed around the author-figure of Jean de Meun" quite early in the poem's history.[200] Who is he, we are left to ask? Is it again the Lover, and in what sense does the miniature suggest that the ostensibly discrete voices, the two poets' and the narrator's and the Lover's, are all one voice? Conceivably even the lectern contributes an unusual nuance, for, although such objects frequently take fanciful and ungainly form, this one has an extraordinarily pronounced droop. It may strike the viewer as detumescent furniture that befits the shrunken spirits of the Lover at this point in the poem, brooding so hopelessly over the apparent loss of Responsiveness's goodwill that he is on the point of despair.

The Lover's Friend Advises (Plate 42)

As in many manuscripts, the illumination of NLW 5016D thins out in Jean's part of the poem. It is a little unusual, however, that no picture slots have been provided for the Lover's second encounter with Reason, who accosts him in his misery and, in a huge discourse, seeks to divert him from infatuation to a less passionate form of love and to calmer reflection. Reason herself, already illustrated in Guillaume's part, was usually represented again here. In addition, subjects in her speech that were sometimes chosen for illustration were the abode and wheel of Fortune, and legends reinforcing Fortune's aberrations, particularly the death of Virginia and the mad antics of Nero.

Reason eventually abandons the Lover in the face of his protest that, whereas she thinks him a fool, he considers himself wise in serving Love, and that he is fed up with her speech and intends to concentrate only on the Rose. Left alone and disconsolate, he only has to remember Friend, "and there he was, sent by God"

---

[199] Bodl., MS Douce 332, fol. 41r; BL, MS Harl. 4425, fol. 127r (Hult, *Self-Fulfilling Prophecies*, figure 5).

[200] Hult, *Self-Fulfilling Prophecies*, 59.

(Horgan 111; we are at liberty to wonder which god). Since Friend finds cause for optimism, not gloom, in events so far, and goes on with advice about all sorts of manipulative strategies of appeasement and guerrilla warfare by which to overcome the guardians of the Rose, one can see why the episode is typically introduced — as in NLW 5016D — with a rubric and miniature on "how Friend comforted the Lover."

Some miniaturists produce a witty effect by including the retreating figure of Reason, from whom the Lover obstinately turns the other way to speak to Friend. More often she has already gone. Then there are just the two men: a scene which can be confusing if Friend is projected as a young man indistinct from the Lover, for the viewer is left glancing from one to the other as though Friend is the alter ego of the poem's narrator.[201] On reflection, such confusion is productive. Not only does it accord with the text's suggestion that the Lover has only to think of Friend and, hey presto, he is there; but it also reintroduces visually the narcissistic discourse which we have found to be so pervasive in the illustrated *Rose*. However, most illustrators deduce from Friend's function as adviser something that the text barely clarifies: they suppose that he is older, perhaps taller, sagaciously bearded even, and someone likely to be more somberly dressed (in a longer robe for instance).[202]

An additional signifier is an "advice" gesture. Thus in Pierpont Morgan Library manuscripts M132 and M324 Friend combines an open-palm neutral conversation gesture (left hand) with a mildly pointing index finger (right hand) which indicates his capacity to direct the Lover, and it is the same gesture which enables us to distinguish Friend in NLW 5016D, Plate 42, despite the smudge damage to this miniature. The figure on the left wearing a long pink gown and hood, but not visibly older than his disciple, points his advice with an elongated finger. The Lover stands on the right engaging in dialogue. It is interesting that he is apparently wearing a short tunic (with red hood) rather than the longer gown otherwise used for him in the manuscript. This prevents us from making categorical deductions about other illustrations in the book on the basis of length of masculine attire.

Amidst the cynicism of Friend's comments, two passages connected with the Jealous Husband — a figment of Friend's imagination — caught the attention of illustrators. One was the Jealous Husband's cynical claim that not even a Lucretia

---

[201] E.g., Vatican, MS Urb lat. 376, fol. 45r (König, *Die Liebe*, 36); CUL, MS Gg. IV. 6c, fol. 49v. On the Friend as alter ego, cf. Kelly's remark that Amis "is Amant telling himself what he wants to know": *Internal Difference*, 106.

[202] Taller and bearded: Bodl., MS e Mus. 65, fol. 56r. Longer robe: Morgan, MS M 324, fol. 50r, and MS M 132, fol. 50r.

would ultimately "defend herself" if a man knew how to take her. This prompts dramatic miniatures of Lucretia's suicide (see figure 7), which, as Lori Walters has suggested, embody a note of female protest launching away from the corrosive verbal context.[203] The other was the Husband's violent attack on his wife which, as we have seen, NLW 5016D transfers to a miniature for Jalousie earlier in the poem.

The Lover Disowned by Wealth (Plate 43)

Amis/Friend is preoccupied with wealth, to the extent of offering a lecture on the origins of the acquisitive instinct. He also cites the authority of Ovid for the view that "the poor man has nothing with which to feed his love" (7955–56, Horgan 122). A corollary is the cynical suggestion that Big Spending (Trop-Doner) is a shortcut into the stronghold of love:[204] but, Friend notes caustically, only Richece/Wealth can give anyone the shortcut, and giving big presents usually leads to ruin anyway.

Not surprisingly, the Lover's next *rite de passage* upon leaving Friend is an immediate encounter with Wealth herself. As if to remind us of the spring of Narcissus, Jean de Meun locates this encounter "beside a bright spring" (*fontenele*, 10021, Horgan 154). Under the shade of an elm tree the narrator sees Wealth, a noble-looking lady, accompanied by her unnamed lover (*son ami*, 10027). The Lover greets them politely "with bent head" and asks the way to Big Spending, only to be told rather haughtily by Wealth that the path is in this very place, and that she is blocking the access. Her response continues to be characterized by haughtiness when she goes on to disparage him as no friend of hers and repudiates the reckless prodigality of lovers.

The iconography of this scene has not attracted much attention, but there are signs that illustrators do respond here to various indications in the text which structure the episode to recall and comment on earlier ones. For one thing, the viewer is bound to notice and reflect upon a participant seemingly incidental in the text yet tantalizing to behold: Wealth's lover. Jean's Amant makes a casual remark disclaiming knowledge of this person's name (10028), an omission which provoked one scribe to invent a genealogy for him (he is Treasure, son of *Aquier Gardant* (ed. Poirion, 10058.01–17).[205] Yet Wealth's partner's anonymity is pre-

---

[203] Walters, "A Parisian Manuscript," 47–48.

[204] "The path of big-presents" is Tuve's expression for Trop-Doner: *Allegorical Imagery*, 260.

[205] The same manuscript earlier names Richece's partner (when she is first introduced in the dance) as Verité.

sumably deliberate. It can have two consequences. Either it makes him an "anyone" partner, as though wealth attaches herself to anyone (a notion explored by the English poet Langland in the account of Mede in *Piers Plowman*), or, as the illuminators often suggest, the figure's reduction to unnamed *ami* levels him with the stereotypical, and not yet named Lover, l'Amant himself. Hence, Wealth's refusal to "know" Amant is partly explicable because she already has an *ami* — one, in fact, whom some illustrators present as a carbon copy of Amant, though he may alternatively be imagined as a more richly-dressed individual.[206]

An implication that Wealth is too preoccupied with her own partner to be interested in Amant is taken to extremes in one New York manuscript (figure 8) where, although she gestures with one hand, her face is turned away to kiss the youth sitting next to her on the bank, whose shoulders her other arm encircles.[207] *Rose* manuscripts not infrequently present sexually suggestive contact between the two: for instance, the man's hand in her lap, or on her knee. Although such figurations increase the sense of Amant's exclusion, it is in fact the Aberystwyth manuscript's comparatively restrained type of representation that is more thoughtfully productive. Here Amant is confronted with a Wealth beside whom is a youth wearing the same colors as he and making the same gestures (even down to the detail of the hand at the midriff). The only distinction is that the partner's attire is knee-length and, as it happens, particularly evocative of the clothes worn in this manuscript by Narcissus (Plate 34). The effect on the viewer is therefore to establish the partner both as a "rival" and as a mirror of Amant, but one who at the same time mirrors Narcissus. Amant sees "himself" as this woman's partner, just as Narcissus sees himself in the well of love, a coincidence deliberately or accidentally reinforced by the presence of three trees in both images, the elm tree specified by Jean as a shade for Wealth being ignored in NLW 5016D (though often attempted elsewhere). On the other hand NLW 5016D does not support the reminiscence by including a spring in the Wealth miniature, whereas other manuscripts do.[208]

Jean's account of this meeting most specifically invokes not so much Narcissus as the earlier action with Oiseuse/Ease. In both cases the Lover seeks entry to a narrow passage. In both cases a female figure presides over the entrance. Wealth

---

[206] Copy: e.g., Bodl., MS Selden Supra 57, fol. 71v; BN, MS fr. 1565, fol. 66r; and especially Morgan, MS M 132, fol. 71v. More richly dressed: e.g., Bodl., MS Douce 332, fol. 95r.

[207] Morgan, MS M 324, fol. 68r.

[208] E.g., Florence, Laurenziana MS Acq. e Doni 153, fol. 121r (Peruzzi, *Codice Laurenziano*, plate II); Morgan, MS M 324, fol. 68r, and MS M 132, fol. 71v; BN, MS fr. 1565, fol. 66r; Bodl., MS e Mus 65, fol. 77v (identical with the Narcissus spring at fols. 12v and 13v in the same manuscript).

CHAPTER TWO

even makes a passing caustic allusion to ease, remarking that Poverty will soon seize the Lover if he goes in the direction of Big Spending, "idle [*oiseus*, 10164] as is your habit" (Horgan 156). The illustrations tend to reduce the visual connection with Ease by attributing a crown and perhaps other signs of prosperity and regality to Wealth (NLW 5016D includes a voluminous fur-trimmed mantle); and in any case the difference between a narrow door in a wall and a narrow "way" in the landscape precludes easy visual cross-reference. Instead, entering timidly upon a grassy knoll sprinkled with flowers, the Lover finds that someone like himself — a nameless mirror-image — *could* be patronized by Wealth (it is what he wants for himself), yet at the same time finds himself rejected. Wealth and Big Spending are not for him. He may be a sensual "fool," but riches are for the few. His rose is not to be purchased with showers of gifts — and Richece is later ejected from Love's army.

One might hazard one more paradoxical suggestion about the Richece miniature. If among the "vices" of this manuscript Greed (Covoitise) entails a threat to masculine wealth through female allure, Wealth's refusal now to admit the Lover qualifies that threat. Or does it? Perhaps the threat is sustained, precisely because Wealth has another playboy in tow. This might emphasize the cynical significance which Sarah Kay observes in the narrative: the Lover "has tried to buy his way to success, and only fails because he lacks the means."[209] The gender insinuations, the nuances of misogyny, flicker on.

Venus Aims to Inflame the Castle (Plate 44)

NLW 5016D has no illustrations for a sizeable part of the text, during which Love summons his "barons," hears what Fraud has to say, and allows Fraud and Constrained Abstinence to open a way into the castle of Jealousy by eliminating Scandal, one of the gatekeepers. There is also a long speech by the Old Woman instructing Responsiveness, before a military attempt is made to capture the tower, though the siege is suspended while Jean develops ideas in Nature's "Confession" and a "sermon" to Love's army by Genius. Representative illustrations for these episodes in the poem will be found in figures 9–14 in this book. In NLW 5016D, illustration resumes near the end of the action.

Cycles of illustration in many *Rose* manuscripts conclude with representations of one or both of two adjacent scenes: Venus taking aim at a sexually explicit female image sculpted on the wall of the tower which incarcerates Bel Acueil/

---

[209] Kay, *The Romance of the Rose*, 42; see also Tuve, *Allegorical Imagery*, 260, and Stakel, *False Roses*, 26.

CHAPTER TWO

Responsiveness and hence withholds the Rose; and Pygmalion fashioning a female figure with which that sculpted image is compared.

Much attention has been paid to the sculptures and to Pygmalion in *Rose* iconography, but perhaps too little to Venus herself. Her role in the poem has seemed to some readers to be overshadowed by that of the male god Amors; she has been thought to exercise only "a severely limited power."[210] Yet the view recently emphasized by Sarah Kay is more accurate: Venus epitomizes women's desire and is an irresistible sexual energy without which the combined efforts of the Lover, God of Love, and allies would be useless.[211] That is reflected in the broader visual structure to which she contributes in Plate 44. After all, her action here visually complements and in effect supersedes that of the God of Love who, at the very inception of the Lover's interest in the Rose, shoots him full of arrows of desire. Just as the male is "attacked" by the male principle of desire, so too the female is attacked ("fired") by the female principle of desire, for, as Jean's poem earlier states, it is Venus *qui les dames espire* (15638) or who "arouses women."[212]

The difference, of course, is that a literal visual imagining of the attack intended by Venus will suggest "a crude reversal of the God of Love's initial penetration of the Lover's heart."[213] Whereas the male victim was imagined as a functioning male youth (albeit that the masculine gaze, the sexualizing masculine eye itself, constitutes his chief function at that point), the female victim is in the text no more than an inert sexual object, a "loophole" (Horgan 320) or arrow-slot (*petitete archiere*, 20762): a sort of architectural vagina, an aperture that Nature has set between thigh-like pillars. While this may well seem to reduce the woman/Rose to the crudity of sheer titillating anatomy, particularly when the text goes on to redefine the "loophole" as a covered "sanctuary" (*un saintuaire*, 20777) within a silver female image supported by the pillars, we should not overlook the fact that the narrative implies that these partly concealed orifices are actually disclosed by Venus alone. It is she who creates the Lover's awareness of nature's secret recess. It takes the "archer" Venus to perceive the secret "archway," as Jean punningly puts it:

---

[210] Theresa Tinkle, *Medieval Venuses and Cupids: Sexuality, Hermeneutics, and English Poetry* (Stanford: Stanford University Press, 1996), 111.

[211] S. Kay, "The Birth of Venus in the *Roman de la Rose*," Exemplaria 9 (1997): 7–37 (here 22).

[212] Adopting a persuasive rendering by Kelly, *Internal Difference and Meanings*, 79, rather than the more bland rendering in both Dahlberg (265) and Horgan (242), that Venus is "the inspiration of ladies." However, Jean de Meun's view of Venus is at times unstable: see lines 10749ff., Horgan 165–66.

[213] Lewis, "Images of Opening," 239.

Chapter Two

puis avise, con bone archiere,
par une petitete archiere
qu'ele vit en la tour reposte (20761–63).

While the Lover, recounting the episode, expresses anticipatory relish for his own investigation of the "sanctuary," and while Jean perhaps draws — as Camille has suggested — on the language of the Song of Songs where a mystical lover is said by the Bride of the song to have "put his hand by the hole in the wall, and my bowels were moved at his touch," in the *Rose* the agent of arousal is actually female.[214]

Readers tend to be confused here by the quasi-phallicism of the carefully-aimed firebrand. Calin describes the brand as a "masculine" metaphor and claims that Venus (along with Nature) assumes "masculine characteristics, as if the notion of sexual . . . liberation forms part of a male world view."[215] But it is worth insisting that the torch's actual trajectory is unknown. Its function proves to be sexually inflammatory, not penetrative. Jean has preserved the mysterious interiority ascribed by Guillaume to the effect of the torch, "whose flame has warmed many a lady" (3407–8) and whose warmth the Rose's Responsiveness was said to "feel" (3455–56, Horgan 52–53) by a process which remains undefined.

The cumulative point seems to be that the female sex organs are as yet stone cold, sacred, reserved, awaiting the spirit of Venus to arouse desire. If the Lover's initiation into love was partly reflexive and narcissistic, so is the Rose's/woman's. Moreover, if the sexualized statuette is in some prior sense a secret which Venus has to reveal, those manuscripts which (like NLW 5016D) do not represent the statuette when they picture the scene with the bow preserve some of the logic of the moment, whether fortuitously or not.

In Plate 44, Venus is a commanding figure standing firmly in a pale violet dress, tight-fitting at waist and bust: there is no attempt to show her "tucking up her skirts," though that is a feature of the immediately ensuing text to which some illuminators respond.[216] Her hairstyle conforms to the standard elegant type in the manuscript, previously noted in such figures as Ease. With no attribute (such as crown or wings) to distinguish her, she can be known only by the bow whose string her elongated fingers so tautly strain, and above all by the *brandons*, the torch-like missile, which is her weapon, although some illustrators miss the point

---

[214] This last important detail is missed by Camille in his brilliant discussion of this episode's "reversal of the normal sacralization of allegory": *Gothic Idol*, 321–22.

[215] William Calin, *A Muse for Heroes: Nine Centuries of the Epic in France* (Toronto: University of Toronto Press, 1983), 136.

[216] See the Valencia MS in Fleming, *Study in Allegory*, figure 41; and Morgan, MS M 132, fol. 148v.

and present a simple arrow instead.[217] Although her representation as woman rather than queen or winged deity is not a rare feature,[218] it is potentially crucial from the viewer's perspective because it tempers the sense of an intervention by an awesome external force. The capitulation of the castle — that stronghold of modesty over which Modesty and Timidity argue futilely with Venus just before the miniature occurs — will seem from such an illustration to be brought about not so much by a deity as by the will of woman herself. The illustration helps us to realize that there is therefore in this episode not only what Daniel Poirion calls a "rehabilitation of female sensuality,"[219] but also a reassertion of female will. The catalyst of arousal remains strictly female.

Venus takes aim at or across a "tower" which recalls the other walled edifices of this manuscript's cycle: a crenellated structure in pink squared masonry with tiled roof and a dark narrow entrance. Her precise target is not clear. Perhaps we are meant to imagine it, somewhere diagonally rightwards and upwards of the picture space. However, since the rubric specifies only that Venus aims a firebrand at the castle in order to set on fire everything within, both rubricator and illustrator may simply have elided the details of the erotic sanctuary. Other manuscripts often do the same,[220] though there is usually some attempt to incorporate "pillars," and later manuscripts increasingly depict a sexualized statuette and aperture for Venus to aim at.[221]

Two explanations for the absence of the eroticised "image" as target can be offered. One is the possibility of scruples about decorum; the other explanation (whether alternative or supplementary to that) is that the "image" is actually an in-

---

[217] E.g., Malibu, Getty Mus. MS 83. MR. 177, fol. 129v; ÖNB, MS 2592, fol. 139v; Bodl., MS Douce 195, fol. 148v; BL, MS Egerton 1069, fol. 140v.

[218] Cf. BL, MS Royal 19. B. XIII, fol. 141v; ÖNB, MS 2592, fols. 139v and 143r; Morgan, MS M 132, fol. 148v. But she is either crowned, or crowned and winged, in, e.g., Morgan, MS M 324, fol. 137v; Malibu, Getty Mus. MS 83. MR. 177, fol. 129v; BL, MS Egerton 1069, fol. 140v; Bodl., MS e Mus. 65, fol. 166r, and MS Douce 195, fol. 148v.

[219] D. Poirion, "Narcisse et Pygmalion dans le *Roman de la Rose*," in *Essays in Honor of Louis Francis Solano*, ed. Raymond J. Cormier and Urban T. Holmes (Chapel Hill: University of North Carolina Press, 1970), 153–65 (here 159).

[220] E.g., Morgan, MS M 324, fol. 137v (closely analogous), and ÖNB, MS 2592, fol. 139v.

[221] Malibu, Getty Mus. MS 83. MR.177, fol. 129v (reproduced in Lewis, "Images of Opening," figure 41) is an example which reduces the castle to a niche revealing female abdomen, pudendum and legs, perhaps humorously exaggerated as McMunn suggests: "Representations of the Erotic," 128.

Chapter Two

serted and therefore dispensable element of the narrative at this point. Moreover, prompted by the omission, we should here like to draw attention to the fact that, although the image as target is recalled just before Venus eventually releases her bowstring, her "brand" is *not* described as hitting that target. The trajectory *does not turn out to be what the reader expects*. Instead, Venus is said to loose her brand "upon the people of the castle, to madden them," though shooting it "with such skill that not one of them could see it, however long they looked" (21221–28, Horgan 327). The prospect of the blazing invasion of an erotic idol's sexual organs suddenly vanishes, during the flight of a weapon which the eye cannot detect, leaving us to contemplate only the result of the action: a conflagration within the castle, which causes the garrison to abandon the defense.

Consequently, illuminators who depicted Venus's missile actually passing through the image's crotch substantially distort Jean's narrative.[222] Misled by such illustrations, or jumping to a conclusion which Jean does not (at this point) give, critics often express or imply the same distortion. One of them reports that the poet "has Venus shoot the masculine, phallic 'arrow' that enters the feminine tower's 'narrow aperture' "; another states that in the poem Venus "shoots her arrow at a loophole between two columns"; another that "she shoots the arrow between the columns."[223] Yet the missile is not actually an arrow, and she never "shoots it *at*" the loophole. We should rather think — like the illuminator of the Oxford manuscript, Douce 195[224] — in terms of some sort of irradiation than of penetration. What Jean has done is to suppress one erotic metaphor, the threat of a violent awakening of female sexuality through phallic penetration, in favor of another erotic metaphor, one which envisages the surrender of female sexual inhibition as a voluntary abandonment of the fort of female modesty without visible external coercion, amidst autonomous flames of desire. The language this speaks is the language used, for example, by Chrétien de Troyes of Laudine in the *Chevalier au lion*: ". . . her own efforts kindled her love, like the log that smokes as soon as the flame is put to it, without anyone blowing or fanning it."[225] Although the poetry of John Gower shows that there came to be available in the Middle

---

[222] E.g., the Valencia manuscript reproduced in Fleming, *Study in Allegory*, figure 41; and BL, MS Egerton 1069, fol. 140v (Lewis, "Images of Opening," figure 42).

[223] Respectively Tinkle, *Medieval Venuses*, 111; Lewis, "Images of Opening," 237; and Ferrante, *Woman as Image*, 115.

[224] Fol. 152v (Dahlberg, trans., figure 56).

[225] ". . . et par li meïsmes s'alume / ensi com la buche qui fume / tant que la flame s'i est mise, / que nus ne la soufle n'atise": Chrétien de Troyes, *The Knight with the Lion, or Yvain*, ed. and trans. William W. Kibler (New York: Garland, 1985), lines 1781–84.

Ages a cliché of "shooting Venus's bow" as a metaphor for penetrative ejaculation, that cliché is not actuated here.[226]

The Aberystwyth miniature may be "right" by luck. In line with a rubric which, following the preceding text, specifies only that Venus "aims a firebrand at the castle in order to set on fire everything within," Plate 44 expresses Venus's intention to set fire to the fort. It presents the encompassing metaphor for a female dispersal of female inhibition, by fire; it does not misrepresent the intangible process by which this will be effected. For whatever reason, the miniature preserves mystery and autonomy in the awakening of female desire — an autonomy which Jean himself sustains even though readers often miss it. Here again, therefore, is an illustration which can accidentally be quite important in interpretative terms, because it happens to respect what some illuminators and critics blur: that is, the text's recognition of female agency in the "storming" of Jealousy's castle.

Pygmalion Sculpts (Plate 45)

The story of Pygmalion intrudes lengthily into the siege narrative at this point, on the pretext that the female "image" at which Venus takes aim outmatches in beauty even the image of a woman whom Pygmalion created in ivory, and whose lifeless form he so adored that he became desperate to vivify it. Scholars have explored numerous implications arising from this "digression": its implications concerning the fantasy and subjectivity of male lust; its explicit recall of Narcissistic infatuation (20846–58); its latent diagnosis of a form of idolatry common to Pygmalion and the Lover.[227] Since it is a segment of the *Rose* which clearly called attention to itself as being ripe for illustration (some picture cycles include more than one miniature on the Pygmalion theme), it is worth asking how far illustrators confirm the suggestiveness of the digression.

The Aberystwyth miniature occurs at the standard textual locus where Pygmalion is introduced as a sculptor working in many media who determines to prove his skill in producing a human likeness. The result is a female form of such beauty as to surpass even legendary women like Helen and Lavinia:

---

[226] Cf. "This Croceus, the bowe bende, / Which Venus tok him forto holde, / And schotte als ofte as evere he wolde," *Confessio Amantis* V. 4860–62: *The English Works of John Gower*, ed. G. C. Macaulay, EETS ES 81–82 (London: Oxford University Press, 1901).

[227] E.g., Tuve, *Allegorical Imagery*, 262–63; Fleming, *Study in Allegory*, 228–38; Robertson, *Preface to Chaucer*, 100–3. For more positive assessments of Pygmalion's love, see Camille, *Gothic Idol*, 325–34; and Kelly, *Internal Difference*, 76–78.

Chapter Two

> He created an ivory image and took such care over the making of it that it was as lovely and beautiful and apparently as alive as the fairest creature living. (20796–99, Horgan 321)

The narrative immediately proceeds with Pygmalion's lament about his predicament when he realizes that he has fallen in love with a deaf and dumb image, one "rigid as a stake" and whose lips are chill (20873–76). After that comes the plangently comic sentiment of numerous attentions he pays to his inert beloved, dressing her up in clothes, jewels, and garlands. We shall adopt for her the name "Galatea" by which she has been known in more recent times.

Illustrations at this point generally adopt one of two models, both of which invoke the concept of monumental sculpture. They show a sculptor working on a female form which is either recumbent on some form of plinth or table, or vertical like a standing statue.[228] The sculptor commonly uses a hammer and chisel or chisel alone on some portion of the image's anatomy, the dominant medium envisaged generally being stone rather than (as in the text) ivory. The more complete the woman's form at which he vigorously chips in this way — especially when it lies before him, and paradoxically even more especially when the body is represented fully clothed as in figure 16 — the more disconcerting is the effect: not so much an effect of creation, as of phallic violence done to a "real" woman's body, to her waist, breasts, abdomen, wherever the chisel is seen to strike. The *Rose* illuminators, wanting to represent the emphatic beauty of the finished product simultaneously with the process of its production from rigid material, seem to involve themselves in problems of illusion which risk implying some kind of sexually sadistic attack on a woman. Whether this means that they detect in the story a comment on the potential brutality of male fantasies of heterosexual desire is therefore an open question.

As can be seen in Plate 45, Galatea may, however, be represented as only partly formed. Here we have a finished neck and head, but the remainder of the body is unworked matter in a sort of mermaid shape. What this probably signifies is that the illustrator has taken one stage further the tendency of the horizontal sculpting model to invoke the art of the funereal monument — those carved images of the dead which lie on top of many medieval stone caskets. (The tendency may be said to be most fulfilled when the recumbent female form lies not on a trestle table but upon a stone sepulchral structure.[229]) The unformed body

---

[228] For the vertical model, see e.g., BL, MS Egerton 881, fol. 165v (Camille, *Gothic Idol*, figure 174); or ÖNB, MS 2592, fol. 140r (Kuhn, "Illustration des *Rosenromans*," plate XI).

[229] For the trestle model see Morgan, MS M 324, fol. 138r and MS M 132, fol. 149r (figure 16); Princeton, Univ. Lib. MS Garrett 126, fol. 146v; BL, MS Yates Thompson 21,

below the shoulders of the woman in NLW 5016D is a visual pun. In one way it signifies formless matter. Unusually here, Galatea's "formlessness" replicates the curved form of unworked ivory, a substance to which (incidentally) the hue of beautiful female skin was often likened. In another way the shape signifies a *dead* body, tightly wrapped in a funereal sheet, as comparison with representations of funerals in manuscripts of the period demonstrates (figure 15).[230] This funereal analogy is clever because it seems to complement two memorable features of the legend. One is the fact that Pygmalion's creation is so lifelike that he confuses himself as to whether she is dead or alive (20896); and the other, really the nub of the story, is that Pygmalion yearns above all to bring the "dead" chill statue to life. In the type of illustration which NLW 5016D exemplifies, both the ambiguity of the statue and his urgent need to resolve it is incorporated into the one representation of Galatea's creation.[231] Where some other manuscripts go on to depict in a separate miniature the responsiveness of Galatea after Pygmalion's impassioned prayer to Venus brings her to life, this manuscript does not need to.

Further hints of the miracle of the vivifying of the statue may strike us. Not only does Galatea's head appear incongruously raised (for which muscular exertion would seem necessary in the absence of any support, as though she is struggling to free herself), but also her gaze can be construed as alive and responsive, though her creator's own eyes are more distantly absorbed. But what exactly is the sculptor doing? Instead of the usual gouging tools, he holds a small vessel in his left hand, while his right hand gently applies to the upraised face, perhaps specifically to the eyebrow, an indeterminate implement which appears to end in a twin point, rather like chopsticks. The possibilities seem to be that he is either using a brush or brushes to apply finishing touches to the statue with paint or cosmetics (a phenomenon paralleled in other contexts[232]), or perhaps plucking the eyebrows with something resembling tweezers. Either way, the effect on the "sculpting" illustration is to soften it and in some sense to expand its field of reference —

---

fol. 136r; Valencia, Univ. lib., MS 387, fol. 141r. For the sepulchral model, see BL, MS Add. 42133, fol. 137r. Funereal resonances are moralistically discussed in V. Egbert, "Pygmalion as Sculptor," *Princeton University Library Chronicle* 28 (1966): 20–23 (here 23).

[230] Besides the funeral of Esclados (figure 16) in *Le Chevalier au lion*, BN, MS fr. 1433, fol. 69v (Hindman, *Sealed in Parchment*, figure 28), see also a corpse in a casket in BL, MS Add. 42130, fol. 157v (Backhouse, *Luttrell Psalter*, figure 6). The corpse-analogy is so strong as to rule out an alternative visual association between Galatea's body and the white-swaddled body of an infant.

[231] Cf. Camille, *Gothic Idol*, 327.

[232] See Camille, *Gothic Idol*, figures 120, 125, 170, for painters working on statues of the Virgin and of a woman. It may be relevant that Nature's creation of humans was imagined to include a kind of "painting": e.g., Chaucer, *Physician's Tale*, VI. 32–36.

to anticipate, for instance, the elaborate attention Pygmalion is to pay to dressing and ornamenting his creation. The illustration is much more dense with implication than at first appears.

The sculptor himself echoes the Lover's previous attire in his longish orangered gown with pink hood and his elegant black shoes. But while visual signals, no less than signals found in the text, may encourage the observer/reader to connect and compare this lover with the poem's other lovers, another contextualizing factor is the positioning of the Pygmalion miniature on the page facing the Venus miniature (Plate 46). Accidentally or not, it is possible to read here a certain complementarity. Venus stands in profile ready to apply her torch to the castle (and to its female "image"). Pygmalion stands in similar profile and applies a more delicate instrument to his "image," an image which the text has specifically compared with Venus's target. The images are not on a single bifolium, so the painter probably did not work on them together. However, looking across the page opening, the viewer will certainly be disposed to move between the miniatures and reflect on their relationship. And this is interesting because the relationship between Pygmalion's action and Venus's is precisely the point of the narrative. The juxtaposing of the miniatures helps to suggest that Pygmalion wants to "ignite" the statue, just as Venus means to ignite the castle in order to render the Rose accessible.

We might read from the two illustrations that masculine desire perverts the impact of Venus (female desire) by seeking to mould the female persona as something acquiescent to masculine subjectivity. Yet the power of Venus's presence on the left counterbalances the male egotism which presumes to construct the female on the right, and therefore seems to qualify what is often thought of as the unrelenting reduction of woman to passive sexual plaything in the closing part of the *Roman*. If the *Rose* strikes some critics as a text reinforcing "the reification of the female as an object and projection of masculine desire,"[233] the representation of Venus and her firebrand with which the Pygmalion/Galatea illustration is paired is a reminder of something which the Pygmalion narrative itself acknowledges — that it is precisely *not* masculine desire which brings feminine desire "alive." Critics have toyed with the question whether the Pygmalion "sculpting" scene articulates something of an ancient stereotype of the male as the active principle, giving "form" to the female who constitutes "matter."[234] If that stereotype is operative, however, the context only goes to show how limited the "forming" power of the male is. The nub of the scene is that Pygmalion cannot vivify the matter which he would presume to form. Of course not: theology held that the crucial animation

---

[233] Jane Chance, "Gender Trouble in the Garden of Deduit: Christine de Pizan Translating the *Rose*," *Romance Languages Annual* 4 (1992): 20–28 (here 20).

[234] Poirion, *Le Roman de la Rose*, 163; Camille, *Gothic Idol*, 306.

came from God. But in the *Rose* it is only Venus — to whom Pygmalion finally prays — who can breathe life into Galatea and hence complete a reciprocation of desires: it is Venus who in the most important sense "in-forms" Galatea.

In one medieval retrospect on the *Rose,* Venus is heard to boast that the whole story "from beginning to end . . . speaks of nothing but me."[235] This was probably intended as a criticism of the concentration on sensual desire in the combined poem. In a literal way the boast is not very applicable to Guillaume's section, where Venus intervenes very briefly and with only temporary effect. Nevertheless, it is interesting testimony to the ultimately pivotal function ascribed to Venus (far more than to masculine Amors) in Jean de Meun's continuation. Jean's poem goes on to conclude with a mockingly salacious abandonment to phallicism. So far as illustration is concerned, NLW 5016D leaves its reader with a different perception. In its Pygmalion there subsists a wry sense of the futile confidence of the masculine ego which would impose a concept of femininity while being incapable of bringing it properly to life. Facing this, in its Venus, there is a recognition that female will is an essential catalyst in the Art of Love.

---

[235] Huot cites this passage from Guillaume de Deguilleveille's *Pelerinage de l'ame* in *The Romance of the Rose and its Medieval Readers,* 227.

Chapter Three

DESCRIPTIONS OF THE MANUSCRIPTS OF THE
ROMAN DE LA ROSE
AT THE NATIONAL LIBRARY OF WALES

The seven manuscripts of *Le Roman de la Rose* at the National Library of Wales, Aberystwyth, all came to the library with the collection of F. W. Bourdillon (1852–1921), purchased in 1922. He calls for a biographical note.

Francis William Bourdillon was the eldest son of Francis Bourdillon, an Anglican clergyman and author of devotional books. The Bourdillons were of Huguenot extraction; the English family maintained contact with French cousins. Francis William spent much of his childhood in Sussex, went to Haileybury College and then to Worcester College, Oxford. After graduation he worked for some years as a private tutor. For most of his life, however, he seems to have been able to live on his means. He married Agnes Smyth and together they settled at Buddington, near Midhurst, in Sussex. There were three children.

Bourdillon showed great devotion to Sussex, to the Alps, to literature, and to books. Three societies provided for his interests, the Sussex Archaeological Society, the Alpine Club and the Bibliographical Society. A collection of his poetry, *Among the Flowers*, published in 1878, was the first of many. Although they do not appear to have met with great public response, he continued until the end of his life to publish small collections, including timely pieces such as an "Ode in Defence of the Matterhorn against the Proposed Railway to its Summit." His work was praised for its purity and delicacy of touch.

It is as a scholar and collector that Bourdillon may be best remembered. Notebooks recording his purchase of books survive for two periods, 1888–89 and 1913–18. By 1888 he was a scholar of repute and an active collector. His taste, reflected in his library, was in the first place for French literature, above all, for French romances, and in the second for English literature.

Bourdillon produced three works of scholarship, all of which have worn well, besides a number of occasional papers: his edition of *Aucassin et Nicolette* (London: Kegan Paul, 1887), with an often reprinted translation; his edition of *Tote listoire*

Chapter Three

de France (London: D. Nutt, 1897), taken from the manuscript in his own library, now NLW MS 5005; and *The Early Editions of the Roman de la Rose* (1906).[1] In these works Bourdillon presents his findings with clarity and elegance.

Medieval manuscripts already feature among Bourdillon's purchases in 1888–89. By the time he came to make the rough list of his manuscripts which survives in NLW MS 5078C, in 1914 or soon after, his collection corresponded closely to that which was acquired after his death by the National Library of Wales. A few notable manuscripts which he had at one time owned he later sold; a number of these are mentioned in a rough list of contents of cupboards and cabinets which he made about 1901 (NLW MS 5073B).

The bulk of Bourdillon's library of over six thousand volumes was bought by the National Library of Wales. The manuscripts are briefly described in the *Handlist* of the library's manuscripts,[2] where they appear as NLW MSS 5001–148. The pencilled numbers of the kind "Bdn 123" which are to be found in the manuscripts and which are referred to in the descriptions below were added at the National Library; they no longer have any function as call-numbers. The collection includes forty medieval manuscripts, mostly French, now NLW MSS 5001–44. Among the remainder are a few post-medieval literary manuscripts, manuscripts relating to Sussex, some fifty of Bourdillon's notebooks, and family material. His printed books included incunabula and, not unexpectedly, a fine collection of early editions of the *Roman de la Rose*. Two valuable portions of Bourdillon's library which were not acquired by the National Library were those which comprised books and drawings by William Blake and publications of the Kelmscott Press.

The National Library intended in the 1920s to publish a catalogue of Bourdillon's library, such as it had acquired. A part of the intended catalogue reached galley proof. A copy of these proofs and the relevant accession register, which together constitute a record of the books acquired, may be consulted in the Printed Books Department of the National Library.

Bourdillon was remembered with affection. A notice of his death in *The Library* refers to the "scholarship and humanity" which he brought to bibliography, enriching his work and endearing him to his friends.[3]

---

[1] *The Early Editions of the Roman de la Rose*, The Bibliographical Society Illustrated Monographs, 14 (1906, repr. Geneva: Slatkine, 1974).

[2] *Handlist of Manuscripts in the National Library of Wales*, vol. 2 (Aberystwyth: National Library of Wales, 1940–).

[3] 4th Series (1920–21): 273–74.

Chapter Three

A note on the form of the descriptions

The following descriptions of the seven manuscripts conform to patterns and conventions which are by now so widespread as to require no explanation. But a few comments on the descriptions may be helpful:

- Each description begins with an attempt to characterize the manuscript in a few words. Among these words occurs "folio," used in its traditional rather than its strict bibliographical sense.
- No attempt to describe texts of the *Roman de la Rose* can begin without reference to Langlois's edition and his study of the manuscripts.[4] The limitations of Langlois's pioneering work require no new comment; Lecoy is judicious in his comments in his own edition.[5] Still, for what they are worth, Langlois's main criteria for classification of texts have here been observed and commented on in relation to the seven Aberystwyth manuscripts; so too have some "remaniements" discussed by Bourdillon himself and by Huot.[6] Beyond recording these features, the descriptions offer some further comments on the text and on lacunae or additions, but without any claim to systematic study in this respect.
- Since Langlois's scholarship on classification is cited, comment on the text in this chapter alone uses the line numbers of Langlois's edition, but with the numbers of Lecoy's edition always supplied in parentheses. However, reference to the text in relation to miniatures is simply by Lecoy's line numbers.
- Citations from the text do not adhere to the capitalization, or lack of capitals, of the manuscript.
- Descriptions of the miniatures are kept to a minimum. For detailed analysis, see Chapter Two.

---

[4] *Le Roman de la* Rose and *Les Manuscrits du Roman de la Rose*.

[5] *Le Roman de la Rose*, I, "Introduction," xxxvii–xxxviii.

[6] Bourdillon, *Early Editions*, and Huot, *The* Romance of the Rose *and its Medieval Readers*, Chaps. 3–5.

Chapter Three

NLW MS 5011E

A large squarish folio, written in two columns, illustrated with two miniatures, s.xv[1] (probably c. 1420–30).

Preparation and writing

Parchment, much of it of poor quality. 153 leaves, bearing foliation of s.xv, i–vii^{xx}xiii. Measure: 335 x 250 mm, written space about 230 x 175 mm. Written in two columns, varying between 34 and 38 lines to the page. Ruled in plummet and crayon. There are ruled columns for line-initials but none for a space between line-initials and text. Collation: 1–14^8, 15^{10} (fols. 113–22), 16–18^8, 19^8 wanting 8 which was very likely blank. Quires 17 and 18 (fols. 131–46) are misbound, and have been from the beginning (see the note of s.xv on fol. 96 drawing attention to the disorder): these two quires should follow quire 12. Catchwords survive but no signatures.

Written in a free *lettre batârde* by a single hand, given to flourishes. There is no punctuation. The ink is pale brown, a darker brown in the latter part; some corrections in the earlier part are made in the darker ink, e.g., on fols. 8r, 9v, 17r–v.

Decoration

There are two quarter-page miniatures (115 x 78 mm) side by side at the head of the text on fol. 1r. One is of the sleeping poet in bed, the other of him washing hands at a fountain. The colors are red, blue, green, and gray. There are simple red frames. The miniatures are probably Parisian work of c. 1420–30 (see above p. 30).

On fol. 1r is an eight-line parti-colored red/blue initial with good penwork. Elsewhere, two-line alternate red and blue initials of romanesque type, without penwork, excepting one on fol. 1r. Headings within the text are in red. Many of the scribe's guide-words for the rubricator survive unerased.

Binding

Limp vellum over pads (not visible) on six bands, with paper pastedowns, perhaps of s.xvii. Ties were provided but are now missing. Wormholes on fols. 1–11 and 132–53 indicate the earlier presence of wooden boards. A paper label on the spine, "Le Roman de la Roze," of s.xviii or xix, conceals an earlier inscription.

2° *fol. Pour les arbres*

Text

Fols. 1r–152v   Maintes gens diens que en songes / Na se non fables et mensonges / ... Ainsi eus la rose vermeille / A tant fu jour et je

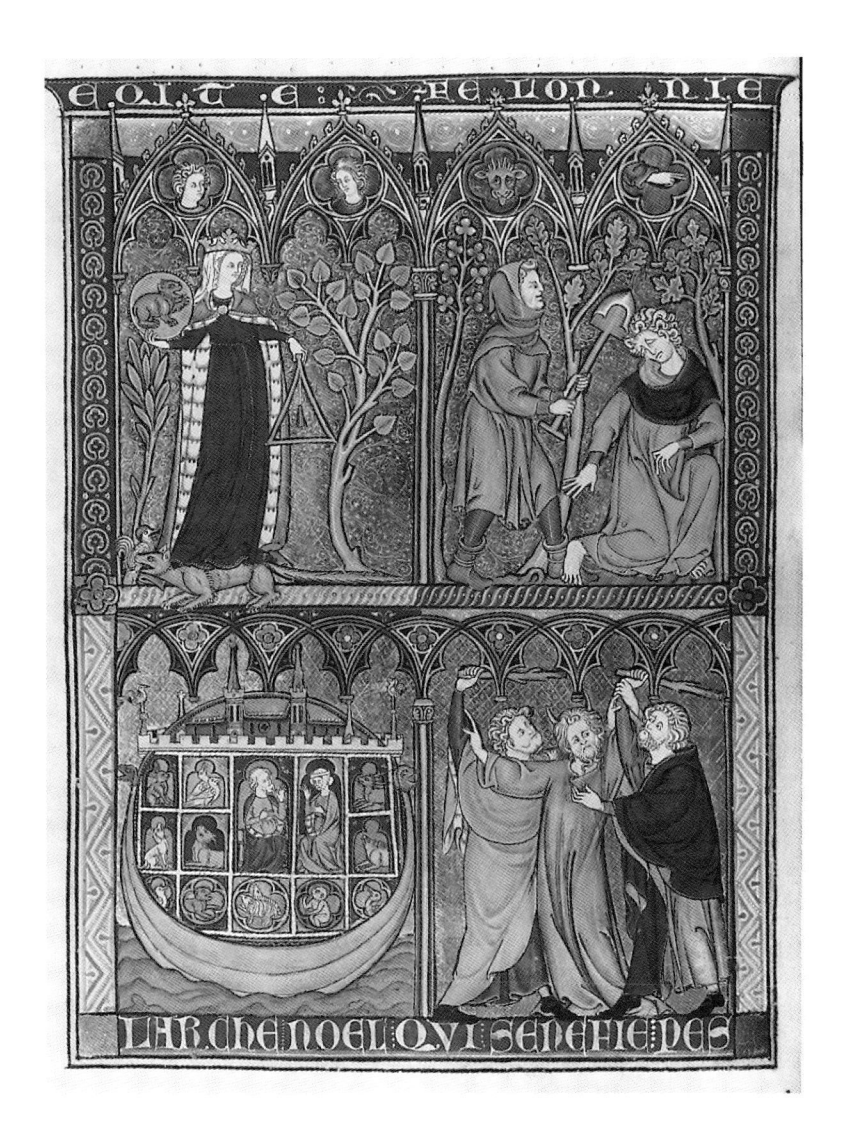

Figure 1: "Equité" and "Felonnie"; *Somme le roi*,
London, BL, MS Add. 28162, fol. 7v (late fourteenth century)
By permission of the British Library.

Figure 2: The poet dreams of a debating theologian and knight;
Le Songe du verger, London, BL, MS Royal 19 C IV, fol. 1v (c. 1378).
By permission of the British Library.

Figure 3: The Duke received by St Peter at the gate of Paradise; the *Grandes Heures* of the Duke of Berry, Paris, BN, MS lat. 919, fol. 96r (1409). By permission of the Bibliothèque nationale de France.

Figure 4: Venus heats Bel Acueil with her firebrand; *Roman de la Rose*, New York, Morgan MS M 132, fol. 30r (c. 1380). By permission of the Pierpont Morgan Library.

ne durroit point a la guerre
a lousse ne lutayne
ne quelle la queust ahayne

D e ce conseil se sont tenues
P uis si sont auant venues
S ont troue le puissant
D essoubz vn aube espin gisant
I l ot en lieu de cheuessel
S oubz son chief de bertint mossel

Figure 5: Pöor and Honte waken Dangiers; *Roman de la Rose*,
Oxford, Bodl. MS e Mus 65, fol. 27v (c. 1390).
By permission of the Bodleian Library.

Figure 6: Jalousie oversees the building of the castle; *Roman de la Rose*,
Oxford, Bodl. MS e Mus 65, fol. 28v (c. 1390).
By permission of the Bodleian Library.

Figure 7: Lucretia's suicide; *Roman de la Rose*,
New York, Morgan MS M 324, fol 592 (c. 1340–50).
By permission of the Pierpont Morgan Library.

Figure 8: The Lover meets Richece and partner; *Roman de la Rose*,
New York, Morgan MS M 324, fol. 68r (c. 1340–50).
By permission of the Pierpont Morgan Library.

Figure 9: The God of Love consults his "barons"; *Roman de la Rose*, Oxford, Bodl. MS e Mus 65, fol. 82v (c. 1390). By permission of the Bodleian Library.

Figure 10: Faus Semblant kills Malebouche: *Roman de la Rose*,
New York, Morgan MS M 132, fol. 90r (c. 1380).
By permission of the Pierpont Morgan Library.

Figure 11: La Vielle with Bel Acueil in the castle; *Roman de la Rose*,
Oxford, Bodl. MS e Mus 65, fol. 98v (c. 1390).
By permission of the Bodleian Library.

Figure 12: Dangiers forces the Lover away from the rose;
Roman de la Rose, New York, Morgan MS M 132, fol. 109v (c. 1380).
By permission of the Pierpont Morgan Library.

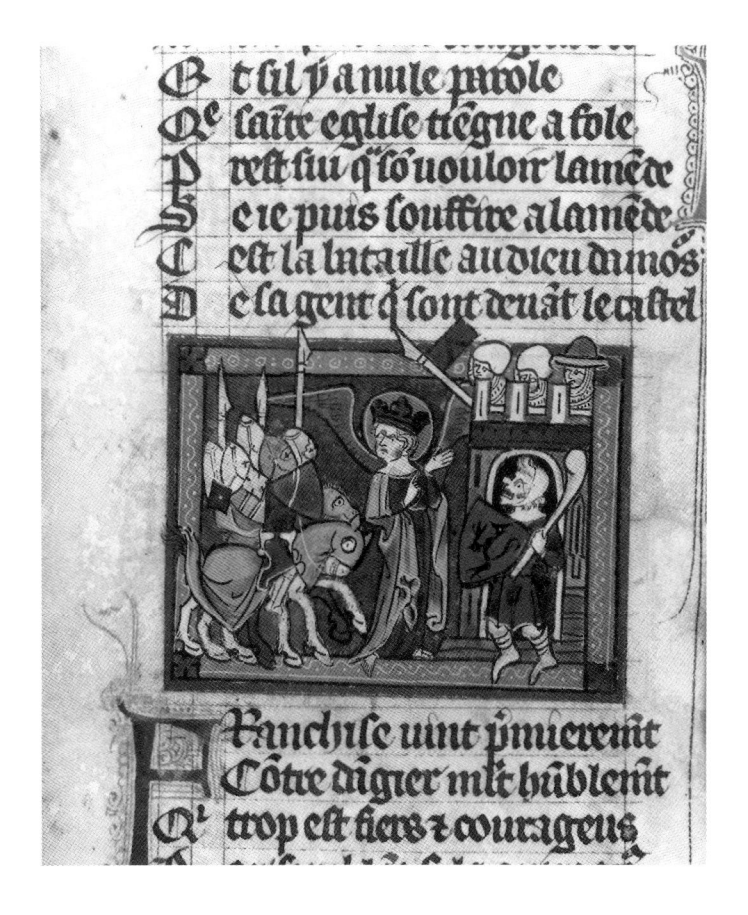

Figure 13: The God of Love instigates the siege; *Roman de la Rose*,
London, BL, MS Royal 20 A XVII, fol. 125r (early fourteenth century).
By permission of the British Library.

Figure 14: Nature confesses to Genius; *Roman de la Rose*,
London, BL, MS Yates Thompson 21, fol. 108r (c. 1380).
By permission of the British Library.

Figure 15: Death and funeral of Esclados; *Le Chevalier au lion*, Paris, BN, MS fr. 1433, fol. 69v (c. 1310–40). By permission of the Bibliothèque nationale de France.

Figure 16: Pygmalion sculpts; *Roman de la Rose*,
New York, Morgan MS M 132, fol. 149r (c. 1380).
By permission of the Pierpont Morgan Library.

mesueille / Explicit le Romant de la Rose / Ou lart damours est toute enclose

The text of Guillaume de Lorris belongs to Langlois's Group II. The reading of his line 2834 (Lecoy 2818) (not *deus*) and the insertion after line 2836 (2820) (*Nez fu saichiez de Normandie . . .*) agree with his sub-group K and L. Lines 109–10 read with his sub-group no. 1. Lines 3019–92 (3003–76) are omitted, a lacuna not recorded by Langlois, perhaps one introduced by carelessness on the part of our scribe or in his exemplar.

The text of Jean de Meun belongs to Langlois's Group II. It belongs with his B manuscripts and includes the interpolations after his line 10518 (10488), of six lines, and after 10830 (10800), of forty lines, given in his edition.[7] The text also includes the interpolated chapter in the discourse of Faus Semblant after line 11222 (11192),[8] comprising lines 1–50 and 57–98 of his text, with an additional two lines after 96.[9]

Fol. 153r   He cle[rc]s quant tu prestres deuiens / plus que angelz adieu auiens / bien doit ta vie estre amendee / . . . toute la foy des crestiens

Eleven lines of verse, contemporary with the main text, possibly added by the scribe of the main text writing more freely.[10]

History

There are many *nota* marks made by two hands of s.xv; on fol. 23v is a note made by a reader of s.xv. There are erased inscriptions of s.xv or xvi on fol. 1r and fol. 153v, the latter beginning "A moy . . .". Inside the upper cover is an unidentified armorial bookplate of s.xix (the arms: a paschal lamb regardant with on a chief three fleurs-de-lis, a motto "Vita sine litteris mors est" and a monogram apparently including the letters C, I, R, L, M, E, and R). Also inside the upper cover are "26225" in pencil; "1500 fr Rahir 1913," no doubt a reference to Édouard Rahir, the Parisian bookseller, and Bourdillon's purchase, in 1913; Bourdillon's 1913 bookplate and, in pencil, "Bdn 164."

---

[7] On the B manuscripts and their "remaniement," see also Huot, *The Romance of the Rose and its Medieval Readers,* Chap. 4.

[8] Printed in Langlois's edition, 3:311–15, and in *Les manuscrits,* 426–30.

[9] See Langlois's edition 3:310.

[10] Not in Arthur Långfors, *Les Incipit des poèmes français antérieurs au xve siécle: Repertoire bibliographique établi à l'aide de notes de M. Paul Meyer* (Paris, 1917).

Chapter Three

NLW MS 5012E

A large folio de-luxe book in virginal condition, never rubricated or illuminated, two quires wanting, s.xv[1].

Preparation and writing

Parchment, of good quality. Foliated i, 1–132; fol. 1 being an old but not original flyleaf. Measure: 335 x 265 mm (written space about 245 x 180 mm). Written in two columns, 38 lines to the page. Lines are ruled in crayon, the frame generally in pale red ink. There are no ruled columns for either line-initials or a space between line-initials and text. Collation: 1–15[8], 16–17[6]. A lacuna in the text between quire 5 and quire 6 would correspond to about 18 leaves, not allowing for miniatures. No signatures or catchwords survive.

Written in a careful upright *lettre bâtarde* by a single hand. There is no punctuation. The ink is brown.

Decoration

Neither rubrication nor illumination were ever begun. The scribe left blank the upper two thirds of fol. 1r and spaces for a long series of (probably) thirty-three single-column miniatures on fols. 2r–5r, 6v–10r, etc. To judge from their locations (using Lecoy's line numbers), the subjects would have been:

fol. 2r	Haine (139)
fol. 2r	Vilanie (156)
fol. 2v	Covoitise (169)
fol. 2v	Avarice (195)
fol. 3r	Envie (235)
fol. 3r	Tritesce (291)
fol. 3v	Vielleice (339)
fol. 4r	Papelardie (407)
fol. 4v	Povrete (441)
fol. 5r	Oiseuse (573)
fol. 6v	the Carole (725)
fol. 6v	Cortoisie (775)
fol. 7r	Deduiz (799)
fol. 7v	Amors (863)
fol. 8r	Biautez (993)
fol. 8v	Richece (1017)
fol. 9r	Largesce (1125)
fol. 9v	Franchise (1189)
fol. 10r	Cortoisie (1227)

fol. 10r   Joinece (1257)
fol. 25r   ?Jalousie rebuking Bel Acueil (3481)
fol. 30r   Reson descending from tower (4199)
fol. 46r   Jalous (9331)
fol. 47v   the origin of kings (9579)
fol. 50v   Richece by a fountain (10021),
fol. 57r   Amors accepts Faus Semblant (10901)
fol. 57v   Faus Semblant addresses the barons (10969)
fol. 67v   Faus Semblant kills Male Bouche (12331)
fol. 83v   ?L'Amant and Bel Acueil (14719)
fol. 86r   ?Jean de Meun's apology (15105)
fol. 96v   Nature's confession (16699)
fol. 114v   Amors vests Genius (19447)
fol. 124r   Pygmalion (20787).

The spaces are of 4–16 lines, the larger ones no doubt intended for miniatures together with rubrics, not miniatures alone. Elsewhere there are spaces of one to three lines for rubrics. There is a space for a four-line initial on fol. 1r and for two-line initials elsewhere. The scribe provided guide-letters for initials but no guidance for rubrics.

Binding
Rough sheep over wooden boards, on six double whittawed thongs, perhaps s.xvi; a centerpiece and a single fillet gold-tooled, of s.xvi or xvii, were perhaps added later. A worm-hole in fol. 1 is not matched in fol. i, the flyleaf. Rebacked at the National Library of Wales.

2° fol. [J]oli gay et plain

Text
Fols. 1r–130v   [M]aintes gens dient que en songes / Na se fables non et mensonges / ... Ainsi euz la rose vermeille / A tant fu jour et si mesueille / Car bien est temps que me repose / Cy fault le rommant de la rose

The lacuna between quires 5 and 6 corresponds to Langlois lines 5882–8563 (Lecoy 5852–8531). The text of Guillaume de Lorris belongs to Langlois's Group II. It does not have the reading *deus* in his line 2834 (2818), nor the insertion which follows his line 2836 (2820). Lines 109–10 read with his variant no. 11.

The text of Jean de Meun, because of the lacuna, lacks Langlois's criterion for distinguishing his Groups I and II. It has however the distinctive features of his B

Chapter Three

manuscripts, which come in his Group I, including the interpolations after his line 4228 (4198), of two lines; after 10518 (10488), of six lines; and after 10830 (10800), of forty lines, all three given in his edition.[11] The text also, however, includes the interpolated chapter in the discourse of Faus Semblant after Langlois line 11222 (11192),[12] comprising lines 1–98 as in the first of his eight groups of this interpolation; and also the Medusa interpolation after Langlois line 20810 (20780) in the full fifty-two lines.[13]

Fols. 130v–31v   [C]es V flesches sont dun affaire / mais elles font plus de mal traire / ... pour reuenir a ma parole / des nobles gens de la carole

Written by the scribe of the main text, beginning at the top of the second column as if this were a free-standing poem. The subject is the five evil arrows of love. There are 164 lines. These are attributed by Langlois to Gui de Mori.[14] They are inserted in a few manuscripts of *Le Roman de la Rose*, including NLW MS 5014D, after Langlois line 975. A text, taken from NLW 5014D, with variant readings from our present manuscript, is printed by Bourdillon.[15]

Fol. 132r–v   Blank

History

There is no annotation of the text or marking by readers before s.xx. Inside the lower cover, "1062.100," of s.xvii or xviii. Inside the upper cover there is a short erased inscription beginning "V[ ]"; and the numbers "40" and "O 353," of s.xviii, and, in pencil, in the lower left-hand corner, "6254," of s.xix. The manuscript was in the library of Henri-François D'Aguesseau (1668–1751), Chancellor of France. A catalogue description of s.xviii/xix written inside the upper cover citing "B B Daguesseau Page 207 Belles lettres Poètes français n° 3160" derives from the sale catalogue of his books.[16] Inside the upper cover and on fol. ir are exten-

---

[11] On the B manuscripts and their "remaniement," see also Huot, *The Romance of the Rose and its Medieval Readers*, Chap. 4.

[12] Printed by Langlois in his edition, 3:311–15, and in *Les manuscrits*, 426–30.

[13] Printed in his edition, 5:107–9, and in *Les manuscrits*, 453–54.

[14] See Ernest Langlois, "Gui de Mori et le Roman de la Rose," *Bibliothèque de l'École des Chartes* 68 (1907): 249–71 (here 265). Huot discusses the "remaniement" of Gui de Mori in *The Romance of the Rose and its Medieval Readers*, Chap. 3.

[15] Bourdillon, *Early Editions*, 176–81.

[16] *Catalogue des livres imprimés et manuscrits, de la bibliothèque de feu Monsieur D'Aguesseau* ... (Paris, 1785), 207.

sive bibliographical notes in French on the text of *Le Roman de la Rose* and on Jean de Meun, of s.xviii/xix. Acquired by Bourdillon not later than c. 1901 (see his list of books and manuscripts in NLW 5073B, fol. 1r; his 1913 bookplate is on fol.i[v], "Bdn 165" in pencil inside the upper cover.

Chapter Three

NLW MS 5013D

A small square folio in modern binding, written in two columns, with eleven miniatures, s.xiv/xv (probably 1380–1400).

Preparation and writing

Parchment. Foliated i, 1–148; fols i and 147–48 are paper flyleaves of s.xix. Measure: 283 x 257 mm; written space c.220 x c.210 mm. Written in two columns, 37–39 lines to the page in quires 1–8, 33–35 in quires 9–10, and 35–39 in quires 11–13. Ruled in plummet. There are ruled columns for line-initials and also for a space between line-initials and text. Collation: 1–12^{12}, 13^2. Catchwords survive, and one single leaf signature, *a iiiii*, small and in red, on fol. 5.

Written in a fairly upright *lettre bâtarde*, by one scribe, relaxing somewhat in quires 9–10. There is no punctuation nor any obvious correction. The ink is dark brown, varying from olive to reddish.

Decoration

On fol. 1r there is a quarter-page miniature (c.100 x 100 mm) of the sleeping poet in bed beneath a rose tree, the page framed, with ivy-leaf branches in the margin. There are ten single-column miniatures (c.60 x 60 mm) on fols. 2r–4v, in simple gold frames with excrescent leaves, also gold, as follows:

fol. 2r	Haine (139)
fol. 2r	Felonie (152)
fol. 2r	Vilanie (156)
fol. 2v	Covoitise (169)
fol. 2v	Avarice (195)
fol. 3r	Envie (235)
fol. 3v	Tritesce (291)
fol. 4r	Vielleice (339)
fol. 4v	Papelardie (405)
fol. 4v	Povreté (439)

The colors used are: red, pink, orange, blue, green, and gray; the background is of blue or vermilion patterned in gold or in the contrasting color. The miniatures are Parisian work of 1380–1400 (see above, pp. 28–29).

Two- or three-line initials are in gold on parti-colored ground of maroon and blue patterned in white. The initials on fol. 1r have been crudely repainted (they had presumably become worn). No spaces were provided by the scribe for rubrics: headings have been written in red in the margins.

CHAPTER THREE

Binding
On five bands, in red straight-grained morocco, decorated with a five-fillet surround, gilt, s.xix, after 1829 ("C.Wise" and "1829" in the watermark of the flyleaves). Wormholes in fols. 1–7 show the earlier presence of wooden boards.

2°*fol. A maintes riches*

Text

Fols 1r–146v   Cy commence le rommans de la roze / Ou lart damours est tout encloze / Maintes gens dient que en songes / Na se fables non et menconges / . . . Ainsi eux la rose vermeille / A tant fu jour et je mesueille / Amen

The text of Guillaume de Lorris belongs to Langlois's Group II. It has both the reading *deux* in Langlois line 2834 (Lecoy 2818) and the insertion *Nez fu sachiez de Normandie* . . . following his line 2836 (2820). Lines 109–10 read with his variant no. 18. Lines 1969–70 (1967–68) are omitted, as in his class L. There is a twelve-line interpolation after Langlois line 1016 for which his edition records no parallel.

The text of Jeun de Meun belongs to Langlois Group II. It belongs to his B manuscripts and includes the interpolations after his line 10518 (10488), of six lines, and after line 10830 (10800), of forty lines, both given in his edition. After Langlois line 4400 (4370) comes the "litany of love" interpolation.[17]

History
There are no significant marks on the text by readers. On fol. 71r in the top right hand corner, probably s.xv, is written "iii^c" (i.e., 300). On fols. 58v, 63r, and 69r there are faint small ink drawings of faces, that on fol. 69r of a man holding a rose perhaps of s.xv or xvi. On fol. 1r is written "[?]De birf" and on fol. 4r, erased, "[?]De musert," both perhaps of s.xvii, both readings uncertain. There are scribbles on fols. 3r and 146r.

This is one of the manuscripts of Joseph Barrois bought by Lord Ashburnham in 1849. Joseph Barrois (1785–1855) and his collection of manuscripts and his unscrupulous dealings in them have been discussed by Delisle.[18] Our manuscript

---

[17] Edited by Huot, *The Romance of the Rose and its Medieval Readers*, Appendix C (365–68).

[18] L. Delisle, *Catalogue des manuscrits des fonds Libri et Barrois* (Paris: Champion, 1888), xxxviii–xlii.

Chapter Three

was numbered CV (105) in Ashburnham's catalogue of the Barrois collection.[19] It was lot 520 in the Ashburnham sale of the Barrois collection by Sotheby's on 10 June 1901 where it was bought by J. & J. Leighton for £110. The note "£210 / L.Ros." on fol.i^v may record the purchase by Bourdillon, though the hand does not seem to be his. "L.Ros." could be Ludwig Rosenthal, the Munich bookseller. Bourdillon's 1913 bookplate is inside the upper cover, and, in pencil on fol. i^r, "Bdn 166."

---

[19] See *Catalogue of the MSS. at Ashburnham Place. Part the second, comprising a collection made by Mr J. Barrois* (London: printed by C. F. Hodgson, n.d.[1853]), and E. A. Bond, *Description of the Ashburnham manuscripts and account of offers of purchase* . . . (London: British Museum [1883]).

Chapter Three

NLW MS 5014D

A small folio, written in two columns, with one miniature, in a fine binding by Lortic, s.xv *med*, but illuminated s.xv².

Preparation and writing

Parchment. Foliated i–iii, 1–149; fols. i–iii and 147–49 were all supplied at the last binding about 1878, fols. i and 149 of blue watered silk on paper, fols. ii–iii and 147–48 of parchment. There is light pencil foliation of s.xix. Measure: 315 x 225 mm; written space c.225 x 155 mm. Written in two columns, 40 lines to the page. Ruled in plummet. There are no ruled columns either for line-initials or between line-initials and text. Collation (judged by catchwords, since the binding is too tight to see the sewings): 1–17⁸, 18¹⁰. In quire 9, the bifolium fols. 67/70 should come between fols. 68/69; the two bifolia were probably misbound from the start, witness the early note on fol. 66v. Catchwords survive but no signatures.

Written in an inelegant *lettre bâtarde* by a single scribe. There is no punctuation. The ink is olive brown.

Decoration

There is a single miniature, half-page, on fol. 1r: within a simple arched frame in gold (152 x 110–32 mm), an interior, on the left the poet sleeping in bed, on the right washing his hands and a servant pouring water. The colors are: red, flesh, blue, turquoise, green, white, gray, and gold pigment. The miniature is probably Parisian work and to be dated 1480–1500 (see above, pp. 30–31); it evidently postdates the writing of the text by a generation or so.

On fol. 1r there is a six-line initial, blue, patterned in white, on a red ground patterned in gold foliage. Elsewhere there are two- and one-line gold initials on parti-colored grounds of maroon/blue, the two colors alternating between interior and exterior of the letter. Headings are in red within the text. The scribe provided guide-letters for initials but no guide-words for headings which he wrote himself. Line-initials are touched in yellow. On fol. 146r, beneath the *explicit*, is a small ink drawing of a rose, evidently by the scribe (Plate 49).

Binding

On five bands, red morocco, richly tooled in blind and in gilt, with doublures of blue morocco, also tooled in gilt, blue washed silk on the facing flyleaves, elaborate gauffering. By Lortic of Paris about 1878 (his label on fol. iᵛ, his stamp at the foot of the upper doublure). The binding is said to have been exhibited at the Paris exhibition of 1878 (NLW MS 5073B, fol. 20r). The rebinding by Lortic was probably the occasion of the repair of the parchment of some leaves, e.g., fols 75, 78, and 80, and the cleansing of marginalia.

CHAPTER THREE

2° fol. Et sachez que bien

Text

Fols. 1r–146r   Maintes gens dient que en songes / Na se fables non et menconges / ... Ainsi eu la rose vermielle / A tant fu jour et je mesueille / Finit le Rommant de la Rose / Ou lart damour est toute enclose / Deo gracias.

The text of Guillaume de Lorris belongs to Langlois Group II. The reading of his line 2834 (Lecoy 2818) (not *deus*) and the insertion after line 2836 (2820) (*Ne fut sachiez de Normandie ...*) agree with his sub-group K and L. The reading of lines 109–10 does not correspond to any given by Langlois: *Descendoit leaue clere et roide / Et venoit bruiant ausi froid*. The text incorporates many of the interpolations of Gui de Mori.[20] Three of the main interpolations are printed from this manuscript by Bourdillon.[21]

The text of Jean de Meun belongs to Langlois Group II. It includes the interpolated chapter in the discourse of Faus Semblant after Langlois line 11222 (11192).[22] Using Langlois's line-numbers, the text of the chapter runs 1–8, 8^{1-20}, 9–12, 12^{1-4}, 13–58, 58^{5-20}, 59–98. It includes also the Medusa interpolation after Langlois line 20810 (20780), in its full 52 lines.[23]

Fol. 146r   O felis ancila dey nos pondere pressor exhonera ... Beate Gonouefe ... gaudentes graciam tuam operante saluemur. Par Christum.

The antiphon for terce on the feast of St Genovefa. Added by a clumsy contemporary hand: the text has been provided with one illuminated initial by the illuminator of the text of the *Roman de la Rose*.[24]

History

The addition, prior to illumination, of the antiphon for St Genovefa, patron saint

---

[20] See Langlois, "Gui de Mori et le *Roman de la Rose*," 271. On the "remaniement" of Gui de Mori, see further Huot, *The Romance of the Rose and its Medieval Readers*, Chap. 3.

[21] Bourdillon, *Early Editions*, 174–84.

[22] Printed by Langlois in his edition, 3:311–15; and in *Les manuscrits*, 426–30.

[23] Printed by Langlois in his edition, 5:107–9, and in *Les manuscrits*, 453–54.

[24] On the antiphon, see U. Chevalier, *Repertorium hymnologicum*, 6 vols. (Louvain and Paris: 1892–1920), no. 30425; V. Leroquais, *Livres d'heures manuscrits de la Bibliothèque Nationale*, 2 vols. (Paris, 1927), 1:306, and 2:118.

of Paris, suggests a Parisian origin. The poor Latin suggests that the owner may have been a layman rather than a cleric. The loss of the original flyleaves and the erasure of marginalia have removed much of the history of the book. The only surviving marginal note, on fol. 66v, of s.xv or xvi, draws attention to the misbinding of the bifolium in quire 9. On fol. 146v is a trace of a drawing in plummet of what appears to be a human head.

The manuscript was acquired in 1873 from the Chateau de Bercy; it was bound by Lortic about 1878 and bought in 1883 by an unknown person, from whom it was bought by J. & J. Leighton, from whom in turn it was bought by Bourdillon in 1893 for £95 (for the descent, see NLW 5073B, fol. 20r). On fol. i^v is Bourdillon's 1913 bookplate; there is no "Bdn" number to be seen.

Chapter Three

NLW MS 5015D

A narrow folio written in single column, decorated, the spaces for miniatures never filled, a good text, s.xv *med*.

Preparation and writing
Parchment. Foliated i–ii, 1–226; fols. i–ii and 225–26 are paper flyleaves of s.xix/xx. There is early foliation, perhaps by the scribe, running i–xi^{xx}iiii, omitting viii and repeating vii^{xx}vi; and there is foliation of s.xvii or xviii, in ink, running 1–83, jumping fol. 40, and continued in pencil 84–216 (on fols. 85–217). Measure: 310 x 150 mm; 240–250 mm column height. Written in one column, 48–55 lines to the page, normally 48 in the early quires. Ruling is in pale red ink. There are no ruled columns either for line-initials or for space between line-initials and text. Collation: 1–12^8, 13^6 (fols. 97–102), 14–27^8, 28^{10}. There are a few surviving leaf signatures of the pattern *ai, aii, aiii, aiiii* on leading leaves of quires (e.g., fols. 20, 33); and also modern pencil quire signatures *a–z, A–E*. There are no catchwords.

Written in an upright *lettre bâtarde* by one scribe. There is scanty punctuation, by point. There are, throughout, correction and revision of the text in darker ink *in rasura*, and additions, notably on fols. 1–3, all made by a second hand of s.xv; evidently another text was at hand. The ink of the original text is pale brown.

Decoration
The spaces provided by the scribe for miniatures are all blank: a quarter-page at the head of fol. 1r and eleven seven-line spaces between fol. 3r and fol. 14v, intended for representations of:

fol. 3r	Avarice (195)
fol. 3v	Envie (235)
fol. 4r	Tritesce (291)
fol. 4v	Vielleice (339)
fol. 5v	Papelardie (407)
fol. 6r	Povreté (441)
fol. 8r	Oiseuse (631)
fol. 12r	Richece (1017)
fol. 13r	Largesce (1125)
fol. 14r	Franchise (1189)
fol. 14v	Cortoisie (1227)

On fol. 1r is a five-line blue initial on maroon ground with gold filigree. All other colored initials are two-line, alternating red and blue, harking back to the arabesque initials of romanesque manuscripts. These initials were done by the hand which added the marginal headings, mostly of speakers' names, in red and blue *lettre bâtarde*. A few of the text-scribe's guide-words for these headings escaped erasure, e.g., on fols. 40r, 162r, and 177v. Line initials are touched in yellow.

Binding
On five bands, in brown morocco, blind-tooled, with stamped panels filled by four parallel strips from a roll designed from an old model; gilt edges. By Ramage of London (stamp at the foot inside the upper cover), s.xix/xx, not later than 1904 (see notes on fol. i).

2° fol. Quant il oyt

Text
Fols. 1r–224v   Aucunes gens dient quen songes / N[a sinon] fables et mensonges / ... Ainsi eu la rose vermeille / Adonc fu iour, et ie mesueille. Explicit.

The letters *a sinon* in the second line are written by the correcting hand over an erasure.

The text of Guillaume de Lorris belongs to Langlois Group I.

The text of Jean de Meun belongs to Langlois Group I. It has none of the omissions which occur in Langlois MS Ac, and in many others.[25] It includes interpolations associated with his B manuscripts after line 4228 (Lecoy 4198), of two lines, and after 10830 (10800), of four lines. It includes the interpolated chapter in the discourse of Faus Semblant after line 11222 (11192),[26] comprising lines 1–50 and 57–98 of Langlois's text.[27] It also includes after Langlois line 20810 (20780) the 52-line Medusa interpolation,[28] including the two lines in Langlois's edition, 43–44, which are omitted in many manuscripts. In NLW MS 5078C, fol. 4r, Bourdillon remarks of our manuscript: "Better text than any of my other MSS."

History
This manuscript evidently remained in France during the sixteenth century. There is contemporary annotation on fols. 47v (noting the omission after Langlois line 4400 [4370] of the "litany of love"[29]), 98r, 100r, and 101r; and on fol. 119r there are pentrials by a French hand probably of s.xvii. On fol. 1r is a largely

---

[25] See Langlois, *Les manuscrits*, 356–57.
[26] Printed by Langlois in his edition, 3:311–15, and in *Les manuscrits*, 426–30.
[27] Manuscripts that share this feature are listed by Langlois in his edition, 3:310.
[28] Printed by Langlois in his edition, 5:107–9, and in *Les manuscrits*, 453–54.
[29] See Huot, *The Romance of the Rose and its Medieval Readers*, Appendix C (365–68).

Chapter Three

erased inscription also probably of s.xvii and the initials or numeral DVI, possibly associated with it. By early in the eighteenth century the manuscript was in England. In the top right hand corner of fol. 1r is the date "27 Januar' 1719/20." Dr Roger Middleton (in a letter to Dr Ceridwen Lloyd-Morgan dated 25 Nov. 1993) has identified the hand as that of Humphrey Wanley: on that date the manuscript was viewed by Wanley for Harley, but returned to the owner, perhaps George Hay, who asked £30 for it.[30] The "4.4.0," also on fol. 1r, of about the same date, probably represents an English price. The manuscript was acquired in 1904 by George Dunn of Woolley Hall (there are notes by him on fols. i and 44r); his book label is inside the upper cover. It was lot 644 in his sale at Sotheby's on 14 February 1913 where it was bought by Bourdillon whose 1913 bookplate is inside the upper cover, as is "Bdn 169" in pencil.

---

[30] See *The Diary of Humphrey Wanley 1715–1726*, ed. C. E. Wright and R. C. Wright, 2 vols. (London: The Bibliographical Society, 1966), 1:24, 29, 194.

CHAPTER THREE

NLW MS 5016D

A small folio in a sixteenth-century binding, written in two columns, supplied with a replacement first leaf, many miniatures, bound with *Le Testament* of Jean de Meun decorated by the same illuminator, s.xiv *med.* (probably c. 1365–75).

Preparation and writing

Parchment. Foliated i, 1–150; fols. i and 150 are paper flyleaves of s.xvi, fols. 1–2 parchment leaves of s.xvi replacing the original first leaf of quire 1. Measure: 282 x 202 mm; written space 205 x 140 mm, 210 x 160 mm in quires 18 and 19. Written in two columns, 42 lines to the page, 43 in quires 18 and 19. Ruled in pale red ink in quires 1–12, the remainder in brown ink. There are ruled columns for line-initials and for a space between line-initials and text. Collation: 1^8 wanting 1 (fols. 3–9), 2^8, 3^8 (4, fol. 21, is a cancel), $4–18^8$, 19^4. There are quire signatures *a–t* in quires 1–17 (omitting *g* and *p* from the sequence); the signatures of quires 14–17 are in darker ink, perhaps by another hand; there are no signatures visible in quires 18 and 19. Signatures are accompanied by one to four horizontal strokes for each of the four leading leaves of the quire. There are catchwords.

There were two scribes, both writing textura, the first wrote fols. 3–136, the second fols. 138–49 (quires 18–19). There is no punctuation. The ink is a warm brown.

The upper inside corners of quires 1 and 19 were damaged by water. From fol. 130 to fol. 149 the upper inner corners of the leaves were repaired with new parchment. This repair derives from a period when the manuscript was still between wooden boards, a period beyond that which preceded the rebinding: there are wormholes in the repair parchment (and not in fol. 150). The damage which necessitated the replacement of the original first leaf may have been caused at the same time.

Decoration

The extent of the text on fol. 2, the replacement leaf, shows that the original must have had a half-page miniature at the head of the text; a blank of a third of a page precedes the text on the present fol. 2r.

There are nineteen single-column miniatures (about 65 x 35–40 mm) in Guillaume de Lorris's text, on fols. 3r–26v, and five in the text of Jean de Meun. They are within frames with foliage excrescence in gold. The ground is of burnished gold or of tessellated gold and color or of a single color patterned in gold; the colors are pale red, pink, vermilion, yellow, blue, green, purple, and white. They are perhaps to be dated 1365–75 (see above, pp. 27–28).

The subjects and locations of the miniatures are as follows:

CHAPTER THREE

fol. 3r   Haine (before 2 interpolated lines, following Lecoy 154)[31]
fol. 3r   Covoitise (169)
fol. 3v   Avarice (195)
fol. 3v   Envie (235)
fol. 4r   Tritesce (291)
fol. 4v   Vielleice (339)
fol. 5r   Papelardie (405)
fol. 5r   Povreté (439)
fol. 5v   *Comment il trouua oyseuse*
              the Lover encounters Oiseuse (495)
fol. 6v   *Comment il deuise a oyseuse son estat*
              (l'Amant "describes his situation to Oiseuse")
              the Lover in the garden with birds (617) (misplaced)
fol. 7r   *Comment elle li ouuri luis du jardin*
              Oiseuse leads the Lover to the garden gate (725)
fol. 8r   *Comment lamant devisoit les oysiaus*
              (l'Amant "describes the birds")
              the Lover (*or* Deduiz/Pleasure?) among trees (863)
fol. 11v   *Comment nercisus morut sur la fontaine*
              Narcissus gazes at the spring (1437)
fol. 13r   *Comment le dieu damours trait a lamant*
              The God of Love shoots an arrow at l'Amant (1679)
fol. 15r   *Comment il fait hommage au dieu damours*
              the Lover performs homage to Amors (1953)
fol. 15r   *Comment il y enferme le cuer a une clef*
              the God of Love locks the Lover's heart (1991)
fol. 20v   *La responce de bel acueil*
              Bel Acueil/Responsiveness reprimands the Lover (2807)
fol. 21r   *Comment raison descendi de sa tour pour parler amant*
              Reason, coming out of her tower, addresses the Lover (2955)
fol. 26v   *Comment ialousie se contient*
              ("how Jealousy behaves")
              the Jealous Husband beats his wife (misplaced) (3779)

---

[31] I.e., the miniature follows Lecoy 154 *son non desus sa teste lui* and precedes two lines interpolated in the manuscript (*Son non je vus dirai maintenant / Car moult jensui bien souvenant*) before 155 *apelee estoit Felonie*. This interpolation is not recorded by Langlois. It reads like an adaptor's imitation of the earlier lines which preface Haïne's portrait, *si vos conterai et dirai / de ces ymages la semblance, / si com moi vient a remenbrance* (136–38).

CHAPTER THREE

fol. 28r   *Ci fine guille de lorris et commence m. jehan de meun,*
           Author at writing desk, representing Jean de Meun (4029)

fol. 47r   *Comment lami reconforte lamant*
           the Friend comforts the Lover (7201)

fol. 64r   *Comment Richesce li enseigne le chemin*
           the Lover meets Richece, who shows him the way (10041)

fol. 129v   *Si [comment] Venus trait ou chastel .i. brandon de feu pour embraser ceulz qui sont dedans*
           Venus aims a brand at the castle to burn up all within (20755)

fol. 130r   *Si commence lystoire de pygmalion et de son ymage*
           Pygmalion's story: he works on his sculpture (20787)

On fol. 138r, at the beginning of *Le Testament*, there is a miniature of the Trinity (c.70 x 80 mm): on a blue ground patterned in gold, red, and white, beneath an arch, is God on a throne, his arms outstretched supporting a cross on which Christ hangs, a dove descending above Christ's head; with full border of bars and ivy-leaf extensions; in vermilion, red, pink, white, blue, and gold.

Associated with miniatures are three-line initials, alternating pink and blue, on a gold ground, infilled with foliage, and with foliage extensions into the margin. Elsewhere, there are two-line initials of gold on a ground either or pink or of blue or of parti-colored of both, all grounds patterned in white. For each stanza of the *Testament* there is a similar one-line initial. On fol. 18v is an initial which had been gilt and burnished and outlined in black but which was overlooked by the colorist. The decoration throughout appears to be by the same hand or hands. Headings are in red and line initials touched in yellow. A guide-word for the rubricator survives on fol. 121r.

Binding

The structure, of five double whittawed thongs, is probably earlier than the present covers if not original. The present covers are of pasteboard covered in black morocco, blind-tooled, with a fillet frame and a monogram formed of two interlocking letters C at the center and in the corners. These covers were added some time not long after 1551: the paper of the flyleaves has a watermark identifiable with Briquet 8091 (example 1551). There are worm-holes from earlier wooden boards in fols. 3–4 and 144–49.

2° *fol. Qui ne me soy*

Text

Fols. 2r–136r   Cy commence le romant de la Rose / Ou lart damours est toute enclose / [A]ucunes gens cuydent quen songes / Nait se

123

Chapter Three

> fables non et mensonges / ... (fol. 2v) Que ioy pres dillecques bruyre / (fol. 3) Qui ne me soy aler deduire / ... (fol. 135v) Ainsi oi la rose vermeille / A tant fu iour et ie mesueille / Et puis que ie fui esueillie / ... Explicit le romans de la rose / (fol. 136r) Nature rit si comme samble / Quant hic et hec ioingent ensamble

The text of fol. 2 is the replacement of s.xvi which may or may not derive from that of the damaged leaf and discarded original first leaf; the script of the replacement is contemporary with the provision of new covers.

The text of Guillaume de Lorris belongs to Langlois Group II. It has the reading *ii* [*deus*] in Langlois line 2834 (Lecoy 2818); lines 2835–36 (2819–20) read *Une semme* [sic] *et .i. vilain homme / Li hons male bouce fe* [sic] *nomme* and are followed by the inserted couplet (*Nes fu sachies en Normandie ...*). Lines 109–10 read *Descendoit ly aue clere et royde / Toute bruiant et aussi froide.*

The text of Jean de Meun belongs to Langlois Group II. It has the apocryphal 24-verse ending (beginning *Et puis que ie fui esueille*) which occurs in Langlois class N.[32] It includes the interpolated chapter in the discourse of Faus Semblant after Langlois line 11222 (11192),[33] in the form of his 7th group,[34] omitting however line 58/28; and also the Medusa interpolation which follows Langlois line 20810 (20780),[35] but omitting lines 43–44 of the text in Langlois's edition.

On fol. 28r, the two parts of the poem are separated by the rubric *Ci fine Guillaume de Lorris / Et commence M. Jehan de Meun.*

Fol. 136r–v   Ci commence le derrain testament / Maistre Ihehan de Meun / Dieux ait lame des trespassez / Car dez biens quil ont amassez / ... Quant uous ne mauez pas creu / A tart uous en repentirez / Explicit le derrenier testament / Maistre Iehan de Meun

This is the text generally known as *Le Codicile* of Jean de Meun. Compared with the edition of Méon,[36] our text omits the second half of stanza 5.

---

[32] See Langlois, *Les manuscrits*, 448, where a text of this ending is printed.
[33] Printed by Langlois in his edition, 3:311–15, and in *Les manuscrits*, 426–30.
[34] Classes M, N, etc.; see Langlois's edition, 3:310.
[35] Printed by Langlois in his edition, 5:107–9, and in *Les manuscrits*, 453–54.
[36] *Le roman de la rose par Guillaume de Lorris et Jehan de Meung*, 4 vols. (Paris: P. N. F. Didot, 1814), 4:117–21.

Chapter Three

Fols. 138r–49v   Li peres et li filz et li sains esperis / Dous dieux en iii personez aorez et chieris / . . . Et li prie humblement que nous soions escript / Ou saint liure de vie que il meismes escript / Amen

Le Testament of Jean de Meun. Printed by Méon and by Gallarati.[37] Compared with Gallarati's edition, our text reverses the order of stanzas 17 and 18, omits stanzas 94, 147, 185–98, adds a stanza after 220, jumps from line 1 of stanza 256 to line 2 of stanza 261 (thus omitting five stanzas), omits stanza 294, reverses the order of stanzas 366 and 367, omits stanzas 380, 402 and 440, adds a stanza after 459, and omits 504.[38]

History

In the lower part of the first column of fol. 136v are perhaps eleven lines of text, written in textura, probably of s.xiv, erased but legible in parts under ultra-violet light. There are no significant marks by medieval readers other than correction of the text on fol. 135r by a hand of perhaps s.xv. On fol. ir is an inscription: "Pour Monsieur de Valentin seigneur de la Rochevalentin, Vitray, le fief de lorme et nostre honorable Secretaire du Roy Maison et couronne de France et de ses finances," s.xvi/xvii; and on fol. 2r, deleted but legible, "Claude Valentin escuyer seigneur de la Rochevalentin Vitray et lorme," in italic script, s.xvi².

On fol. 128r a hand of perhaps s.xviii has added an omitted line of text. On fol. 149v is a deleted inscription. On fol. 1r is a cutting from an English catalogue of s.xviii/xix. Inside the upper cover is a scribbled note "from King Charles's Library with his initals [*sic*] stamp'd" and booksellers' marks and a price, "6.6.0," in ink, and, in pencil, "No. 1," all s.xviii/xix. On fol.iv is a note on the text signed "[?]H^y H A," s.xix. Owned by H. W. F. Hunter Arundel of Barjang Tower, Dumfries; it was lot 224 in his sale at Sotheby's on 6 April 1914 where it was bought by Bourdillon for £141. His 1913 bookplate is inside the upper cover, and "Bdn 170" in pencil.

---

[37] Méon, *Le roman de la rose par Guillaume de Lorris et Jehan de Meung*, 4:1–116; S. B. Gallarati, *Le Testament Maistre Jehan de Meun: un caso letterario* (Alessandria: Edizioni dell' Orso, 1989).

[38] On the manuscript tradition of *Le Testament*, see S. B. Gallarati, "Nota bibliografica sulla tradizione manoscritta del *Testament* di Jean de Meun," *Revue romane* (Copenhagen), 13 (1978): 2–35, where 116 manuscripts are listed (NLW 5016 on p. 23).

CHAPTER THREE

NLW MS 5017D

A small folio in modern binding, written in two columns by "Stephanus Arnulphi clericus," with eleven miniatures, s.xiv[1] (probably 1330–50).

Preparation and writing
Parchment. Foliated i–iii, 1–148; fols. i–ii and 147–48 are modern and of paper, fols. iii and 146 modern and of parchment. Measure: 290 x 210 mm; written space 225 x 170 mm. Written in two columns, 38 lines to the page. Ruled in crayon, with ruled columns both for line-initials and for space between line-initials and text. Collation: 1–18^8, fol. 145 a singleton. There are quire signatures of the pattern *a, aa, aaa, aaaa* in ink visible up to quire 13 (beginning in quire 2, quire 1 signed *o*); in quire 10 additional signatures in red occur in the top right-hand corners; in quires 16–18 there are leaf signatures in plummet. There are catchwords.

Written by one hand in a loose textura, without punctuation. The ink is pale brown.

Decoration
On fol. 1r is a half-page miniature (155 x 75 mm) of the sleeping poet in bed, Dangiers, holding a key and a branch, standing at the foot of the bed, a rose tree in the background, a tower (?the garden gate) to the right; the whole page has a bar frame, with foliage excrescence; a burnished gold ground; the colors are vermilion, pink, blue, green, yellow, white, and gray.

Subsequently there are ten six- or seven-line single-column miniatures (c.65 x 40 mm), framed, but without marginal excrescence. On the miniatures, probably Parisian work to be dated 1330–50 (see above, pp. 26–27). The subjects and locations are as follows:

fol. 2r	Haine (139)
fol. 2r	Vilanie (157)
fol. 2r	Covoitise (169)
fol. 2v	Avarice (195)
fol. 2v	Envie (235)
fol. 3r	Tritesce (291)
fol. 3v	Vielleice (339)
fol. 4r	Papelardie (405)
fol. 4r	Povreté (439)
fol. 6v	the *carole* (775)

All are on grounds of burnished gold, or of tessellated gold and color, or of color and color patterned in white.

Chapter Three

There is a six-line initial on fol. 1r, blue, patterned in white and infilled with foliage on a gold ground; elsewhere, two-line gold initials on a parti-colored ground of blue and pink patterned in white. There are headings in red up to fol. 78r but none thereafter. The scribe's guide-words for the rubricator survive, e.g., on fols 2r, 5v, 14r, and 32r. The initials of lines are touched in yellow.

Binding

On five bands, dark blue straight-grained morocco; a gold-tooled floral border and gold tooling on the spine; pink watered silk doublures and endleaves; gilt-edged. At the foot of the spine is the stamp: REL. P. BOZERIAN. Bozerian was active in Paris from 1795 to 1810.[39] There are worm-holes in fols. 1–18 and 134–45, evidence of earlier wooden boards. The binding is too tight to allow a view of the early sewing holes.

2° fol. lors men alay

Text

Fols. 1r–145r   Maintes gens dient quen songes / Na se fables non et mensonges / ... Ainssi oy la rose vermeille / A tant fu iour et ie mesueille / Explicit le rommanz de la rose / Ou lart damours est toute enclose / Stephanus qui scripsit clericus / Arnulphi sit benedictus

The text of Guillaume de Lorris belongs to Langlois Group II. It does not have the reading *deus* in Langlois line 2834 (Lecoy 2818), nor the insertion following his line 2836 (2820). Lines 109–10 read *Descendoit liaue fiere et raide / Elle estoit clere et aussi froide.*

The text of Jean de Meun belongs to Langlois group II. It includes the two-line interpolation after Langlois line 4228 (4198) which is characteristic of his B manuscripts but lacks others of their features. There is a lacuna not recorded by Langlois, corresponding to his lines 4201–24 (4171–94), no doubt arising from an error by our scribe or in his exemplar. It includes the interpolated chapter in the discourse of Faus Semblant after Langlois line 11222 (11192),[40] in the form which occurs in those manuscripts of his 7th group which omit lines 58/28–29.[41] Following Langlois line 20810 (20780) is the Medusa interpolation,[42] in-

---

[39] C. Ramsden, *French Bookbinders 1789–1848* (London: Lund Humphreys, 1950), 41.
[40] Printed by Langlois in his edition, 3:311–15, and in *Les manuscrits*, 426–30.
[41] Langlois edition, 3:310.
[42] Langlois, edition, 5:107–9, and *Les manuscrits*, 453–54.

cluding the two additional lines 43–44 printed in his edition, which occur only in a few manuscripts.

History

The manuscript was written by "Stephanus Arnulphi clericus," a scribe not recorded by the Benedictins du Bouveret.[43] However, a note of sale in a *Summa Azonis* records that book's purchase in 1348 from a certain *librarius* living in the Rue Neuve Notre-Dame at Paris, named *Stephanus Arnulphi*.[44] (This Stephanus Arnulphi, or Etienne Ernoul, was also among sixty-four named members of the university booktrade in a document of 1368.) There is annotation of s.xv or xvi on fols. 26r and 28r, the latter noting the division of texts of Guillaume de Lorris and Jean de Meun. The rebinding in Paris about 1800 no doubt led to the loss of early flyleaves and marks of ownership. On fols. ii and 148r are mostly-erased notes in French of s.xix; on fol. 148r are two price marks of English booksellers or owners, in pencil, and others erased, and the initials "P S," all of s.xix. The manuscript was sold at Sotheby's on 8 April 1914, lot 778, the property of Kendall Hazeldine of Woldingham, Surrey, and was bought by Bourdillon for £85; his 1913 bookplate is on fol.iv, together with "Bdn 171" in pencil.

— *Daniel Huws*

---

[43] *Colophons des manuscrits occidentaux, des origines aux XVIe siècle* by the Benedictins du Bouveret, 5 vols. (Fribourg: Editions universitaires, 1965–75).

[44] "Iste liber est Johannis Juvenis de Pontisara licenciati in legibus, et emit a quodam librario commoranti Parisius in vico Novo qui vocabatur Stephanus Arnulphi, anno CCC XLVIII"; BN, MS lat. 8943, fol. 126r. Information about Stephanus Arnulphi has been most generously supplied by Mary and Richard Rouse: see further their catalogue *Manuscripts and Their Makers: Commercial Book Producers in Medieval Paris 1200–1500*, 2 vols. (Turnhout: Harvey Miller, 2000).

Bibliography

Alexander, Jonathan. *Medieval Illuminators and their Methods of Work*. New Haven: Yale University Press, 1992.

Alford, John. *Piers Plowman: A Glossary of Legal Diction*. Cambridge: D. S. Brewer, 1988.

Allen, Peter L. *The Art of Love: Amatory Fiction from Ovid to "The Romance of the Rose"*. Philadelphia: University of Pennsylvania Press, 1992.

Alvar, Carlos. "Oiseuse, Vénus, Luxure: Trois dames et un miroir." *Romania* 106 (1985): 108–17.

Andersen, Flemming G., et al., eds., *Medieval Iconography and Narrative: A Symposium*. Odense: Odense University Press, 1980.

Andrew, Malcolm, and Ronald Waldron, eds., *Poems of the Pearl Manuscript*. London: Edward Arnold, 1978.

Arden, Heather. *The Romance of the Rose*. Boston: Twayne, 1987.

———. *The Roman de la Rose: An Annotated Bibliography*. New York and London: Garland, 1993.

———. "Women as Readers, Women as Text in the *Roman de la Rose*." In *Women, the Book, and the Worldly*, ed. Lesley Smith and Jane H. M. Taylor, 111–17. Cambridge: D. S. Brewer, 1995.

Ashburnham, Lord. *Catalogue of the MSS at Ashburnham Place. Part the Second, comprising a collection made by Mr J. Barrois*. London: C. F. Hodgson, n.d.

Avril, François. *Manuscript Painting at the Court of France: The Fourteenth Century*. London: Chatto and Windus, 1978.

———. "Les Manuscrits enluminés de Guillaume de Machaut, Essai de chronologie." In *Guillaume de Machaut: Colloque–Table Ronde*, 117–33. Paris: Klincksieck, 1982.

———, and Nicole Reynaud. *Les Manuscrits à peintures en France, 1440–1520*. Paris: Flammarion, and the Bibliothèque nationale de France, 1995.

Backhouse, Janet. *The Luttrell Psalter*. London: The British Library, 1989.

Barasch, Moshe. *Gestures of Despair in Medieval and Early Renaissance Art*. New York: New York University Press, 1971.

———. *Giotto and the Language of Gesture*. Cambridge: Cambridge University Press, 1987.

Bibliography

Batany, J. "Miniature, allégorie, idéologie: 'Oiseuse' et la mystique monacale récupérée par la 'classe de loisir'." In *Guillaume de Lorris, Études sur le* Roman de la Rose, ed. J. Dufournet, 7–36. Paris: Champion, 1984.

Blamires, Alcuin. *The Case for Women in Medieval Culture*. Oxford: Clarendon Press, 1997.

———. "The 'Religion of Love' in Chaucer's *Troilus and Criseyde* and Medieval Visual Art." In *Word and Visual Imagination: Studies in the Interaction of English Literature and the Visual Arts*, ed. Karl Höltgen, P. Daly and W. Lottes, 11–31. Erlangen: Universitätsbibliothek, 1988.

———, with Karen Pratt and C. W. Marx, eds. *Woman Defamed and Woman Defended*. Oxford: Clarendon Press, 1992.

Bond, E. A. *Description of the Ashburnham Manuscripts and Account of Offers of Purchase*. London: British Museum, 1883.

Bouché, Thérèse. "Burlesque et renouvellement des formes: L'Attaque du Château dans le *Roman de la Rose* de Jean de Meun." In *Farai Chansoneta Novele: Hommage à Jean-Charles Payen*, 87–98. Caen: Centre de Publications de l'Université de Caen, 1989.

Bourdillon, Francis. *The Early Editions of the Roman de la Rose*. The Bibliographical Society Illustrated Monographs, 14. London: Chiswick Press, 1906; repr. Geneva: Slatkine, 1974.

Braeger, Peter C. "The Illustrations in New College MS 266 for Gower's Conversion Tales." In *John Gower: Recent Readings*, ed. R. F. Yeager, 275–310. Kalamazoo, MI: Western Michigan University, 1984.

Braet, Herman. "*Le Roman de la Rose*, espace du regard." *Studi Francesi* 35 (1991): 1–11.

Branner, Robert. *Manuscript Painting in Paris during the Reign of Saint Louis*. Berkeley and Los Angeles: University of California Press, 1977.

———. "The 'Soissons Bible' Paintshop in Thirteenth-Century Paris." *Speculum* 44 (1969): 13–35.

Brent, Beat. "Le texte et l'image dans la *Vie des saints* au Moyen Âge: rôle du concepteur et rôle du peintre." In *Texte et image*, Actes du Colloque International de Chantilly, Oct. 13–15, 1982, 31–40. Paris: Les Belles Lettres, 1984.

Brook, Leslie C. "Jalousie and Jealousy in Jean de Meun's *Rose*." *Romance Quarterly* 41 (1994): 59–70.

Brown, Michelle P. *Understanding Illuminated Manuscripts*. London: The J. Paul Getty Museum and the British Library, 1994.

Brownlee, Kevin. "Pygmalion, Mimesis, and the Multiple Endings of the *Roman de la Rose*." In *Rereading Allegory: Essays in Memory of Daniel Poirion*, ed. Sahar Amer and Noah D. Guynn. *Yale French Studies* 95 (1999): 193–211.

———, and Sylvia Huot, eds. *Rethinking the* Romance of the Rose. Philadelphia: University of Pennsylvania Press, 1992.

BIBLIOGRAPHY

Burnley, David. *Courtliness and Literature in Medieval England*. Harlow, England: Addison Wesley Longman, 1998.

Busby, Keith, Terry Nixon, Alison Stones, and Lori Walters. *Les Manuscrits de Chrétien de Troyes*. 2 vols. Amsterdam and Atlanta: Editions Rodopi, 1993.

Cahoon, Leslie. "Raping the Rose: Jean de Meun's Reading of Ovid's *Amores*." *Classical and Modern Literature* 6 (1985–86): 261–85.

Calin, William. *A Muse for Heroes: Nine Centuries of the Epic in France*. Toronto: University of Toronto Press, 1983.

Calkins, Robert. "Stages of Execution: Procedures of Illumination as Revealed in an Unfinished Book of Hours." *Gesta* 17 (1978): 61–70.

Camille, Michael. *The Gothic Idol: Ideology and Image-Making in Medieval Art*. Cambridge: Cambridge University Press, 1989.

———. "Gothic Signs and the Surplus: The Kiss on the Cathedral." In *Contexts: Style and Values in Medieval Art and Literature*, ed. Daniel Poirion and Nancy F. Regalado, 151–70. *Yale French Studies*, special number. New Haven: Yale University Press, 1991.

———. *Image on the Edge: The Margins of Medieval Art*. London: Reaktion Books, 1992.

Catalogue des livres imprimés et manuscrits, de la bibliothèque de feu Monsieur D'Aguesseau. Paris, 1785.

Chance, Jane. "Gender Trouble in the Garden of Deduit: Christine de Pizan Translating the *Rose*." *Romance Languages Annual* 4 (1992): 20–28.

Chaucer, Geoffrey. *The Riverside Chaucer*, 3rd ed., ed. Larry Benson. Boston: Houghton Mifflin and Oxford: Oxford University Press, 1987.

Chevalier, U. *Repertorium hymnologicum*. 6 vols. Louvain and Paris, 1892–1920.

Chrétien de Troyes. *The Knight with the Lion, or Yvain*, ed. and trans. William W. Kibler. New York: Garland, 1985.

Christianson, C. Paul. "Evidence for the Study of London's Late Medieval Manuscript-Book Trade." In *Book Production and Publishing in Britain 1375–1475*, ed. Derek Pearsall and Jeremy Griffiths, 87–108. Cambridge: Cambridge University Press, 1989.

Colophons des manuscrits occidentaux, des origines aux XVIe siécle by the Benedictins du Bouveret. 5 vols. Fribourg: Editions universitaires, 1965–75.

Coomaraswamy, Ananda K. "Mediaeval Aesthetic II: St. Thomas Aquinas on Dionysius, and a Note on the Relation of Beauty to Truth." *Art Bulletin* 20 (1938): 66–77.

Dahlberg, Charles. "Love and the *Roman de la Rose*." *Speculum* 44 (1969): 568–84.

De Hamel, Christopher. *Medieval Craftsmen: Scribes and Illuminators*. London: British Museum, 1992.

———. *A History of Illuminated Manuscripts*. 2nd ed. London: Phaidon, 1994.

Delisle, Leopold. *Catalogue des manuscrits des fonds Libri et Barrois*. Paris: Champion, 1888.

Bibliography

De Winter, Patrick M. *La Bibliothèque de Philippe le Hardi Duc de Bourgogne (1364–1404)*. Paris: Éditions du Centre National de la Recherche Scientifique, 1985.

Diamond, Joan. "Manufacture and Market in Parisian Book Illumination around 1300." In Elisabeth Liskar, ed., *Europäische Kunst um 1300*, Akten des XXV. Internationalen Kongresses für Kunstgeschichte Wien 4–10 September 1983, 6: 101–10. Vienna: Bohlau, 1986.

Donovan, Claire. *The de Brailes Hours: Shaping the Book of Hours in Thirteenth-Century Oxford*. Toronto: University of Toronto Press, 1991.

Duby, Georges, ed. *A History of Private Life*. 2 vols. 2: *Revelations of the Medieval World*, trans. Arthur Goldhammer. Cambridge, MA: Belknap Press of Harvard University Press, 1988.

Earp, Lawrence. *Guillaume de Machaut: A Guide to Research*. New York and London: Garland, 1995.

Egbert, Virginia W. "Pygmalion as Sculptor." *Princeton University Library Chronicle* 28 (1966): 20–23.

Ferrante, Joan. *Woman as Image in Medieval Literature from the Twelfth Century to Dante*. New York: Columbia University Press, 1975.

Fleming, John V. *The* Roman de la Rose: *A Study in Allegory and Iconography*. Princeton, NJ: Princeton University Press, 1969.

———. "Further Reflections on Oiseuse's Mirror." *Zeitschrift für Romanische Philologie* 100 (1984): 26–40.

Francis, W. Nelson, ed. *The Book of Vices and Virtues*. EETS OS 217. London: Oxford University Press, 1942.

Friedman, John B. "L'iconographie de Vénus et de son miroir à la fin du Moyen âge." In *L'Erotisme au Moyen Age*, ed. Bruno Roy, 51–82. Montreal: Aurore, 1977.

Gallarati, S. B. "Nota bibliografica sulla tradizione manoscritta del *Testament* di Jean de Meun." *Revue romane* (Copenhagen) 13 (1978): 2–35.

Garnier, François. *Le Langage de l'image au Moyen Âge: Signification et symbolique*. Paris: Le Léopard d'Or, 1982.

Gaunt, Simon. "Bel Acueil and the Improper Allegory of the *Romance of the Rose*." *New Medieval Literatures* 2 (1998): 65–93.

Gombrich, Ernst H. "Ritualized Gesture and Expression in Art." In idem, *The Image and the Eye: Further Studies in the Psychology of Pictorial Representation*, 63–77. Oxford: Phaidon, 1982.

Gower, John. *The English Works of John Gower*, ed. G. C. Macaulay, EETS ES 81–82. London: Oxford University Press, 1901.

Guillaume de Lorris and Jean de Meun. *Le Roman de la Rose par Guillaume de Lorris et Jehan de Meung*, ed. D. Méon. 4 vols. Paris: Didot, 1814.

———. *Le Roman de la Rose*, ed. Ernest Langlois. SATF, 5 vols. Paris: Champion, 1914–24.

Bibliography

———. *Le Roman de la Rose*, ed. Félix Lecoy. 3 vols. Classiques Français du Moyen Age. Paris: Champion, 1965–70.

———. *The Romance of the Rose*, trans. Harry W. Robbins, ed. Charles W. Dunn. New York: Dutton, 1963.

———. *The Romance of the Rose by Guillaume de Lorris and Jean de Meun*, trans. Charles Dahlberg. Princeton: Princeton University Press, 1971; 3rd ed., 1995.

———. *The Romance of the Rose*, trans. Frances Horgan. World's Classics. Oxford: Oxford University Press, 1994.

Gunn, Alan M. F. *The Mirror of Love: A Reinterpretation of* The Romance of the Rose. Lubbock, TX: Texas Tech Press, 1952.

Hair, Paul. *Before the Bawdy Court*. London: Elek, 1972.

Hedeman, Anne D. *The Royal Image: Illustrations of the* Grandes Chroniques de France, *1274–1422*. Berkeley and Los Angeles: University of California Press, 1991.

Hicks, Eric. "Donner à voir: Guillaume de Lorris ou le Roman Impossible." *Etudes de Lettres* 37 (1994): 93–104; trans. as "*Donner à voir:* Guillaume de Lorris or the Impossible Romance." In *Rereading Allegory: Essays in Memory of Daniel Poirion*, ed. Sahar Amer and Noah D. Guynn. *Yale French Studies* 95 (1999): 65–80.

Hill, Thomas D. "Narcissus, Pygmalion, and the Castration of Saturn: Two Mythographical Themes in the *Roman de la Rose*." *Studies in Philology* 71 (1974): 404–26.

Hindman, Sandra. *Sealed in Parchment: Rereadings of Knighthood in the Illuminated Manuscripts of Chrétien de Troyes*. Chicago: University of Chicago Press, 1994.

Hult, David. "The Allegorical Fountain: Narcissus in the *Roman de la Rose*." *Romanic Review* 72 (1981): 125–48.

———. *Self-Fulfilling Prophecies: Readership and Authority in the First* Romance of the Rose. Cambridge: Cambridge University Press, 1986.

Huot, Sylvia. "The Scribe as Editor: Rubrication as Critical Apparatus in Two Manuscripts of the *Roman de la Rose*." *L'Esprit Créateur* 27 (1987): 67–78.

———. *The* Romance of the Rose *and its Medieval Readers: Interpretation, Reception, Manuscript Transmission*. Cambridge: Cambridge University Press, 1993.

Jean de Meun. *See also* Guillaume de Lorris.

———. *Le Testament Maistre Jehan de Meun: un caso letterario*, ed. S. B. Gallarati. Alessandria: Edizioni dell'Orso, 1989.

Jehan Le Fèvre. *Les Lamentations de Matheolus*, ed. A. G. Van Hamel. Paris: Bouillon, 1892/1905.

Kay, Sarah. *The* Romance of the Rose. Critical Guides to French Texts, 110. London: Grant and Cutler, 1995.

———. "The Birth of Venus in the *Roman de la Rose*." *Exemplaria* 9 (1997): 7–37.

Kelly, Douglas. *Internal Difference and Meanings in the* Roman de la Rose. Madison: University of Wisconsin Press, 1995.

BIBLIOGRAPHY

———. "'Li chastiaus ... Qu'Amors prist puis par ses esforz': The Conclusion of Guillaume de Lorris's *Rose*." In *A Medieval Miscellany*, ed. Norris J. Lacy, 61–78. Lawrence, KS: University of Kansas Press, 1972.

Kelly, Thomas E., and Thomas H. Ohlgren. "Paths to Memory: Iconographic Indices to *Roman de la Rose* and *Prose Lancelot* Manuscripts in the Bodleian Library." *Visual Resources* 3 (1983): 1–15.

Kenton, Warren. *Astrology: The Celestial Mirror*. New York: Avon, and London: Thames and Hudson, 1974.

Kolb, H. "Oiseuse, die Dame mit dem Spiegel." *Germanisch-Romanische Monatsschrift* 15 (1965): 139–49.

König, Eberhard. *Der Rosenroman des Berthaud d'Achy: Codex Urbinatus Latinus 376*, with an Appendix by Gabriele Bartz, facsimile and commentary. 2 vols. Codices e Vaticanis selecti, 71. Zurich: Belser Verlag, 1987.

———. *Die Liebe im Zeichen der Rose: Die Handschriften des Rosenromans in der Vatikanischen Bibliothek*. Stuttgart and Zurich: Belser Verlag, 1992.

Kuhn, Alfred. "Die Illustration des *Rosenromans*." *Jahrbuch der Kunsthistorischen Sammlungen des allerhöchsten Kaiserhauses* 31.1 (1912): 1–66.

Långfors, Arthur. *Les incipit des poèmes français antérieurs au xve siècle: Répertoire bibliographique établi à l'aide des notes de M. Paul Meyer*. Paris: Champion, 1917.

Langland, William. *The Vision of Piers Plowman, a Critical Edition of the B-Text*, ed. A. V. C. Schmidt. London: Dent, 1978.

Langlois, Ernest. "Gui de Mori et le *Roman de la Rose*." *Bibliothèque de l'École des Chartes* 68 (1907): 1–23.

———. *Les Manuscrits du Roman de la Rose: Description et classement*. Paris: Champion, Lille: Tallandier, 1910; repr. Geneva: Slatkine, 1974.

Lawton, Lesley. "The Illustration of Late Medieval Secular Texts, with Special Reference to Lydgate's *Troy Book*." In *Manuscripts and Readers in Fifteenth-Century England*, ed. Derek Pearsall, 41–69. Cambridge: D. S. Brewer, 1983.

le Goff, Jacques. "The Symbolic Ritual of Vassalage." In idem, *Time, Work and Culture in the Middle Ages*, trans. Arthur Goldhammer, 237–87. Chicago: University of Chicago Press, 1980.

Leroquais, V. *Les Livres d'heures manuscrits de la Bibliothèque Nationale*. 2 vols. Paris, 1927.

Lewis, C. S. *The Allegory of Love*. Oxford: Oxford University Press, 1936.

Lewis, Suzanne. "Images of Opening, Penetration and Closure in the *Roman de la Rose*." *Word and Image* 8 (1992): 215–42.

Luria, Maxwell. *A Reader's Guide to the Roman de la Rose*. Hamden, CT: Archon, 1982.

McMunn, Meradith. "Representations of the Erotic in Some Illustrated Manuscripts of the *Roman de la Rose*." *Romance Languages Annual* 4 (1992): 125–30.

———. "The Iconography of Dangier in the Illustrated Manuscripts of the *Roman de la Rose." Romance Languages Annual* 5 (1994): 86–91.

———. "Animal Imagery in Texts and Illustrations of the *Roman de la Rose.*" *Reinardus: Yearbook of the International Reynard Society* 9 (1996): 87–108 and plates 1–16.

———. "In Love and War: Images of Warfare in the Illustrated Manuscripts of the *Roman de la Rose.*" In *Chivalry, Knighthood, and War in the Middle Ages*, ed. Susan Ridyard, *Sewanee Mediaeval Studies* 9 (Sewanee, TN: University of the South, 1999), 165–93.

Marie de France. *Lais*, ed. A. Ewert (Oxford: Blackwell, 1978).

———. *The Lais of Marie de France*, trans. Glyn S. Burgess and Keith Busby. Harmondsworth: Penguin, 1986.

Marks, Richard, and Nigel Morgan. *The Golden Age of English Manuscript Painting, 1200–1500*. London: Chatto and Windus, 1981.

Martin, Priscilla. *Chaucer's Women: Nuns, Wives and Amazons*. Basingstoke: Macmillan, 1990.

Meiss, Millard. *French Painting in the Time of Jean de Berry: The Late Fourteenth Century and the Patronage of the Duke*. 2 vols. London: Thames & Hudson, 1969.

———. *French Painting in the Time of Jean de Berry: The Limbourgs and their Contemporaries*. 2 vols. London: Thames & Hudson, 1974.

Ménard, Philippe. "Les Représentations des vices sur les murs du verger du *Roman de la Rose*: la texte et les enluminures." In *Texte et Image*, Actes du Colloque international de Chantilly, 1982, 177–90. Paris: Les Belles Lettres, 1984.

Müller, Ulrich, ed. *Die grosse Heidelberger "Manessische" Liederhandschrift*. Goppingen: Kümmerle, 1971.

Newton, Stella. *Fashion in the Age of the Black Prince*. Woodbridge: Boydell and Brewer, 1980.

Nichols, Steven J. "Ekphrasis, Iconoclasm, and Desire." In *Rethinking the Romance of the Rose*, ed. Brownlee and Huot, 133–66.

Ovid. *The Art of Love and Other Poems*, ed. and trans. J. H. Mozley. 2nd ed. revised by G. P. Goold. Cambridge, MA: Harvard University Press, 1979.

Panofsky, Erwin. "Blind Cupid." In idem, *Studies in Iconology*, 95–128. New York: Harper and Row, 1962.

Pearsall, Derek, ed. *Manuscripts and Readers in Fifteenth Century England*. Cambridge: D. S. Brewer, 1983.

———, and Jeremy Griffiths, eds. *Book Production and Publishing in Britain 1375–1475*. Cambridge: Cambridge University Press, 1989.

Peruzzi, Simonetta Mazzoni. *Il Codice Laurenziano Acquisti e Doni 153 del "Roman de la Rose."* Società Dantesca Italiana, Quaderno 3. Florence: Sansoni, 1986.

Pickford, C. E. "An Arthurian Manuscript in the John Rylands Library." *Bulletin of the John Rylands Library* 31 (1948): 318–44.

Bibliography

Poirion, Daniel. "Narcisse et Pygmalion dans le *Roman de la Rose*." In *Essays in Honor of Louis Francis Solano*, ed. Raymond J. Cormier and Urban T. Holmes, 153–65. Chapel Hill: University of North Carolina Press, 1970.

———. *Le Roman de la Rose*. Connaissance des Lettres. Paris: Hatier, 1973.

Ramsden, C. *French Bookbinders 1789–1848*. London: Lund Humphreys, 1950.

Richards, Earl Jeffrey. "Reflections on Oiseuse's Mirror: Iconographic Tradition, Luxuria and the *Roman de la Rose*." *Zeitschrift für Romanische Philologie* 98 (1982): 296–311.

Riddy, Felicity. "Engendering Pity in the *Franklin's Tale*." In *Feminist Readings in Middle English Literature*, ed. Ruth Evans and Lesley Johnson, 54–71. London: Routledge, 1994.

Ringbom, Sixten. "Some Pictorial Conventions for the Recounting of Thoughts and Experiences in Late Medieval Art." In *Medieval Iconography and Narrative: A Symposium*, ed. Flemming G. Andersen et al., 38–69.

Robertson, D. W., Jr. *A Preface to Chaucer*. Princeton: Princeton University Press, 1962.

Rouse, Richard H., and Mary A. Rouse. *Manuscripts and Their Makers: Commercial Book Producers in Medieval Paris 1200–1500*. 2 vols. Turnhout: Harvey Miller, 2000.

Rushing, James A. *Images of Adventure: Ywain in the Visual Arts*. Philadelphia: University of Pennsylvania Press, 1995.

Sadlek, Gregory M. "Interpreting Guillaume de Lorris's Oiseuse: Geoffrey Chaucer as Witness." *South Central Review* 10 (1993): 22–37.

Salter, Elizabeth, and Derek Pearsall. "Pictorial Illustration of Late Medieval Poetic Texts: The Role of the Frontispiece." In *Medieval Iconography and Narrative: A Symposium*, ed. Flemming G. Andersen et al., 100–23.

Sandler, Lucy F. *The Peterborough Psalter in Brussels and Other Fenland Manuscripts*. London: Harvey Miller, 1974.

———. *The Psalter of Robert de Lisle*. Oxford: Harvey Miller, 1982.

Schultz, Alwin. *Das Höfische Leben zur zeit der Minnesinger*. 2 vols. 1889, repr. Osnabrück: Zeller, 1965.

Scott, Kathleen L. "Design, Decoration and Illustration." In *Book Production and Publishing in Britain 1375–1475*, ed. Derek Pearsall and Jeremy Griffiths, 31–64.

Scott, Margaret. *Late Gothic Europe 1400–1500*. The History of Dress Series. London: Mills and Boon; and New Jersey: Humanities Press, 1980.

Spearing, A. C. *The Medieval Poet as Voyeur: Looking and Listening in Medieval Love-Narratives*. Cambridge: Cambridge University Press, 1993.

Spencer, Judith, trans. *The Four Seasons of the House of Cerruti*. New York: Facts on File, 1984.

Stakel, Susan. *False Roses: Structures of Duality and Deceit in Jean de Meun's "Roman*

Bibliography

de la Rose." Stanford French and Italian Studies, 69. Saratoga, CA: Anma Libri, 1991.

Sterling, Charles. *La peinture médiévale à Paris, 1300–1500.* Paris: Bibliothèque des Arts, 1987.

Stirnemann, Patricia. "Nouvelles pratiques en matière d'enluminure au temps de Philippe Auguste." In *La France de Philippe Auguste: Le temps des mutations,* ed. Robert-Henri Bautier, 955–80. Colloques internationaux du CNRS, 602. Paris, 1982.

Stones, Alison. "Secular Manuscript Illumination in France." In *Medieval Manuscripts and Textual Criticism,* ed. Christopher Kleinhenz, 83–102. Chapel Hill: University of North Carolina Press, 1976.

Thomas, Marcel. *The Golden Age: Manuscript Painting at the Time of Jean, Duc de Berry.* London: Chatto and Windus, 1979.

Tinkle, Theresa. *Medieval Venuses and Cupids: Sexuality, Hermeneutics, and English Poetry.* Stanford, CA: Stanford University Press, 1996.

Tuve, Rosemond. *Allegorical Imagery: Some Mediaeval Books and Their Posterity.* Princeton, NJ: Princeton University Press, 1966.

Voelkle, William M. *The Pierpont Morgan Library: Masterpieces of Medieval Painting.* Chicago: University of Chicago Press, 1980.

Walters, Lori. "A Parisian Manuscript of the *Romance of the Rose.*" *Princeton University Library Chronicle* 51 (1989): 31–55.

———. "Author Portraits and Textual Demarcation in Manuscripts of the *Romance of the Rose.*" In *Rethinking the* Romance of the Rose, ed. Brownlee and Huot, 359–73. Philadelphia: University of Pennsylvania Press, 1992.

———. "Illuminating the *Rose*: Gui de Mori and the Illustrations of MS 101 of the Municipal Library, Tournai." In *Rethinking the* Romance of the Rose, ed. Brownlee and Huot, 167–200. Philadelphia: University of Pennsylvania Press, 1992.

Warner, George, and Julius Gilson. *Catalogue of Western MSS in the Old Royal and Kings' Collections.* 4 vols. vol. II. London: British Museum, 1921.

Wright, C. E., and R. C., eds. *The Diary of Humphrey Wanley 1715–1726.* 2 vols. London: The Bibliographical Society, 1966.